EVOLVING CITIES

To Olga, my mother

Evolving Cities

Geocomputation in Territorial Planning

Edited by

LIDIA DIAPPI
Polytechnic of Milan, Italy

Routledge
Taylor & Francis Group

LONDON AND NEW YORK

First published 2004 by Ashgate Publishing

Published 2016 by Routledge
2 Park Square, Milton Park, Abingdon, Oxfordshire OX14 4RN
711 Third Avenue, New York, NY 10017, USA

First issued in paperback 2016

Routledge is an imprint of the Taylor & Francis Group, an informa business

British Library Cataloguing in Publication Data
Evolving cities : geocomputation in territorial planning. -
    (Urban and regional planning and development)
    1. City planning - Data processing 2. Geographic information
    systems 3. Land use, Urban - Mathematical models 4. Cities
    and towns - Growth - Mathematical models 5. Neural networks
    (Computer science)
    I. Diappi, Lidia
    307.1'216'0285

Library of Congress Cataloging-in-Publication Data
Evolving cities : geocomputation in territorial planning / [edited by] Lidia Diappi.
    p. cm. -- (Urban and regional planning and development series)
    Includes index.
    ISBN 0-7546-4194-5
    1. Information storage and retrieval systems--City planning. 2. Information storage and
retrieval systems--Regional planning. 3. Geographic information systems. I. Diappi, Lidia.
II. Urban and regional planning and development.

Z699.5.C55E96 2004
307.1'216'028563--dc22
                                                                    2004047676

ISBN 13: 978-1-138-26660-5 (pbk)
ISBN 13: 978-0-7546-4194-0 (hbk)

Contents

List of Figures

List of Tables

List of Contributors

Paola Bolchi
Dept. of Architecture and Planning, Politecnico di Milano, via Bonardi 3 - 20133
Milano. e-mail: paola.bolchi@polimi.it

Francesco Bonchi
Dept. of Informatics, Università di Pisa, via F. Buonarroti 2 - 56127 Pisa
e-mail: bonchi@di.unipi.it

Massimo Buscema
Semeion Center, via Sersale 117/119 - 00100 Roma
e-mail: m.buscema@semeion.it

Grazia Concilio
Dept. Architecture and Planning, Politecnico di Bari, via Orabona 4 - 70125 Bari
e-mail: g.concilio@poliba.it

Emilia Conte
Dept. Architecture and Planning, Politecnico di Bari, via Orabona 4 - 70125 Bari
e-mail: conte@poliba.it

Lidia Diappi
Dept. of Architecture and Planning, Politecnico di Milano, via Bonardi 3 - 20133
Milano. e-mail: lidia.diappi@polimi.it

Manfred Fischer
Dept. of Economic Geography & Geoinformatics, Vienna University of Economics
and Business Administration, Rossauer Lände 23/1 - 1090 Vienna
e-mail: manfred.fisher@wu-wien.ac.at

Roberto Gianassi
via Pimentel 1 – 50013 Campibisenzio (Fi)
e-mail: gianassi@tele2.it

Silvio Griguolo
Dept. of Planning, Università Iuav di Venezia , S. Croce 1957 - 30135 Venezia
e-mail: silvio@cidoc.iuav.it

Katerina Hlavackova-Schindler
Institute for Computer–Aided Automation (PRIP), Vienna University of
Technology, Favoritenstrasse 9 - 1040 Vienna
e-mail: kat@prip.tuwien.ac.at

Silvana Lombardo
Dept. of Civil Engineering, Università di Pisa, via Diotisalvi 2 - 56126 Pisa
e-mail: s.lombardo@ing.unipi.it

Kai Nagel
Institute for Scientific Computing, Dept. of Computer Science, ETZ Zürich - 8092
Zürich. e-mail: nagel@inf.ethz.ch

Michela Ottanà
via Cattaneo 4 - 20020 Arconate (Mi)

Serena Pecori
Dept. of Civil Engineering, Università di Pisa, via Diotisalvi 2 - 56126 Pisa
e-mail: s.pecori@ing.unipi.it

Bryan Raney
Institute for Scientific Computing, Dept. of Computer Science, ETZ Zürich - 8092
Zürich. e-mail: raney@inf.ethz.ch

Alessandro Santucci
Dept. of Civil Engineering, Università di Pisa, via Diotisalvi 2 - 56126 Pisa
e-mail: alsantucc@tiscai.it

Ferdinando Semboloni
Dept. of City and Regional Planning, Università degli Studi di Firenze, via Micheli
2 - 50121 Firenze
e-mail: semboloni@urba.arch.unifi.it

Chris Webster
Dept. of City and Regional Planning, Cardiff University-Cardiff CF10 3WA
e-mail: webster@cf.ac.uk

Foreword

This book stems from a Research Project financed by the Italian Ministry of University and Scientific Research (MIUR) which has been carried out in the period 1999-2002. The Project, entitled "Knowledge Engineering in Planning Process" was aimed at developing Artificial Intelligent technologies in analysis, project and evaluation in territorial planning. This approach, which has recently been defined "Geocomputation" in the scientific literature, constitutes an emerging paradigm in territorial sciences.

Many different Italian partners participated in the Project:

Lidia Diappi, Coordinator (Polytechnic of Milan), Giovanni Rabino (Polytechnic of Milan), Silvana Lombardo (University of Pisa), Emilia Conte (Polytechnic of Bari), Ferdinando Semboloni (University of Florence), Silvio Griguolo (University of Venice).

The final research results were presented in a workshop which took place in Milan in November 2001. In addition to the parties of the project, the meeting hosted speakers internationally well known as the cutting edge of researchers in the field. Among them: Mike Batty (Centre for Advanced Spatial Analysis (CASA)-UCL-London), Dino Borri (Polytechnic of Bari), Chris Webster (Cardiff University), Kai Nagel (Computer Science Institüt- Zurich), Katerina Hlavackova-Schindler (Vienna University of Economic and Business Administration), Lena Sanders (CNRS, Paris), Paul Torrence (CASA-UCL, London).

The proposed book collects the proceedings of this concluding workshop. We are grateful to all those who have contributed to the present volume. Without their willingness to participate, this endeavour could never have been realized.

We wish also to express our gratitude for support from our home institutions, and the generous financial backing by the MIUR Ministry.

Milan, 1 February 2004

Lidia Diappi
Polytechnic of Milan

Chapter 1

Introduction

Lidia Diappi

We seek a learning system that turns expert behavior into fuzzy rules. We seek a system which learns fuzzy rules from experience.
Bart Kosko

Emergent Territorial Phenomena

There have been a number of significant changes affecting the field of territorial planning which have become increasingly evident over recent decades.

The present work identifies some of the main changes.

- The first distinctive feature is the growing dispersion of settlements. This phenomenon, described as diffused city (Secchi, 2001), metapole (Ascher, 1995) or urban glue (Hall, 1999) does not so much involve a spreading outwards of large cities, but rather a gradual urbanisation of the territory between cities. Understanding the factors underlying these new locational impulses and finding their hidden aspects is an important challenge inspiring various contributions to this book, particularly in the second part.
- The increasing mobility within this new urban morphology has occurred along routes which follow a process more closely resembling percolation in a porous fragmented fabric (Secchi, 2001) than the orderly flows channelled into road networks, as traditional transport models interpret.
- The new settlement processes and greater mobility can also be described in terms of increasing globalisation. But globalisation also results in greater emphasis on the local, since the process is driven by differences. The diffused city and globalisation induce a mutually supportive process of standardisation and differentiation. Standardisation occurs as one tends to find the same type of economic actors, services and opportunities in every city and country. Differentiation occurs because what drives the circulation of people, goods and ideas is ultimately the difference between territories.
- The increasing autonomy of individuals means there is a proliferation in choices and behaviours, even though they may be expressed within increasingly socialised and complex systems. The flexibility in working hours, the

increasing autonomy of family members, new technologies, from mobile phones to portable PCs, enable ever increasing individual management of time and space.

This does not only mean that urban planning practice has had to address new priorities. It has also had to examine new techniques for analysis and evaluation, together with procedures for monitoring and control. In a situation marked by growing uncertainty, forecasts are inevitably subject to increasing limitations. The conception and implementation of design and management principles in planning therefore require much better understanding of phenomena than in the past, with the factors affecting the evolution of the city and society being identified. New hypotheses, new models and a new scale for examining phenomena are needed. This can be effectively achieved by making use of the large databases in high-dimensional space which are now available. It is necessary to once again observe, investigate behaviours, classify and create models starting from observations on an individual level. This book provides a clear demonstration of how this can be done, by integrating GIS (Geographical Information Systems) databases with the powerful tools offered by the new processing abilities of the Geocomputation approach.

What is Geocomputation?

This book aims to show the potential for building knowledge of territorial phenomena using the new tools of Geocomputation (Openshaw and Abrahart, 2000; Fischer and Leung, 2001; Longley et al., 2001).

Geocomputation (GC) is an emerging paradigm which has the potential to dramatically improve the effectiveness of urban studies through the use of computational intelligence technologies (CIT).

The most widely accepted definitions of GC emphasise the role of new technologies in processing large databases. For Stan Openshaw (2000), father of this neologism, GC is "an approach based on high performance computing to solve currently unsolvable or even unknown problems".

Longley defines GC as "...(the) application of computationally intensive approaches to the problem of physical and human geography. In some important respects the term GC is synonymous with geographic information science, although it has often put greater emphasis upon the use of high performance computers" (Longley et al., 2001).

For Helen Couclelis GC is "...the eclectic application of computational methods and tools to solve geographical problems and to explain geographical phenomena" (Couclelis, 1998). A more specific definition is given by Fischer and Leung who, in addition to the greater computational efficiency and "fuzziness" provided by computational intelligence technologies, state that GC can:

improve the quality of research results by utilizing computationally intensive procedures to reduce the number of assumptions and remove the simplifications imposed by computational constraints that are no longer relevant (Fischer and Leung, 2001, p. 5).

In our view Geocomputing includes approaches to human reasoning that try to make use of the human tolerance to incompleteness, uncertainty, imprecision and fuzziness in decision, making processes. In addition to neural networks and adaptive fuzzy systems, it also incorporates evolutionary computation, cellular automata, expert systems and probabilistic reasoning. Geocomputing is especially concerned with combinations of these methodologies and introduces the spatial dimension developed and structured by GIS into soft computing techniques (Zadeh, 1965).

Many innovative features characterise this approach:

- The first concerns identification of the rules. The well established body of theories and models developed since the beginning of the 1960s is based on explicit rule formulation of assumptions derived deductively from theories. The goal of learning is to formulate explicit rules (propositions, hypotheses, etc.) which generalise in a very succinct manner. Powerful mechanisms, with considerable innate knowledge of a domain, formulate general hypothetical rules by analysing particular cases and then formulate explicit generalisations. The Geocomputation approach is completely different, since it assumes that information processing should itself be able to find out the rules through learning.
- The second major difference concerns the scale of description, i.e. the level of resolution of the system. The micro-scale description, which characterises the GC approach, with agents representing individual decision units, is suitable for articulating micro-spatial, socio-economic assumptions and other well formed behavioural theories of urban processes, including land use change. This is because many GC tools use parallel distributed computing, which is particularly suited for describing interactions between subjects. This permits the generation of a new, socially-based type of knowledge which can greatly increase effectiveness in analysis, simulation and planning.
- Finally Geocomputation offers opportunities to reconstruct missing information, because it is based on "…substituting a vast amount of computation as a substitute for missing knowledge or theory and even to augment intelligence" (Openshaw, 2000). Geocomputation is something more than a set of methods and techniques for sophisticated data processing. It is, to some extent, a different approach for understanding phenomena compared to the traditional model building approach.

About this Book

The present volume aims to make a scientific contribution to the Geocomputation approach in urban planning, with a specific focus on the development of Distributed

Artificial Intelligence principles and techniques (Werner, 1996) as a support to planning. Neural Networks (NN), Multi-Agent Systems (MAS) and Evolutionary Algorithms (EA), in particular, allow the knowledge level to be increased by multiplying the information capacity of the GIS and offering a new approach to territorial modelling.

PART I: The Spatial Investigation Capabilities of Neural Networks

The first part of the book is devoted to the investigative potential of neural networks. The most prominent feature of NNs is their ability to learn from examples. Using so-called learning algorithms they solve problems by processing a set of training data. Some types of neural network are comparable to statistical regression or discriminant models. However they do not explicitly make assumptions on the distribution of their training data, or on the relationship between their input and output variables. Another basic question refers to the stored knowledge that gives rise to a specified pattern of activation. In parallel distributed processing (PDP) models, the patterns themselves are not stored. Instead, what is stored are the connection strengths between units that allow these patterns to be recreated.

From a statistical point of view, neural networks are non-parametric models, and for some it can be shown that they are universal function approximators. There is a drawback of NNs, which can pose a problem for some applications. In general it cannot be proved that a NN works as expected. Due to its distributed nature, the solution that a NN has learned cannot be expressed explicitly. A neural network learns, but a user cannot learn from the network. For the user it is simply a black box.

The strong points of neural networks are their learning capabilities and their distributed structure which allows for highly parallel software or hardware implementations.

The second chapter by *Silvio Griguolo* shows the power of neural networks as pattern recognisers. Neural networks are universally recognised as efficient classifiers for multi-dimensional problems involving pattern recognition of massive quantities of data for remotely-sensed imagery.

There may be a range of different objectives such as land cover recognition based on a set of radiometric bands; eco-climatic zoning or crop monitoring based on time series of images, mostly representing some kind of Vegetation Index; or the singling out of specific objects of interest, like roads, building, etc., based on the relationships between the features of pixels and the characteristics of their neighbourhoods.

The approach can be supervised or unsupervised, depending on the problem: neural networks are available for both cases. It is commonly acknowledged that, thanks to their independence from a particular data model, they quite often perform better than statistical classifiers.

In the specific case of land cover classification, it is well known that radiometric information alone is insufficient to achieve soundly reliable recognition. The use of suitable ancillary information is necessary to solve dubious cases, and this is commonly done by defining a specific set of rules that are applied as a post-classification stage. It is easy to show that this way of proceeding has some drawbacks that cannot be overlooked.

The paper presents a method of land cover recognition that operates via a supervised neural network and uses the available ancillary information during the assignment process itself and not as a separate step. The approach is operational and is illustrated by means of an application described in detail.

Chapter 3, by *Manfred Fischer* and *Katerina Hlavackova-Schindler*, presents two new approaches using neural networks and statistical optimisation to solve the parameter estimation problem, one of the main issues in neural spatial interaction modelling. Current practice is dominated by gradient-based local minimization techniques. They efficiently find local minima and work best in unimodal minimization problems, but can fail in multimodal problems. Global search procedures provide an alternative optimisation scheme which allows an escape from local minima.

This contribution presents two global optimisation methods, Differential Evolution and Alopex. Differential Evolution was introduced as an efficient direct search method for optimising real-valued multi-modal objective functions. Alopex, the second alternative of an appropriate global search method for spatial interaction modelling applications, was introduced in its original version as early as 1973 by Tzanakou and Hart. Little is known about the behaviour of either global search procedure in real world applications. Both methods were successfully tested on Austrian inter-regional telecommunication traffic data by the authors.

This work evaluates both methods for robustness when applied in the neural spatial interaction context with respect to common benchmark models and measured in terms of in-sample and out-of-sample performance. A benchmark comparison of both methods for robustness and generalisation performance, when applied on a neural network model against backpropagation of conjugate gradients and measured by their in-sample and out-of-sample performance, is based on Austrian inter-regional telecommunication traffic data.

Chapter 4, written by *Lidia Diappi*, *Massimo Buscema* and *Michela Ottanà*, addresses the problem of evaluating the complex facets of urban sustainability in Italian cities.

The question to be posed is the following: is it possible to evaluate urban sustainability in cities with different contexts, with major dissimilarities in terms of environmental conditions, social welfare and economic indicators, as well as dynamics of growth and decline? Since the cities differ with respect to institutional, historical, cultural and economic variables, there is no uniform scale for measuring sustainability and the process of urban ranking is rather arbitrary. With this in mind, suitable indicators to investigate the relationships between the different properties of cities and the various patterns of development have resulted in a better understanding of the influence of different attributes. Since sustainability should be defined as a positive co-evolution of social, economic and environmental systems, the complex interactions among the phenomena give rise to positive and negative externalities described by a set of indicators.

The complexity of the interactions requires highly efficient investigation tools and presents the opportunity for a new methodology of scientific investigation using Self-Reflexive Neural Networks (SRNN). These networks are a useful instrument for investigative and analogic questioning of the data base. Once the SRNN has learned the structure of weights from the DB, by querying the network with maximisation or minimisation of specific groups of attributes, it can read the related properties and rank the cities according to this urban profile.

PART II: Land Use Dynamics through Artificial Intelligence Tools

The second part of the book shifts attention to different studies for assessing land use change. The various authors adopt a wide range of approaches with Intelligent Computing accompanying more established statistical or modelling approaches.

In Chapter 5, written by *Silvana Lombardo, Francesco Bonchi* and *Serena Pecori*, a cognitive system is presented which is based on Data Mining and Knowledge Discovery in Database Process. This method merges concepts and techniques from many different research areas, such as statistics and machine learning, with the aim of extracting knowledge on the role played by urban/territorial factors in spatial evolution. The methodology of data mining tools is examined to investigate the underlying features of land use dynamics in a metropolitan context (Rome) and in an urban-agricultural context (the Pisa area).

Chapter 6, written by *Francesco Bonchi, Silvana Lombardo, Serena Pecori* and *Alessandro Santucci*, presents the experimental results of the above method.

In Chapter 7, *Ferdinando Semboloni* shows a method for extracting the rules of the urban spatio-temporal dynamic from a limited set of data. This method is based on a GIS at two temporal thresholds concerning the spatial distribution of relevant variables in a city. The simplest spatial rules which reproduce the situation at time t_2, based on the situation at time t_1, are identified through a neural network. Then the weights of the neural network are corrected by a set of parameters, calibrated by using Simulated Annealing in order to generate the spatial dynamic at different time steps. The method was experimentally tested on the case study of Rome.

The final chapter of Part II, Chapter 8, written by *Lidia Diappi* and *Paola Bolchi*, moves to GC modelling through a dynamic model of urbanisation. The model is based on transition rules learned from an autopoietic neural network (SOM, Self-Organizing Maps) which processes land use changes occurring in the area being studied over a certain period. A stochastic model then allocates the land use changes in the subsequent period (forecast) by applying learned rules.

SOM processing allows the typologies of transformation to be identified, i.e. the classes of area which are transformed in the same way and which give rise to territorial morphologies; this is an interesting by-product of the approach.

The model assumes that territorial micro-transformations occur according to a local logic, i.e. to use, accessibility, presence of services and conditions of centrality, periphericity or isolation of each territorial "cell" relative to its neighbourhood. The method presented here aims to combine the significant investigative power of NNs in organising knowledge with a stochastic simulation model able to produce urbanisation scenarios based on rules learned by NNs.

PART III: Multi-Agent Systems: Interactions among Actors and Their Behaviours

Simulating real processes using Multi-Agent Systems means building up a complex system from individual decision units having a certain degree of autonomy and which interact with one another according to certain rules. It can be defined as "... a weakly connected network of agents which act together to resolve problems that exceed their individual capacity to resolve them..." (Durfee et al., 1989;). Originally created to resolve problems in information science, the approach is now widely used in economics to evaluate the problems of competition or cooperation among markets, in ecology to study the evolutionary dynamics of species and in urban studies to evaluate such things as competition between cities (Benenson & Portugali, 1997) or the various demographic weights of cities in a region, starting from the behaviour of individual families (Aschan-Leygonie et al., 2000). Transport and mobility, as the contribution of Nagel and Raney in this book shows, are issues particularly suited to MAS treatment since they simulate different settlement behaviours and the reciprocal effects of individual journeys on infrastructure. The way multi-agent systems are structured demonstrates the power of the approach: it builds a model starting at the level of a single agent relative to other agents and can then allow cooperation, negotiation and competition processes to develop, so forming a model of the system at a more aggregated level.

Chapter 9, by *Kai Nagel* and *Bryan Raney*, presents an innovative approach where the classical modules in transportation modelling (activity generation, mode choice and routing, simulation and testing, learning and feedback) are revised in an MAS framework. Each traveller is represented individually with his own set of plans and strategies, that are loaded into the simulation modules.

Using advanced computational methods, in particular parallel computing, it is shown how it is possible to implement these modules for large metropolitan areas with 10 million inhabitants or more. A partial implementation of this approach is presented for Swiss morning peak traffic.

In Chapter 10 by *Grazia Concilio* and *Emilia Conte*, MAS techniques shift to decision support systems (DSS) in order to study the architecture of a knowledge-based multi-agent DSS for monitoring the compatibility of urban activities, and particularly of traffic induced by such activities, in relation to the generation or presence of atmospheric pollutants. The system is proposed to support the task of technicians in a city's traffic agency, and especially decisions regarding data validation and action strategies.

The urban level was considered suitable for developing this research, so Bari, a medium-sized city in Southern Italy, was selected as the case study. Investigations were carried out into the specific decision-making mechanisms used by municipal environmental monitoring; the actors in decisional processes, their roles and levels of action were identified using the technique of semi-structured interviews.

The most significant outcomes focused on knowledge acquisition, and how it could be represented and formalised through decisional routines and the topic of learning at both levels of human decision makers and machines.

In Chapter 11, *Chris Webster* demonstrates the use of a simple cellular automaton to represent a model of neighbourhood evolution based on theoretical ideas from the new institutional economics. The urban neighbourhood is viewed as a constantly evolving nexus of contracts (informal institutions) the purpose of which are to constrain competition over jointly consumed resources. Neighbourhoods are joint consumption spheres and spheres of joint agreement (or contract) over the allocation rules that govern joint consumption. More formally, contracts may be thought of as emerging to create and protect the right to consume private and public goods and services (property rights). The cellular automata simulation demonstrates how voluntarily-organised public realms (spheres of "private planning") can emerge naturally through bilateral neighbour agreements. It illustrates the chaotic nature of neighbourhood evolution however, showing that neighbourhood growth (spread of contracts) can equilibrate in several states: a citywide stable neighbourhood, fragmented stable neighbourhoods, fragmented unstable neighbourhoods or fragmented anarchy.

References

Aschan-Leygonie, C., Mathian, H., Sanders, L., Mäkilä, K. (2000), "A spatial simulation of population dynamics in Southern France: a model integrating individual decisions and spatial constraints", in G. Ballot, G. Weisbuch (eds), *Applications of Simulations to Social Sciences*, Hermès, Paris, pp. 109-125.

Ascher, F. (1995), *Métapolis ou l'avenir des villes*, Ed. Odile Jacob, Paris.

Batty, M. (2001), "Cellular Dynamics: Modelling Urban Growth as a Spatial Epidemic", in M.M. Fischer, Y. Leung (eds), *Geocomputational Modelling: Techniques and Applications*, Springer Verlag, Berlin, pp.109-141.

Benenson, I. Portugali, J. (1997), "Agent-based Simulations of City Dynamics in a GIS Environnment", in S.C. Hurtle, A.U. Frank (eds.), *Spatial Information Theory: A Theoretical Basis for GIS*, Springer Verlag, Berlin, pp. 501-502.

Couclelis, H. (1998), "Geocomputation in context", in P.A. Longley, S.M. Brooks, R. McDonnell, B. Macmillan (eds.), *Geocomputation, a Primer*, John Wiley & Son, Chichester, England.

Durfee, E.H., Lesser, V.R., Corkill, D.D. (1989), "Trends in cooperative distributed problem solving", IEEE Trans. Knowl. Data Eng., KOE-11 (1), pp. 63-83.

Fischer, M.M., Leung, Y. (2001), (eds), *Geocomputational Modelling: Techniques and Applications*, Springer Verlag, Berlin, Heidelberg, New York.

Hall, P. (1999), "The future of the cities", *Computers, Environment and Urban Systems*, vol. 23, 3, pp. 173-185.

Longley, P.A., Goodchild, M.F., Maguire, D.J., Rhind, D.W. (2001), *Geographic Information Systems and Science*, John Wiley & Son, Chichester, England.

Mitchell, W. J. (1999), *E-topia*, MIT Press, Cambridge, Mass; London, England.

Openshaw, S. (2000), "Geocomputation", in S. Openshaw, R.J. Abrahart (eds), *Geocomputation*, Taylor & Francis, London.

Openshaw, S., Abrahart, R.J. (2000), *Geocomputation*, Taylor & Francis, London.

Secchi, B. (2001), "Agir sur la ville dispersée: la ville invisible qui échappe aux aménageurs", in A. Masboungi (ed.) *Fabriquer la ville*, La Documentation française, Paris.

Werner, E. (1996), *Logical Foundations of Distributed Artificial Intelligence*, John Wiley & Son, Chichester, England.

Zadeh, L. A. (1965), "Fuzzy Sets", *Information and Control*, 8, pp. 338-353.

PART I
THE SPATIAL INVESTIGATION
CAPABILITIES OF NEURAL
NETWORKS

Chapter 2

Neural Classifiers for Land Cover Recognition: Merging Radiometric and Ancillary Information[1]

Silvio Griguolo

The Domain: Knowledge and Control of Territorial Phenomena

Human activity has always been a cause of changes to the surface of the Earth. These modifications have particularly accelerated during the second half of the twentieth century, stimulated by increasingly rapid economic development and a demographic explosion. The fragility of the environment now appears alarming: the greenhouse effect; the reduction of equatorial forests – the planet's large lungs – with the consequent release of millions of tons of carbon dioxide into the atmosphere; increasing desertification…these are only some of the results, visible to everybody.

Unfortunately, traditional techniques like air photo surveys involve a long delay (at least one year) between capture and actual availability of the collected information: this is the time required for cartographic restitution, still the most common way of distributing territorial information. This delay is certainly an obstacle for the monitoring and management of regions characterised by increasingly rapid change.

Alternatively, data sensed by the Earth Resource Observation Satellites (particularly SPOT, LANDSAT and NOAA) enable the continuous monitoring of environmental transformations. They provide useful information in real time on land use changes, on the extension and type of vegetation cover, on built-up areas, on water and air quality, etc. For decision-making purposes, such information must be rapidly processed and made available in usable form.

A systematic use of remotely-sensed data can help to achieve the concept of almost *interactive* planning and management activity.

[1] This chapter was written in the frame of research on "Knowledge Engineering in Planning Process", co-financed by the Italian Ministry of Scientific Research (MIUR) and co-ordinated by L. Diappi, Polytechnic of Milan. The introductory section partially re-uses some of the author's other papers, mentioned in the References.

Characteristics of Remotely-Sensed Data

Remotely-sensed data differ from other types of territorial data mostly because:

- the region of interest is periodically observed by the satellite and this permits a regular data updating;
- elementary areas on the ground, represented as points (*pixels*) in the output images, emit, reflect or diffuse electromagnetic energy. The sensors mounted on the satellite platform measure this energy on a *set of radiometric channels*, whose frequency is selected according to the features to be focused. The information collected is *numeric* and *multidimensional*.

Satellite data is digital, not analogue: data can be directly processed to extract synthetic and immediately usable information. In particular, the ground elementary units, the *pixels*, can be clustered in homogeneous groups, with the purpose of simplifying, ordering and making their characteristics and behaviour easier to understand.

A *classified* satellite image[2] is the result of a complex analytical operation, shown schematically in Figure 2.1, aimed at synthesising the information conveyed by a set of input images (collected on different radiometric channels, or at different dates – in brief, representing different raster descriptions of the region of interest). It can be imported into a GIS project and used as a raster layer.

Since the beginning of the 1970s, the availability of images of the same region, observed at regular intervals, has opened wide perspectives for monitoring. Thanks to the improved technical level of the sensors mounted on orbital platforms, precisely geo-referenced images are being issued both at the urban/regional and continental scale. In practice, this makes available a kind of dynamic description of the region of interest, overcoming the limitations of cartography based on air photos.

Efficient software tools are necessary to analyse remotely-sensed data, embedding information derived from other sources into the process. The necessary steps can be summarised as follows:

- acquisition of remotely-sensed data, together with other supplementary information;
- image processing, in order to extract and synthesise the information useful for the objectives of the analysis;
- presentation of the outcome, and its integration into a suitable management tool, such as a GIS.

---

[2] In a *classified image* every pixel (point of the image corresponding to a well-identified area on the ground, whose size depends on the sensor's resolution) takes a value that represents the code of the class to which it belongs.

Some aspects, and some decisions to be taken during the research, depend on the scale. For example, a land cover classification is usually *hard*, i.e. each pixel is assigned to one and only one target theme, or maybe to none of them if it appears to be too different from them all. Advantages and drawbacks are evident: extreme (often excessive) synthesis on one hand, imprecision on the other. The imprecision is due to the fact that a pixel is frequently a mix of different themes, and this depends on the scale at which it is observed.

A set of themes appropriate for an analysis of large areas, based on NOAA-AVHRR or SPOT-VEGETATION images, may not be pertinent when processing LANDSAT-TM or SPOT images, with a pixel size of 30 or 20 metres respectively, or IKONOS images, with 1 metre resolution. At a lower scale, small objects of different nature that co-exist in the same pixel generate an averaged signal, while they can be separately captured at a larger scale. A pixel classified as *"sparse vegetation"* at the resolution of 1 km splits up into a set of trees, bushes, grassland or bare soil in a 20m image; an area classified as *"low density built-up"* in a 30m LANDSAT-TM image allows the separate recognition of roofs, gardens, asphalted surfaces, plus a certain number of mixed intermediate classes, in an IKONOS image.

The latter situation, characteristic of urban areas, may require a texture-based supplementary analysis, capable of recognising the various spatial patterns representing meaningful organisations of elementary objects. The recognition of complex textures, operated by the human brain (the visual interpreter) on the basis of shapes and colours, is fast and sufficiently reliable. However, an algorithmic procedure, coded and run on a computer to perform the same task, will be inefficient and output results that will generally require massive ex-post controls.

This, more than pixel-by-pixel classification problems, adequately tackled by statistical classifiers, appears to be a promising domain of application for neural networks.

As an alternative to hard classifications, fuzzy methods can be used to recognise mixes of features, assigning each pixel to a plurality of themes and quantifying the belonging rates. For example, the LMM method (Linear Mixture Modelling, Frew, 1990) assumes that the descriptive pattern of each pixel can be expressed as a linear combination of a limited number of elementary types, the *end members*, that in a land cover application can represent some basic types of covers like *water*, *forest*, *built-up*, etc.

Input: p images of the same region
(radiometric bands, synthetic neo-channels,
multitemporal series of images...)

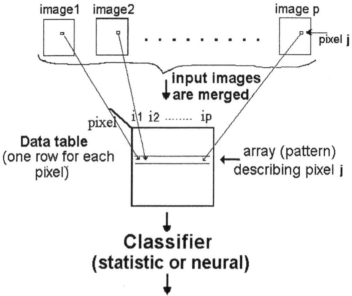

Classifier
(statistic or neural)

Result: a classified map whose classes
consist of pixels with similar features

Figure 2.1 Construction of a Classified Image

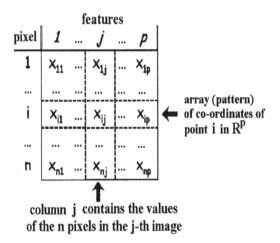

Figure 2.2a The Data Table

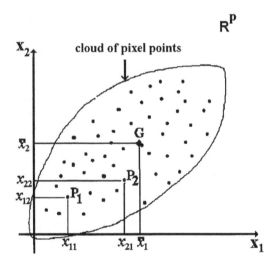

Figure 2.2b The Cloud of Pixel-points in the Feature Space
Only two axes are shown for simplicity.

Classifying Remotely-Sensed Imagery

Generalities

The geographic region to be classified is described by a set of p radiometric channels, directly observed, or synthetic neo-channels (Principal Components, some kind of Vegetation Index,[3] etc.), computed from the observed reflectances.

Each elementary ground areal unit, corresponding to an image pixel, is described by a vector (its *pattern*) whose p components (its *features*) are drawn in order from the input images (Figure 2.1). A pixel is a geo-referenced unit and its *features* capture the aspects to be focused, relevant for the particular problem.

The *data table* to be analysed is obtained by merging the p input images. It has p columns (Figure 2.2a) and each row describes a pixel that can be seen as a point in a p-dimensional space, the *feature space* (Figure 2.2b). The co-ordinates of a pixel-point are the components of its pattern.

Unfortunately there is not a fixed correspondence among the possible patterns, that fill more or less continuously the feature space, and the *land cover types*, that are labels that mirror our need for synthesis and characterise wide and often irregularly-shaped regions of the feature space.

To cope with this, a *post-classification step* is commonly performed, with the objective of improving a classification by eliminating some of its inconsistencies. Post-classification requires the definition of a suitable set of decision rules, that control the re-assignment to the classes of those pixels whose first assignment does not appear reliable. During this phase, available *ancillary databases* are necessary to cope with the insufficiency of radiometric data.

The common opinion that radiometric information *alone* is insufficient to achieve reliable recognition is based on visual interpretation practice, long used in remote sensing. On deriving a thematic map from satellite images, human interpreters always take into account not only the radiometric data, but also the available cartographic information (elevation maps, soil maps,...), their knowledge of local vegetation species, etc.

The recourse to ancillary information is always necessary to improve the quality of an automatic classification, whether it is obtained by *statistical or neural* methods.

To summarise, radiometric information is far from complete and must be complemented with data from other sources. This can be done:

---

[3] The NDVI (Normalised Difference Vegetation Index) is the most frequently used Vegetation Index. It is computed from the Red (R) and Near InfraRed (NIR) channels:

$$NDVI = \frac{NIR - R}{NIR + R}$$

The NDVI is a good indicator of the amount of healthy vegetal biomass present in each pixel. By definition it takes values in $[-1..1]$: its value lies between 0.1 and 0.7 for vegetated areas, is negative for water and about zero for clouds and bare soil.

- immediately after producing the classified image, as a successive step aimed at improving its quality (post-classification);
- at the same time as the classified image is produced, as will be shown below;
- within a GIS, capable of integrating different aspects.

Clustering and Classification: Some Methodological Considerations

The automatic recognition of the elements of interest in a scene has always been a focus in remote sensing applications. The commonly used *false colour images,*[4] visually interpreted by expert operators, limit to three the number of (neo)channels that can be simultaneously used. Even if the three channels most relevant for the objectives of the research are carefully chosen, it is clear that an exhaustive description should generally be based on a higher number of channels: it is a waste to ignore them if they are available. Automatic clustering can use all the available raster descriptions (channels or neo-channels) that appear to be relevant.

In addition to this, there are types of analyses that *must* take a high number of channels as input: for example, multitemporal analyses, in which satellite images making up a time series are processed in order to analyse the cycle of a variable of interest (often, some kind of Vegetation Index) in each pixel. The number of input images can easily be as high as 36, or even 52 when images are produced with weekly cadence. Similar cases can only be dealt with automatically.

More and more space is being dedicated to automatic clustering procedures in Remote Sensing handbooks. Just to mention a few, good chapters on this subject can be found in the classic Lillesand and Kiefer (1987), in Bonn and Rochon (1996), in Mather (1999), Gibson (2000) and above all in Tso and Mather (2001), largely focused on neural network applications to remote sensing. A very detailed treatment of image classification, also including neural methods, can be found in Richards and Xiuping (1999).

A classification can be carried out with *statistical* or *neural* tools, and according to a *supervised* or *unsupervised* approach.

Neural methods differ from their statistical counterpart in that they do not operate according to a pre-defined model. They are in general capable of handling any type of data distribution, and capturing non-linear relationships among the variables, while, for example, Principal Components Analysis or minimum-distance clustering methods cannot.

The only hypotheses are those implicit in the net architecture. However, this is not a minor question: the definition of the most appropriate net architecture for a given problem is always a long and sometimes not very successful operation.

The *supervised* approach, both in the neural and statistical context, requires the availability of a *training set*, i.e. a set of units *whose class is explicitly indicated.* This is the case when the *target classes* (or *themes*) are given *a priori* (e.g.: *built-*

---

[4] *False colour images* merge the information conveyed by three radiometric or synthetic channels: the value in each channel is assumed as the intensity of one of the three fundamental colours red, green, blue (RGB).

up, roads, water, sparse vegetation...): by examining the training set, the classifier can derive some statistical parameters, or some discriminating functions, or the weights of a neural Backpropagation net...in short, it learns a way to reproduce as best as possible the assignments indicated as correct for the training pixels. In the operational phase this knowledge is then used to classify, on the basis of their vectors of attributes, other statistical units whose class is undefined.

Instead, in the *unsupervised* case no *a priori* class is defined. Pixels are *clustered* automatically, according to the similarity of their patterns, in a number of classes decided by the analyst, or determined by the algorithm itself at runtime. Each class must be as homogeneous as possible.

Notice that the optimisation concept pursued by the two approaches is not the same.

- In the *supervised case*, the training pixels representing the various themes correspond to clearly interpretable behaviours. If they are carefully selected, all pixels relating to the same theme (say, *built-up areas*) can be expected to have similar patterns and lie sufficiently close to one another in the feature space.

  Yet, characters vary in a continuous way in the feature space, and a *real pixel* represents a ground area where several themes are often present, depending on the resolution. A mixed pixel is assigned to the theme closest to it in the feature space, often oversimplifying and with a relevant loss of information. Groups with high internal dispersion may result, certainly not an optimum from the statistical viewpoint, according to which the internal compactness of the classes is usually the pursued objective.

  Thus, *apparent* interpretative neatness, characterised by semantically clear labels, is often associated with an excessive inhomogeneity of the output groups and a high level of confusion.

- On the other hand, in the *unsupervised case* the *construction* of the classes follows a criterion of statistical optimisation. The resulting partition is more objective, and strictly determined by the way the statistical units are distributed in the feature space. The total internal variance of the classes, assumed as a measure of their overall internal dispersion, must be a minimum: to achieve this, the algorithm will segment the feature space locating the class centres in the denser regions of the cloud. The classes obtained, though optimal from the statistical point of view, are generally not easily interpretable according to common sense. For example, instead of two neat classes interpretable as *forest* and *grassland*, three classes may result, that correspond to mixtures of *forest* and *grassland* in different proportions. The result is determined by the features of the most frequent pixels, that are often mixed.

To summarise, real situations are always to some extent confused. With a supervised classifier the meaning of the classes is clear in the analyst's mind, but the classification obtained is often correctly interpretable only following a fuzzy logic, even if the training set was carefully selected.

Table 2.1 shows the components of the activation vector computed by the classifier (in this case, a neural network) for a random pixel. The thirteen (non-normalised) components of the activation vector computed by the net can be thought to capture the presence of each target theme in the pixel mix.

Table 2.1 Example of an Activation Vector Computed by the Net

In a *hard* classification the pixel would be simply labelled as *irrigated*, but from a fuzzy point of view it can be considered a mix with some proportion of *arable* and *olive grove*.

Arable	Irrigated	Rice paddies	Vineyards	Orchards	Olive groves	Pastures	Broadleaf forest	Coniferous Forest	Mixed forest	Grassland	Shrubs	Barren
0.19	0.50	0.0	0.0	0.0	0.21	0.0	0.0	0.0	0.0	0.0	0.0	0.0

The training set must be as consistent as possible: it should not include pixels presented to the classifier with an erroneous label. The training pixels relative to a theme can (better, they *should*) be sparse around their common class centre in the feature space, as this helps the classifier to derive the level of tolerance allowed for a correct assignment, teaching it to *generalise*. But the training set should not include *outliers*, i.e. units closest to the centre of a class to which they are not declared to belong. This erroneous information would interfere with the training process, confusing the classifiers.[5]

Image processing software usually enables the analyst to select the training pixels by delimiting a set of areas with the mouse, attaching to each of them a class label, based on the analyst's knowledge of the site. As an area is seldom perfectly homogeneous, it may occur that some of its pixels are quite different from their neighbours, and are located far from them in the feature space: they should be singled out as outliers, and removed from the training set.

Neural Classifiers

Doubtless, the eyes-brain combination is the best image interpretation system we know, much better than any computer when it is a question of recognising complex patterns or detecting particular objects out of a confusing background. Unfortunately, this great tool is too slow when what is required is systematic assignment of

---

[5] Training problems caused by outliers are more severe in the statistical case if the Mahalanobis distance is adopted. The reason is that its computation makes use of variance-covariance matrices, that depend on the *squares* of differences: this enhances the impact of outliers.

each pixel of a large scene to an appropriate land cover class, basing this on a high number of input images. Automatic classification is necessary.

The application of neural networks to the classification of remotely-sensed images has started to develop only in the last decade, thanks to the availability of faster computers and increased mass storage.

A good review of the history of Artificial Neural Networks (ANN) can be found in Simpson (1990). Theory, types of Nets and applications are dealt with in many good books: McClelland and Rumelhart (1986), Pao (1990), Schalkoff R. (1992), Bishop (1996), Ripley (1996) and many others.

Neurones and Networks

ANN derive from a simplified mathematical model of the biological neurone, proposed in 1943 by McCullock and Pitts, who showed that in theory an ANN could compute any mathematical or logical function.

Neurones are interconnected units making up a complex structure. The large computing capability of biological systems is due to a high number of such simple units, operating in parallel and forming an extremely complex and densely connected network: the human brain consists of about 100 billion neurones, each connected to around ten thousand other neurones.

The high number of connections among neurones generates an extremely complex circulation of electric signals in the brain: we cannot yet tell exactly how it works. Maybe we could, if the neurones were fewer in number, and not so interconnected...but, as Mather (1999) ironically remarks, if our brain had fewer neurones it would also be too stupid to deal with the problem. It can be guessed that self-consciousness arises above a critical level of net complexity.

The *formal neurone*, schematically shown in Figure 2.3, models the way its biological counterpart works. A pattern x (input) is presented to the neurone, with components x_i whose values mostly lie in $[0..1]$ in ANN real applications. The array x can represent either a p-component external stimulus, or a pattern of signals elaborated by other neurones.

A weight w_i, that can be positive or negative, is associated with each connection: weights are used to compute a weighted sum of the input pattern components: if the result is greater than a suitable threshold Δ, the neurone produces an output Y (whose value can also lie in $[0..1]$). Y can be modified by applying a simple *nonlinear* function (often a *sigmoid*) to it, that converts it into the actual output value O in $[0..1]$. This can be the input to other units, connected in cascade with the one just considered.

In 1949 Donald Hebb, a psychologist, put forward the hypothesis that in biological systems inter-neuronal connections through which frequent electric discharges occur become more permeable, thus configuring privileged paths for signals. This idea suggested a method for training ANN by changing the weights associated with connections.

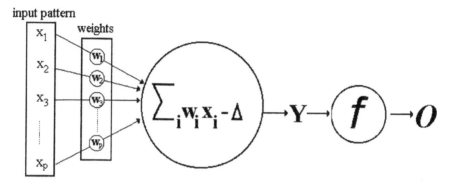

input pattern

Figure 2.3 Schema of How a Formal Neurone Works

The first type of ANN had only one layer of processing neurones, plus a passive input layer, used only for the presentation of input patterns (Single-Layer Perceptron): it was capable of solving only linearly-separable problems, in which hyperplanes are used as bounding surfaces to separate classes in the feature space. This limitation, stressed in a crucial book by Minsky and Papert (1969), resulted in reduced research funding, until the Multi-Layer Perceptron (MLP) was proposed, which proved able also to solve non-linearly separable problems. Figure 2.4 shows the net with two layers of adaptive weights (three layers of units, but remember that the nodes in the input layer are not processing units: they simply represent the input values).

Though applications using perceptrons with a higher number of layers can be found in the literature (an example is Kanellopoulos et al., 1991), it has been proved that "*networks with sigmoidal non-linearities and two layers of weights can approximate any decision boundary to an arbitrary accuracy*" (Bishop, 1995, chap. 4). Any function can be computed with any desired accuracy by such a network: the advantage of using more than one hidden layer of units can be improved efficiency (fewer total weights to do the job, for example), not the level of the results obtainable.

ANN and Expert Systems differ in that the latter apply a hierarchy of explicit rules, while ANN operate below the cognitive level, with no symbolic processing. This is what a human expert often does, coping with a problem that he/she has learnt to solve without explicit verbalisation.

The interest directed at ANN is due to some advantages they have over other types of classifiers: they learn adaptively from a set of examples (the *training set*); they are not constrained by rigid formal rules and show a high tolerance of incomplete or imprecise information. Once trained, a network can classify new units very quickly, practically in real time.

An ANN can be considered as *a non-parametric and non-linear regression technique*, with no need of any *a priori* model for data. By repeatedly examining the training set it determines the best fitting function, without any need to indicate it explicitly.

In short, an ANN is a system that maps *non-linear* input pattern x to output patterns y:

$y = f(x,w)$, where w is the matrix of weights and f is a non-linear function.

The strong point of ANN is not *precision*. What would be a handicap in accounting applications, that require high computational precision, is an advantage in pattern recognition applications, where the desired answer is qualitative (*this pattern is assigned to that class...*). Similar input patterns cause similar outputs, and the network will generally assign similar units to the same class. Also noise-affected or distorted patterns will often be classified correctly: the network is highly noise-tolerant. On the other hand, a *precise* (analytic) solution often simply does not exist, and example-derived knowledge is the only way out.

ANN can *generalise*: when presented with a pattern different from those used during training, a network can assign it correctly if an appropriate class exists.

Summarising, a neural network has the following advantages over a statistical classifier.

1. *No need to specify the statistical distribution of input data:* this overcomes the difficulty in estimating parameters when the training set has a limited size. Moreover, data of different nature and derived from other sources can be merged with radiometric information to make up more complex input patterns.

2. *Generalisation capability*: it can recognise patterns similar, albeit not identical, to those used for training. The reason is that the *relevant* components of the problem are automatically captured and coded into weight values during training.

3. *Tolerance to the noise* affecting the training set (not to outliers, i.e. to totally erroneous information!).

Obviously, there are also some drawbacks.

1. *Incertitude in the determination of the most appropriate architecture*: how many layers? How many neurones in the hidden layers? Which nodes should be connected? What value should the learning coefficient have, and how should it vary with time? There is no certain rule, even though useful discussions and empirical criteria are available (Kavzoglu, 2001). A net strives to adapt itself to data anyway and to find a reasonable solution, but it is not simple to decide *a priori* what might be the best architecture.

   Paola and Schowengerdt (1997) found empirical evidence that a net oversized with respect to the problem to be faced loses capability to generalise. Hence the utility of *pruning*, i.e. of eliminating the connections associated with almost null weight values (Kavzoglu and Mather, 1999). This incidentally also has the advantage of decreasing the computation time. As remarked in Maren (1991), this is a typical case where "*the form follows the function*":

the structure of a net strictly depends on the features of the problem it should deal with.

2. *A training time* extremely longer than that requested by a statistical classifier: an ANN is trained iteratively, not via a direct parameter computation. Once a net is trained, however, the assignment of the units submitted to it is very fast.

3. When training, a net can be stuck in a *local optimum of limited interest*, or oscillate continuously.

4. *Danger of overtraining* (see also point 1 above): the net can learn to match every small and unimportant feature of the training set so well that it loses the capability to generalise. If it has a very large number of connections, and the cases in the training set are relatively few, a net can always activate the weights sufficient to reproduce the desired output exactly. The essential information is not recognised as such and separated from noise. This is an obstacle to generalisation capability. In order to avoid overtraining, the training set must be numerous (when compared to the number of weights) and its units well distributed in the feature space.

Schematically, a training and a recognition stage can be distinguished (Hecht-Nielsen, 1990).

- In the *training stage* – a kind of programming carried out without providing a set of explicit rules – the net learns from a sample extracted from the data that will be later processed.

- In the *recognition stage* (the operational one), the net processes all input patterns using the internal structure it has developed during training.

Supervised Training: Backpropagation

In a *supervised* classification each statistical unit is assigned to one and only one class, chosen among *a set of classes defined a priori*. The units must have a numeric description, and the reality is therefore suitably modelled by associating with each unit a vector of attributes (its *features*), that describe problem-relevant aspects.

The question can then be expressed as follows: given an input sample of n patterns, find the weight values able to best produce the desired outputs. This process is called *training*, as the system learns the set of weights w_{ij} from the sample patterns.

The Multi-Layer Perceptron, trained with the *Backpropagation* method, is the best known and the most frequently used network architecture. The MLP is obtained by adding to a perceptron, that has only an input and an output layer and is unable to solve non-linearly separable problems, some intermediate (*hidden*) layers, usually one or two (Figure 2.4). The MLP can be trained to perform a given task by means of a method known as Backpropagation (of errors), based on the

Generalised Delta Rule (McClelland and Rumelhart, 1986, chap. 8; Bishop 1996, chap.6), a generalisation of the Delta Rule based on Least Mean Square proposed by Widrow and Hoff in 1960. The delta rule conforms to the Minimum Disturbance Principle: weights are modified so as to reduce the output error for the current pattern, trying to disturb as little as possible the responses already learned.

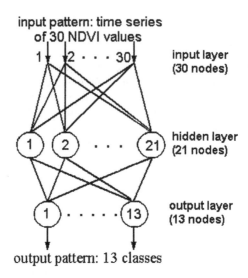

Figure 2.4 The Three-layer Feedforward Backpropagation Net (Used for the Exercise Described in next Section)
As the input images are 30, each pixel is represented by a vector with 30 components. The target themes are 13, therefore the output layer consists of 13 nodes, each representing a theme. For a pixel being classified, each output node takes a value that measures the affinity between the pixel and the theme associated with the node.

Actually, the Backpropagation method was initially proposed by Werbos (1974), but his work was largely ignored. It was then independently re-proposed by several other researchers, until McClelland and Rumelhart's final version.

The net is presented with a set of examples, each consisting of a descriptive pattern and the corresponding desired output pattern. For each pattern the output generated by the net, that depends on the current values of its weights, is compared with the expected output: the weights are modified so as to reduce the difference.

All examples included in the training set are repeatedly presented, and weights modified recursively, until the net can reproduce the desired output sufficiently well.

Weights can be updated after presenting each single pattern, or at the end of each *epoch*, i.e. after one presentation of all training units.

The Backpropagation procedure has proved valid for training nets with several layers to carry out various tasks, specially when the relationship between input and output is not linear, and training data are numerous. Unfortunately a very high number of presentation cycles is usually necessary, which makes the training process quite slow. A faster variant is the *Conjugate Gradient Method*, proposed by Johansson et al. (1992).

Teuwo Kohonen's Self-Organizing Maps (SOM)

Teuwo Kohonen (1995, 2001) proposed a particular type of ANN suitable for *unsupervised clustering*: the net is presented only with a set of input patterns, that are clustered according to their similarity.

In his most common formulation, a SOM consists of a bi-dimensional set of neurones, interconnected so as to form a rectangular or hexagonal grid (the *map*). The main difference with respect to other ANN stays in the way it learns.

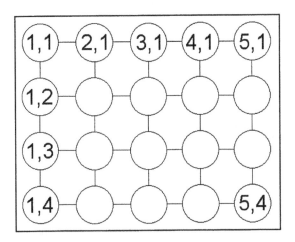

Figure 2.5 Example of a SOM with Rectangular Topology

Each node, with co-ordinates (i, j) in the map, is associated with a reference vector $m_{i,j}$, its *codebook*, having the same size as the input patterns to be clustered.

Each input pattern x is compared with all codebooks m_{ij} and assigned to the most similar one, i.e. the one closest to x in the feature space according to a suitable metrics, usually the Euclidean one. Then the winner, and the nodes lying near to it in the map, are modified so as to reinforce their similarity with x. In general, denoting with m_k the kth component of the codebook m to be modified, with x_k the corresponding component of the input pattern, with t the time when the pattern is presented, the value of the kth component at the time t+1 is:

$$m_k(t+1) = m_k(t) + h(t)[x_k(t) - m_k(t)] \qquad \forall \, k$$

The function $h(t)$, known as *neighbourhood function*, varies with the distance (on the map) between the node being modified and the winner, and with the time elapsed from the beginning of training. If $h(t)$ has the form shown in Figure 2.6, all nodes having a distance not greater than a from the winner undergo the same modification effect. Different forms of $h(t)$ can cause corrections decreasing with the distance, or inhibitive effects beyond a given distance, etc. Anyway, $h(t)$ always decreases with t in order to stabilise the net.

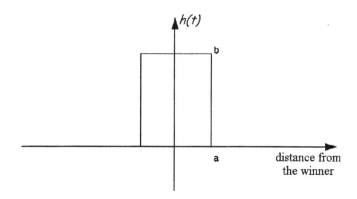

Figure 2.6 Homogeneous Neighbourhood Function
The correction affects all neurones lying on the map at a distance not greater than a from the winner.

The initial values of the codebooks m_{ij} are chosen randomly, or by regularly scanning the feature space. At the start of the training both the value of the learning coefficient, included in the $h(t)$ function, and the neighbourhood radius are quite high; this causes strong changes in the codebooks, something similar to what occurs initially with *simulated annealing* methods. These two parameters decrease with time, and slowly some codebooks emerge that satisfactorily capture the characters of the training patterns. To an increasing extent, while the training continues, similar patterns lead to the same winner and are assigned to the same class.

Once the net is trained, other statistical units can be examined, and assigned to one of the classes that spontaneously emerged. In particular, by presenting to the net patterns whose meaning is known, and observing to which node they are assigned, it is possible to attach some suitable labels to the various nodes (*map calibration*), thus helping interpretation.

While training, a SOM autonomously develops an internal organisation that causes similar input patterns to activate the same node of the map, or adjacent nodes, keeping inactive those far away. Typical applications are exploratory: it is expected that the net will *alone* discover some interesting things about a population of units described by non-structured patterns.

In addition to Kohonen's mentioned books, also Carpenter and Grossberg (1991) can be usefully referred to.

An Exercise: Land Cover Classification via a Feedforward Backpropagation Net

This section presents a quite complex application that illustrates some of the problems mentioned before. It focuses on the selection of a good training set, and on how available ancillary information can be used to orient the assignment of pixels to the classes.

A first statistical version of the methodology described in this section was conceived and utilised during research financed by the European Commission.[6] Among other ancillary information, that research used a 275m raster map of CORINE:[7] a 1100m PELCOM pixel included 16 CORINE pixels exactly.

Later, in another research co-financed by MIUR (the Italian Ministry of Scientific Research) the methodology was modified and implemented via a neural network, with improved results. A sample land cover classification of Southern Italy was presented in Griguolo (2001). The example presented here deals with the North Eastern part of the Mediterranean Region and uses as input a time series of more geometrically precise images, collected by the SPOT4-VEGETATION sensor.[8]

The information in CORINE was used to extract from the VEGETATION images a set of presumably almost *pure* pixels: i.e., pixels that consisted of CORINE sub-pixel largely (at least 14 out of 16) belonging to the same theme. They were

---

[6] The PELCOM (Pan-Europe Land Cover Monitoring) project was financed in the 4th Framework, Environment and Climate. Its goal was the creation of a raster land cover map of the European continent at the 1.1 km scale, based on NOAA-AVHRR images. Once completed, the map was used as one of the inputs in the construction of some environmental and meteorological dynamic models at the continental scale. The PELCOM legend included 13 main target themes while some other themes, like *internal water, wetlands* and *urban,* were derived from existing masks. The results were published in several papers, in particular Mucher et al., 1999 and 2001 (the PELCOM final report).

[7] CORINE (*Co-ORdination of INformation on the Environment*, CEC 1993), built under the supervision of the *European Environment Agency*, is the most detailed existing database, at the 1:100.000 scale, of the land cover of a large part of the European continent. CORINE was produced through visual interpretation of high resolution imagery (LANDSAT-TM and SPOT-XS). Its legend included 44 classes, mostly oriented towards Landscape and Ecology.

[8] SPOT4-VEGETATION images (at 1km resolution) have been available since 1998, when the SPOT4 platform was launched. The geometrical quality is very good, and steady over time, so that VGT images are particularly suitable for multitemporal applications. Thanks to financial support by the European Commission, France, Italy, Belgium and Sweden, all 10-day syntheses (radiometric bands and NDVI) can be freely downloaded from the site http://free.vgt.vito.be. Files available from that site are in HDF format and zipped: a utility program to extract a sub-region at will from a whole set of distribution zipped archives, masking clouds, can be downloaded from http://cidoc.iuav.it/~silvio/crop_vgt.html.

assumed as candidates for the preparation of the training and validation sets, according to the procedure described below.

The Images, the Net and the Software

The region analysed here is a window of 750x800 pixels, centred on Greece. The input is a series of 30 ten-day (dekadal) NDVI images, observed from February to November 2001 by the SPOT4-VGT sensor. Images captured in January and December 2001 were used only for smoothing, owing to a high presence of clouds. As VGT images are distributed at the scale of 1km and in long/lat projection, while all ancillary information, derived from the PELCOM research, was at the 1.1 km scale, and in the Albers projection, the VGT images were re-projected to Albers, 1.1 km.

The objective was to create a classified map of land covers, based on pixels' yearly NDVI profiles. The classification should be carried out separately on homogeneous strata: in fact, when a region is too large, similar profiles observed in different parts of it can correspond to different land cover; conversely, the same land cover type can be represented by different NDVI profiles in different areas. For example, in mild-weather North Italy *arable land* shows a maximum of vegetation presence in summer, while in that season the same theme is characterised by a vegetation minimum in South Italy, which is much hotter and drier. The two regions cannot be classified jointly. The same is true in our example: the climate is very different in South Greece and in the interior of the Balkan peninsula, and these regions should be split into sufficiently homogeneous strata before being analysed [9]... so this should be regarded as a rough example.

After merging the input images (Figure 2.1), each pixel was represented by a time series of 30 values. Each pixel's series was checked for the presence of missing values (clouds) and completed by interpolation when possible: it was then smoothed via a moving average of order 3, eventually obtaining the input data table.

Thirteen assignment themes (the *target classes*) were assumed: they coincide with the target legend of the PELCOM research, though some themes are actually not considered in this analysis due to the scarce number of pure pixels available to train the net.

The Multi-Layer Feedforward Perceptron shown in Figure 2.4 was used, trained by Backpropagation. The input layer has 30 nodes, to which the 30 components of each pattern are presented; the output layer consists of 13 nodes, one for each target class; the hidden layer has 21 nodes.

The software freely available on the Internet (see some short notes in the References) is generally suitable for processing a low number of statistical units, while remote sensing applications generally deal with a very high number of pixels. The training set is also often numerous.

General purpose packages, like SNNS (Stuttgarter Neuronale Netze Symulator) or the Rochester Simulator, can implement a high variety of net architectures, yet this generality entails consistent overheads that burden execution. For this reason,

---

[9] The PELCOM research adopted the stratification proposed by the FIRS European Project (Kennedy et al., 1993).

and to implement the original *knowledge-based* method described below, it was expedient to write some problem-specific software, able to deal directly and efficiently with binary images.

Three programs were used in sequence, each of them automatically reading the output of the one that precedes.

1. The first prepares the input and output sets for training and validation, in binary format.

2. The second trains the net on a set of pixels that are candidates for training or validation. While training, the net progressively detects and eliminates outliers from each class. The net trained on the training set is saved to file, while the one developed to clean the validation set from outliers is not used further.

3. The last program loads the previously trained net from file and assigns all pixels, iteratively striving to match the *a priori* knowledge. The classified image is saved to file, together with some other useful statistics.

Minor programs are used to carry out some complementary operations, like validation.

Input NDVI values are proportionally recoded from [0..255] to [0..1], so that each pattern presented to the net consists of 30 components between 0 and 1.

An output pattern is an activation vector with 13 components, each associated with one of the target themes. For pixels included in the training set, the component relative to the theme to which the pixel belongs is set to 1, the others to 0. When it assigns a pixel whose theme is unknown, the net computes an activation pattern consisting of a value for each output node (theme) and the pixel is assigned to the theme with maximum activation value.

Notice that the information offered by an output activation pattern has a kind of *fuzzy* flavour: as each *real* pixel is actually a mix of the basic themes included in the training set, its activation pattern computed by the net can be thought to represent its relative similarity with the various themes included in the training set. Though it is eventually assigned to the prevalent class, thus obtaining a hard classification, the information computed by the net is much more complex and rich. In particular, the activation pattern can indicate that a pixel is not sufficiently similar to *any* target class, and that further investigation is necessary.

The supervised classification sequence consists of the following steps.

1. Two iterative selections are carried out *separately* on two sets of presumably *pure* pixels, aimed at producing two sets that offer a reliable representation of the target themes. One of them will be used to train the neural classifier, the other to validate the final classification.

2. All pixels are assigned to the classes, using the available *a priori* knowledge during the assignment procedure.

3. The quality of the classification is assessed.

The Iterative Selection of the Training Pixels

By repeatedly examining the training set, formed by pairs of vectors representing an input pattern and the corresponding desired output, the net gradually modifies its internal parameters and learns to compute, for each input pattern, the associated output. In our example only the weights are adapted, but some examples exist in the literature in which the net architecture itself is modified.

Obviously, a good matching can be achieved only if the training set is not internally contradictory, as happens when pixels with identical or very similar descriptions are declared to belong to very different themes. Hence the extreme care necessary in the selection of a good training set: as far as possible, unreliable cases must be eliminated. In order to capture possibly existing non-linear relations, the net itself should select the training set pixels, by adapting a procedure already conceived for a statistical classifier and described in Griguolo (2000).

The Net makes use of a Backpropagation procedure with momentum[10] to correct its weights *after the presentation of each pixel*. The analyst sets the learning- and momentum-controlling coefficients, as well as the stopping conditions. The transfer function is a logistic.

Several learning cycles are carried out. For each of them the analyst decides how many times the learning set is presented to the net (60 presentations per cycle in our exercise). As the pixel to be presented is chosen randomly each time, its frequency of presentation is actually variable, ranging in our case between 50 and 70 per cycle approximately.

---

[10] In the learning with *momentum* the correction applied to a weight depends also on its change during the preceding iteration. It can be proved that this generally quickens the learning process, eliminating some disadvantages.

How to select a reliable set of training pixels

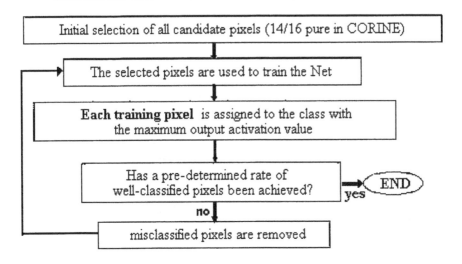

Figure 2.7 The Flowchart of the Training Set Selection

The *overall error* (defined as the sum over all training pixels of the squared differences between the computed activation array and the target array) is computed at the end of each cycle. If its value is less than that computed in the preceding cycle the net is saved and the learning process continues. If the error has not decreased, the last saved net is re-loaded and the learning process continues, looking for some other evolutionary path that may lead to an error decreasing. The random presentation of pixels and the fact that weights are updated after each presentation ensure a different evolution. The learning is terminated when the global error does not decrease any more for a number of consecutive cycles set by the analyst (five in our case).

The selection is carried out according to the scheme shown in Figure 2.7. Each time the unreliable pixels, that confuse the net and keep high the global error, are eliminated. They can be pixels misclassified in CORINE, or characterised by a highly confusing mix of themes, or subject to geometric errors, etc.

The eliminated pixels are those lying off the diagonal of the confusion matrix shown in Table 2.2. Their character according to CORINE is not confirmed by the control assignment performed by the net after being partially trained. For each theme, pixels retained after completing the procedure can be thought to make up a homogeneous and reliable core: they are used to train the net on the iteration that follows.

Table 2.2 shows the situation after the first learning phase, that encompassed 14 cycles. In each cycle all 2079 candidate pixels were presented 60 times to the net. The overall error decreased only from 3092 to 2973. The learning was far from satisfactory: the net was confused by too many *outliers*, whose descriptive patterns did not match the theme to which they were declared to belong.

Table 2.2 The *Confusion Matrix* After the First Iteration

	Arable	Irrigated	Vineyards	Orchards	Olive groves	Broadleaf forests	Coniferous forests	Mixed forests	Grassland	Scleroph., shrubs	Total
Arable	**538**	19	1	0	0	0	0	0	14	0	572
Irrigated	22	**538**	0	0	0	0	0	0	2	0	562
Vineyards	1	1	**31**	0	4	0	1	0	7	2	47
Orchards	0	7	0	**31**	7	5	2	9	0	2	63
Olive groves	0	0	0	3	**64**	0	1	2	1	1	72
Broadleaf	1	0	0	0	0	**242**	1	6	2	1	253
Coniferous	0	1	0	4	8	3	**41**	26	5	5	93
Mixed forests	0	0	0	1	10	8	6	**31**	2	2	60
Grassland	13	0	5	0	1	1	0	2	**249**	2	274
Sclerophyllous vegetation, shrubs	1	0	0	3	34	0	0	3	8	**44**	83
Total	576	566	37	42	118	259	52	79	290	60	2079

Table 2.2, known as the *confusion matrix*, shows how the net classified the pixels used to train it: the row gives the theme to which pixels in each cell are assigned by the net, while the column gives their class according to CORINE. In general, the percentage of misclassified pixels is higher for the themes for which fewer training pixels are available.

Out of the 2079 *presumably pure* pixels initially considered, the 270 misclassified ones, lying off the main diagonal of Table 2.2, were excluded.

The training continued according to the scheme shown in Figure 2.7, discarding from the training set at the end of each phase the pixels whose theme was not confirmed. Note that not all errors are equally severe, as some themes have a high degree of similarity. For example, in Table 2.2 the assignment to a different type of forest is quite tolerable, due to the mix probably occurring in each pixel.

The elimination of the 270 unreliable pixels reduced the global error computed at the beginning of the second phase from 2973 to only 223. In this example the training/selection overall process lasted three phases, each consisting of about 20 cycles of 60 complete presentations. Eventually, the value of the residual global error was reduced to 160. Table 2.3 shows the final situation: all retained training pixels were correctly classified, and the residual global error is the result of slight differences between target and computed output vectors, insufficient to produce a wrong assignment.[11] This was considered satisfactory and the selection procedure terminated.

Table 2.3 The Distribution of Pure Pixels to be Used for Training: the Final Situation when the Iterative Selection is Concluded

	Arable	Irrigated	Vineyards	Orchards	Olive groves	Broadleaf forests	Coniferous forests	Mixed forests	Grassland	Scleroph, shrubs	Total
Arable	**538**	0	0	0	0	0	0	0	0	0	538
Irrigated	0	**535**	0	0	0	0	0	0	0	0	535
Vineyards	0	0	**31**	0	0	0	0	0	0	0	31
Orchards	0	0	0	**31**	0	0	0	0	0	0	31
Olive groves	0	0	0	0	**63**	0	0	0	0	0	63
Broadleaf	0	0	0	0	0	**242**	0	0	0	0	242
Coniferous	0	0	0	0	0	0	**40**	0	0	0	40
Mixed forests	0	0	0	0	0	0	0	**28**	**0**	0	28
Grassland	0	0	0	0	0	0	0	**0**	**0**	0	249
Sclerophyllous vegetation, shrubs	0	0	0	0	0	0	0	**0**	**0**	43	43
Total	538	535	31	31	63	242	40	28	249	43	1800

The same selection procedure was then *separately* applied to the second half of the pixels, *pure* according to CORINE, that had been put apart to be used for post-classification validation. In this case four selection phases were necessary, and 1744 pixels were finally retained.

It is worth remarking that the iterative selection procedure proposed in this section is totally independent of the particular characteristics of the analysis being carried out. It can be applied to any set of pixels suspected of including *outliers*, in

---

[11] The residual global error is positive even though all training pixels are correctly assigned by the classifier being trained, as generally the computed output patterns do not perfectly match the target patterns, in which only the value of the component relative to the target theme is 1, all others being 0. The net could continue learning, striving to better match pure output pattern, also when all pixels are already correctly assigned.

order to exclude them. The only hypothesis is that a sufficient number of the pixels indicated as representative of each theme be actually appropriate and can be assumed as a reliable core, while outliers are more or less casually spread around this core in the feature space.

The "Knowledge-Based" Classification Phase

Classifications computed taking into account only the radiometric information are generally unsatisfactory. The mix of themes occurring in a pixel generally makes results uncertain: the rarest themes often appear to be spread in an almost casual way over the classified map; some themes appear at implausible elevations, etc. In order to make the classification useful and internally consistent it is necessary to improve it through the use of some suitable decision rules.

Decision rules are used to change the assignment of some pixels, so as to force results to better match the available auxiliary information. It must be noted that these rules should be applied *simultaneously and not sequentially*, otherwise the results would depend on the (arbitrary) order in which themes are processed during reassignment. The rules should therefore be applied iteratively, keeping open the possibility of undoing some of the changes already operated. This is clearly not easy.

In order to cope with this difficulty, we thought of embedding the most relevant ancillary information into the assignment procedure itself. Most of the post-classification decision rules we can devise depend on the way target themes are distributed over elevation. Such distributions can be easily computed from CORINE and a raster DTM (some examples in Figure 2.8): they enabled us to construct a *knowledge-based classification*, in which the ancillary information is directly used when pixels are assigned to themes.

This eliminated the need for explicitly formulating a set of decision rules. The results were excellent, but it must be noted that in this case both the analysis sequence and the software that implements it strongly depend upon the particular nature and structure of the data. As far as possible, this dependence should be attenuated to make the method more generally useful.

Each pixel, that a statistical classifier would assign to the theme from which its Euclidean or Mahalanobis distance is minimum, is now assigned by the net to the theme with the maximum activation value. Assignments are reviewed iteratively: at each step the activation arrays are corrected so as to keep into account (albeit not rigidly, as we will see) and progressively match the constraints implicit in the available ancillary information.

The objective is to construct a classification based on the remotely-sensed information, but also bound to reproduce the CORINE-derived distribution of the themes over suitable elevation ranges. It is worth remarking that, in order to apply the method, all that is requested is a matrix representation of some kind of distribution of the target themes, derived from the available ancillary information. The matrix depends on the classification to be constructed, and on the available ancillary data: it can describe the distribution of various crops over some type of administrative units (regions, provinces or municipalities), or the proportion of built-up/non built-up area per census tract, etc. In general, any type of information can be used that is known *a priori* and should be matched, at least in principle, by the classification results.

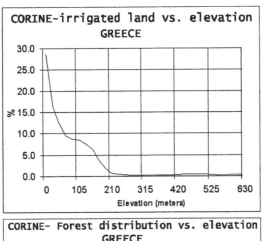

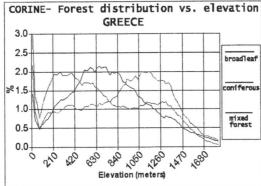

Figure 2.8 Sample Distribution of Some Themes Over Elevation, from CORINE and a Raster DTM

The assignment algorithm is described here below in some detail. The net is supposed to have been trained by a set of pixels selected as described in the preceding section.

1. The *Target* table **T**, that expresses as a matrix the available ancillary information, is defined and computed. Themes are cross-tabulated with one or more categorical variables, on the basis of published administrative or census data, or of specific computations if other kind of data is available. In our exercise, the distribution of our 13 target themes over 12 suitably defined elevation ranges was computed from CORINE. The result is a contingency table whose generic entry T_{ij} (i=1..n_ranges and j=1..n_themes) represents the frequency

of theme **j** over the **i**-th elevation range. The count units are 275m CORINE pixels.

2. Each pixel's pattern is presented to the net, that computes the corresponding output pattern. The pixel is assigned to the theme with maximum activation: The activation arrays are computed only once for all pixels and stored to file, to be re-used during all following iterations. The *Current* table **C** is computed, with exactly the same structure and meaning as **T**, but based on classification results. There are at this point two tables:

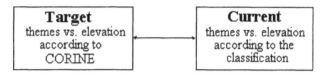

Target	**Current**
themes vs. elevation according to CORINE	themes vs. elevation according to the classification

and they generally do not coincide.

3. A table of *correction factors* CF_{ij} is defined, also sized *n_ranges* x *n_themes* like **T** and **C**. Each correction factor refers to a cell: CF_{ij} is used to correct the component of the activation array relative to theme **j**, for all pixels whose elevation range is **i**.
    The correction factors are initialised to 1, or to a conventional value meaning *impossible* when the corresponding entry T_{ij} of the target table **T** is empty, i.e. when no pixel of theme **j** exists at elevation **i** in CORINE.

Now a cycle of iterations is started, aimed at orienting the assignments, though not in a rigid way, so as to reduce the global distance between tables *Current* and *Target*:

•   the classification is iteratively modified, so as to force the computed table *Current* to match as far as possible the knowledge base represented by *Target*;

•   at the same time *Target* is also modified, albeit to a lesser extent, bringing it nearer to *Current* in order to allow for possible changes occurred in reality.

Here below, the common structure of the two tables *Target* and *Current* is shown:

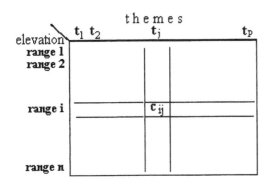

n suitably defined elevation ranges;

p target themes;

C_{ij} is the frequency of theme j at the elevation range i in the *Current* table C;

At each iteration, the probability that a pixel at elevation i be assigned to the theme j is

- increased if $C_{ij} < T_{ij}$

- decreased if $C_{ij} > T_{ij}$

Then, each iteration cycles through the following steps 4 and 5.

4. For each pixel to be assigned:

    • the activation array computed initially (purely based on radiometric data) is re-read from the binary file where it was stored, and each of its components is corrected by multiplying it by the appropriate (according to both theme and range) correction factor CF_{ij};

    • the pixel is assigned to the theme with the *maximum corrected activation value*.

5. After re-assigning all pixels:

    • the *Current* table is updated;

    • the correction factors CF_{ij} are recomputed, so as to further force C towards T on the following iteration. The correction operated is

    $$CF_{ij} \leftarrow CF_{ij} * (1 - alpha \frac{C_{ij} - T_{ij}}{(C_{ij} + T_{ij})/2})$$

    • also the *Target* table is similarly modified by moving its generic entry T_{ij} closer to C_{ij}:

    $$T_{ij} \leftarrow T_{ij} * (1 + k * alpha \frac{C_{ij} - T_{ij}}{(C_{ij} + T_{ij})/2})$$

    where *k* is a constant between 0 and 0.5, whose value is set by the analyst.

In brief, the current classification is modified so as to ease the reproduction of the themes vs. elevation table computed from CORINE; at the same time, this latter table is also modified, in order to take into some account the empirical evidence expressed by the radiometric data.

The number of iterations and the starting value *alpha0* of the correction coefficient are chosen by the analyst. The value of this coefficient is steadily decreased
during the procedure:

$$alpha = alpha0 \frac{(NIterations - current\_iteration)}{NIterations}$$

where *NIterations* is the pre-defined number of iterations, *current_iteration* is the
ordinal number of the current one (the first is 0) and *alpha0* is the initial value set
by the analyst. We used values of *alpha0* in [0.1...0.3], while a number of iterations between 40 and 100 generally proved to be sufficient for a satisfactory
convergence.

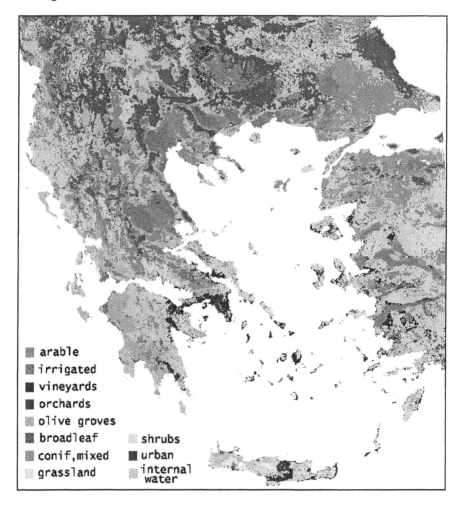

Figure 2.9 The Classified Map Issued by the *Knowledge-based* Iterative Procedure

After updating the tables **C**, **T** and **CF**, another assignment/correction cycle is started from step 4.

The Correction Factors CF_{ij} can be seen as continuously updated probabilities, derived from non-rigid *a priori* knowledge. In this sense, the approach can be considered bayesian-like.

As is obvious, *the theme to which the pixel being processed belongs in CORINE does not directly affect the assignment.* Only the tables **T** and **C** are considered, which represent some *target* and *current* aggregate distributions of the themes over the elevation ranges.

Figure 2.9 shows the classified map obtained after 100 iterations.

Validation

The validation test was done on half of the *pure* pixels, selected as described in the preceding section, Table 2.4 shows the confusion matrix. Notice that this is a validation *relative to CORINE*, not to the absolute ground truth. Coniferous and mixed forests have been merged.

Table 2.4 The Confusion Matrix for the Validation Pixels
> For each cell the column shows the pixels' theme in CORINE;
> the row gives the theme to which pixels are assigned by the ANN.

	Arable	Irrigated	Vineyards	Orchards	Olive groves	Broadleaf forests	Coniferous, mixed	Grassland	Scleroph., shrubs	Total	Reliability
Arable	521	4	0	0	0	0	0	8	0	533	97.8%
Irrigated	4	544	1	0	0	0	0	0	0	549	99.1%
Vineyards	0	0	24	0	0	0	0	4	0	28	85.7%
Orchards	0	0	1	23	1	0	0	0	0	25	92.0%
Olive groves	0	0	0	0	61	0	3	1	3	68	89.7%
Broadleaf forests	0	0	0	0	0	219	0	0	0	219	100%
Coniferous-mixed	0	0	0	0	0	5	71	0	0	76	93.4%
Grassland	3	1	0	0	0	3	4	179	1	191	93.7%
Sclerophyllous veget., shrubs	0	0	8	0	1	1	2	4	49	65	75.4%
Total	528	549	34	23	63	228	80	196	53	1754	
Accuracy %	98.7	99.1	70.6	100	96.8	96.1	88.6	91.3	92.5		

The *reliability* of the classification (for a theme) is the percentage of pixels assigned to that theme by the classifier that belong to the theme also according to the reference truth.

The *accuracy* is the percentage of pixels belonging to a theme according to the reference truth that are correctly assigned to that theme by the classifier.

Validation pixels, that are *pure*, are generally very well recognised, with a satisfactory or even excellent level of accuracy and reliability for all themes. Themes for which the accuracy is lower are those for which few training pixels were available, as could be expected.

The overall rate of well-classified pixels is 96.4%: a very high value, when compared with rates of around 80% usually obtained in similar analyses.

Some Additional Considerations

Nearly every issue of the main Remote Sensing magazines published during the last decade has included at least one application of ANN. From common land cover classification to the analysis of temporal series of images, from texture analyses to sensor fusion, from crop monitoring to tropical fire detection, from oceanography to meteorology, from the study of polar caps to the classification of clouds...the possible applications are countless.

The three-layer perceptron trained via Backpropagation used in our empirical example is the net most frequently used for supervised applications, followed by Kohonen's SOM for the unsupervised case. Also other types of nets have been applied to RS problems, especially fuzzy ARTMAP, Hopfield networks and CounterPropagation.

Fuzzy ARTMAP are based on the Adaptive Resonance Theory (ART). Some versions of ART are suitable for unsupervised pattern recognition, while fuzzy ARTMAP has been used for supervised pattern recognition on satellite images, and can deal with both binary and analogue input data. ARTMAP presents some similarity with SOM, in that nodes behave competitively and only the winner's weights are modified during the learning stage. A *vigilance parameter* is used to control the compactness of the clusters generated, so there is no need to decide *a priori* how many clusters to request. By changing the vigilance parameter, clusters with only a few units can be created, and this makes ARTMAP nets quite different from other unsupervised classifiers, like ISODATA or SOM, that tend not to allocate a specific cluster for a few units, even if very peculiar (a way to skirt this difficulty is proposed in Griguolo et al., 1997).

While a wide consensus exists on the higher accuracy achieved by neural methods, views are divergent when the compared efficiency of various ANN types is in question. According to a comparison among MLP, SOM, Fuzzy ARTMAP and CounterPropagation Networks, whose results are reported in Tso and Mather (2001), MLP gives the best results. ARTMAP appeared to train faster but its accuracy was not so good, contrary to what is claimed by Carpenter et al. (1997) or Mannan et al. (1998), according to whose opinion ARTMAP performs better than other methods, MLP included. The question is open but difficult to solve, as different nets give their best in different types of problems, and comparisons of results are often context-specific.

Several works have tried to compare the performance of statistical and neural classifiers (Benediktsson et al., 1990; Paola and Schowengerdt, 1995b; and many others). Such comparisons are difficult to carry out, and sometimes meaningless, because the results strongly depend on initial conditions, which are usually set randomly, and from which an optimum is reached that is usually only a *local one*.

The literature offers several examples of hybrid architectures, with different types of nets being coupled in original ways (the CounterPropagation is a simple case). An excellent review is offered by Paola and Schowengerdt (1995a), but some additional titles mentioned in the References give a panoramic view of the many types of ANN used in Remote Sensing applications.

A recent and interesting book by Fischer and Leung (2001) deals with the application of ANN to regional problems. Two chapters in particular are dedicated to the classification of satellite images. Kanellopoulos et al. (1997) focuses totally on the use of ANN in Remote Sensing applications.

ANN are a powerful tool, whose use is now made easier by increasingly faster computation capabilities. Patents for industrial applications number in the thousands. The theory is well mastered, and further progress depends only on the design of increasingly powerful multi-processor chips, capable of high parallel computation.

References

References mentioned in the text

Benediktsson, A., Swain, P.M., Ersoy, O.K. (1990), "Neural Networks versus Statistical Methods in Classification of Multisource Remote Sensing Data", *IEEE Transactions on GeoScience and Remote Sensing*, Vol. 28, n.4, pp. 540-552.

Bishop, M.C. (1995), *Neural Networks for Pattern Recognition*, Clarendon Press, Oxford.

Bonn, F., Rochon, G. (1996), *Précis de Télédétection*, Vol. 1, Presse de l'Université, Québec.

Carpenter, G.A., Grossberg, S., (eds) (1991) *Self-Organizing Neural Networks*, MIT Press, Cambridge, Mass.

Carpenter, G.A., Gjaja, M.N., Gopal, S., Woodcock, C.E. (1997), "ART neural networks for remote sensing: vegetation classification from Landsat TM and terrain data", *IEEE Transactions on Geoscience and Remote Sensing*, Vol. 35, pp. 308-325.

CEC (1993) *CORINE Land Cover Technical Guide*, European Union, Directorate-Generale Environment, Nuclear Safety and Civil Protection. Luxembourg.

Fischer, M.M., Leung, Y. (eds), (2001), *Geocomputational Modelling*, Springer Verlag, Berlin.

Frew, J. E. (1990), *The Image Processing Workbench*, PhD Thesis, University of California, Santa Barbara.

Gibson, P.J. (2000), *Introductory Remote Sensing – Digital Image Processing and Applications*, Routledge, London.

Griguolo, S. (2000), "Land Cover Recognition: an Example of Knowledge-based Classification", in Cankut Ormeci (ed.), *International Symposium on Remote Sensing & Integrated Technologies*, Istanbul Technical University, Istanbul, pp. 183-194.

Griguolo, S. (2001), "Neural Classification of Remotely-Sensed Images for Regional Knowledge: Embedding Ancillary Information", *Proceedings of the Conference INPUT 2001* (on CD), Tremiti Islands, June.

Griguolo, S., Cremasco, C., Ponso, M. (1997), "Immagini satellitari e riconoscimento automatico delle coperture al suolo: due metodi a confronto e qualche nuova idea su come controllarli", *Proceedings of the 18th Italian Conference of Regional Science*, Siracusa, pp. 300-324.

Hebb, D. (1949), *The Organization of Behavior: a Neuropsychological Theory*, John Wiley & Sons, New York.

Hecht-Nielsen, R. (1990) *Neurocomputing*, Addison-Wesley, New York.

Johansson, E.M.. Dowla, F.U., Goodman, D.M. (1992), "Backpropagation learning for multilayer feed-forward neural networks using the conjugate gradient method", *International Journal of Neural Systems*, 2 (4), pp. 291-301.

Kanellopoulos, I., Varfis, A., Wilkinson, G.G., Mégier, J. (1991), "Classification of Remotely-Sensed Satellite Images Using Multi-Layer Perceptron Networks"', in Kohonen T., Mäkisara K., Simula O. e Kangas J. (eds.), *Proceedings of the 1991 International Conference on Artificial Neural Networks (ICANN-91)*, Elsevier Science Publications (North-Holland), pp. 1067-1070.

Kanellopoulos, I., Wilkinson, G., Roli, F., Austin, J. (eds) (1997), *Neurocomputing in Remote Sensing Data Analysis*, Springer Verlag, Heidelberg.

Kavzoglu, T. (2001), "An investigation on the design and use of feed-forward artificial neural networks in the classification of remotely-sensed images", PhD Thesis, School of Geography, University of Nottingham.

Kavzoglu, T., Mather, P.M. (1999), "Pruning Artificial Neural Networks: an example using land cover classification of multi-sensor images", *International Journal of Remote Sensing*, **20**, pp. 2787-2803.

Kennedy, P., Folving, S., McCormick, N. (1993), "An introduction to the FIRS project", *Proceedings of the International Conference on Satellite Technology and GIS for Mediterranean Forest Mapping and Fire Management*, Thessaloniki, Greece, pp. 294-304.

Kohonen, T. (1995) *SOM_PAK - The Self-Organising Map Program Package*, University of Technology, Helsinki-Finland.

Kohonen, T. (2001) *Self Organising Maps*, Third Edition, Springer, Berlin.

Lillesand, T.M., Kiefer, R.W. (1987), *Remote Sensing and Image Interpretation*, Wiley, New York.

Mannan, B., Roy, J., Ray, A.K. (1998), "Fuzzy ARTMAP supervised classification of multispectral remotely-sensed images", *International Journal of Remote Sensing*, vol. 19, pp. 767-774.

Maren, A.J. (1991), "A Logical Topology of Neural Networks", *Proceedings of the Second Workshop on Neural Networks*, February.

Mather, P.M. (1999), *Computer Processing of Remotely-Sensed Images*, Wiley & Sons, Chichester.

McClelland, J.L., Rumelhart, D.E. (1986), *Parallel Distributed Processing*, 2 vol., MIT Press, Cambridge, Mass.

McCullock, W., Pitts, W. (1943), "A Logical Calculus of the Ideas Immanent in Nervous Activity", *Bulletin of Mathematical Biophysics*, **5**, pp. 115-133.

Minsky, M.L., Papert, S. (1969), *Perceptrons: An Introduction to Computational Geometry*. MIT Press Cambridge, Mass.

Mucher, C.A., Champeaux, J.L., Steinnocher, K.T., Griguolo, S., Wester, K., Loudjani, P. (1999), "Land Cover Characterization for Environmental Monitoring of pan-Europe", in Nieuwenhuis G.J.A., Vaughan R.A., Molenaar M. (eds.), *Operational Remote Sensing for Sustainable Development*, A.A. Balkema, Rotterdam, pp.107-112.

Mucher, C.A., Steinnocher, K.T., Champeaux, J.L., Griguolo, S., Wester, K., Heunks, C., Winiwater, W., Kressler, F.P., Goutorbe, J.P., ten Brink, B., van Katwijk, V., Furberg, O., Perdigao, V., Nieuwenhuis, G.J.A. (2001*), Development of a consistent methodology to derive land cover information on a European scale from remote sensing for environmental modelling – the PELCOM Final Report*, Centre for Geo-Information (CGI), Wageningen University. 160 pp. The Report can be downloaded from the page http://cgi.girs.wageningen-ur.nl/cgi/projects/eu/pelcom/download/FINALREP.ZIP.

Pao, Y.H. (1990), *Adaptive Pattern Recognition and Neural Networks*, Addison-Wesley, New York.

Paola, J., Schowengerdt, R.A. (1995a), "A review and analysis of backpropagation neural networks for classification of remotely-sensed multi-spectral imagery", *International Journal of Remote Sensing*, 16, pp. 3033-3058.

Paola, J., Schowengerdt, R.A. (1995b), "A detailed comparison of backpropagation neural networks and maximum likelihood classifiers for urban land use classification", *IEEE Transactions on Geoscience and Remote Sensing*, 33, pp. 981-996.

Paola, J., Schowengerdt R.A. (1997), "The effect of neural network structure on multispectral land-use/land-cover classification", *Photogrammetric Engineering and Remote Sensing*, 63, pp. 535-544.

Richards, J. A., Xiuping, Jia, 1999, *Remote Sensing Digital Image Analysis: An Introduction*, Springer Verlag, Berlin.

Ripley, B.D. (1996), *Pattern Recognition and Neural Networks*, Cambridge University Press, Cambridge, UK.

Schalkoff, R. (1992) *Pattern Recognition - Statistical, Structural and Neural Approaches*, Wiley, New York.

Simpson, P.K. (1990), *Artificial Neural Systems: Foundations, Paradigms, Applications and Implementations*, Pergamon Press, New York.

Tso, B., Mather, P.M. (2001), *Classification Methods for Remotely Sensed Data*, Taylor and Francis, London (specially focused on Neural Networks applications).

Werbos, P.J. (1974), "Beyond regression: New tools for prediction and analysis in the behavioral sciences", Masters thesis, Harvard University, Boston, Mass.

Widrow, B., Hoff, M. E. (1960), "Adaptive switching circuits", in *1960 IRE WESCON Convention Record*, IRE, New York, 96-104.

A short note on other useful material

- Two very good tutorials on Remote Sensing, among many others present on the Internet, are those available from NASA (that also consider the use of NN for image processing) at http://rst.gsfc.nasa.gov/TofC/Coverpage.html and from the Canada Centre for Remote Sensing at: www.ccrs.nrcan.gc.ca\ccrs\homepg.pl.11.html.

- The Remote Sensing FAQ, (SATFAQ), with very interesting information and links, can be accessed at http://www.geog.nott.ac.uk/remote/satfaq.html.

- The NN FAQ, maintained by Warren S. Sarle, can be downloaded from ftp://ftp.sas.com/pub/neural/FAQ.html.

- The Neuroprose FTP Archive, at Ohio University, stores many papers on ANN and their applications.
  The page is ftp://archive.cis.ohio-state.edu/pub/neuroprose.
- A rich collection of papers and public domain software is available at Finnish University Network: ftp://ftp.funet.fi/pub/sci/neural. Many pages on ANN existing on the Internet can be accessed from here.
- The *International Journal of Remote Sensing* (IJRS) has dedicated a special issue (volume 18, n. 4, 1997) to *"Neural Networks in Remote Sensing"*.
- SNNS (Stuttgarter Neuronale Netze Symulator), one of the most interesting and complete ANN packages available on the Internet, can be freely downloaded from the page: http://www-ra.informatik.uni-tuebingen.de/SNNS/.

Some other interesting links:

- http://europa.eu.int/en/comm/eurostat/research/supcom.95/16/result/final-report.html, (final report of some European research on the use of ANN in satellite image processing).
- http://www.geog.nott.ac.uk/~mather/useful_links.html (links in Prof. Paul Mather's page, University of Nottingham).
- http://www.members.tripod.com/~kavzoglu/kavzoglu.htm A very rich page, with plenty of links for both RS and NN. All Kavzoglu's publications on the classification of RS images via NNs (many of them in collaboration with P. Mather) can be downloaded, in particular his PhD thesis dealing with guidelines to design and use ANN effectively.
- http://www.fme.vutbr.cz/html/MECH/LINKS/nnlinks.html (various links on ANN).
- http://stargate.jpl.nasa.gov:1083/html/wpz.htm (applications of ANN to Remote Sensing).

Chapter 3

Spatial Interaction Modelling: Neural Network Methods and Global Optimization

Manfred Fischer and Katerina Hlavackova-Schindler

Introduction

The development of spatial interaction models is one of the most significant contributions of spatial analysis to social science literature. In more recent years, technological innovations in many areas have strongly influenced the research of spatial interaction modelling. The powerful and fast computing environment has brought many scholars to spatial interaction theory once again, by utilizing evolutionary computation to breed novel forms of spatial interaction models [see, for example Fischer and Gopal, (1994); Fischer, Hlavackova-Schindler and Reismann, (1999a and 1999b); Bergkvist, (2000); Reggiani and Tritapepe, (2000); Mozolin, Thill and Usery, (2000)] leading to neural spatial interaction models. Although the neural spatial interaction models have been inspired by neuroscience, they are more closely related to conventional spatial interaction of the gravity type than they are to neurobiological models.

Learning from examples, the problem which neural networks were designed to solve, is one of the most important research topics in artificial intelligence. A possible way to formalize learning from examples is to assume the existence of a function representing the set of examples and, thus, enabling generalization. This can be called a function reconstruction from sparse data (or in mathematical terms, approximation or interpolation problem). Within this general framework, the main issues of interest are the representational power of a given network model and the procedures for obtaining the optimal network parameters. In this contribution, the second issue, network training (i.e. parameter estimation), will be addressed.

Many training (learning) methods find their roots in function minimization algorithms, which can be classified as local or global minimization algorithms. Local minimization algorithms, such as the gradient descent and the conjugate gradient methods (for more details, see Fischer and Staufer, 1999), are fast, but usually converge to local minima. In contrast, global minimization algorithms have heuristic strategies for escaping from local minima.

Stochastic global search methods rely on probability to make decisions. The simplest probabilistic algorithm uses restarts to bring a search out of local minima when little improvement can be made locally. More advanced random search methods rely on probability to indicate whether a search should ascend from a local minimum (for example, simulated annealing), when it accepts uphill movements. Other stochastic search methods rely on probability to decide which intermediate points to interpolate as new starting points, such as random recombinations and mutations in evolutionary algorithms.

In this chapter we consider two novel approaches to parameter estimation, the Differential Evolution Method (DEM), recently introduced by Storn and Price (1996, 1997), and Alopex, originally introduced by Tzanakou and Harth in 1973, and compare their performance to the benchmark model of backpropagation of conjugate gradients in a neural spatial interaction modelling environment.

The structure of this chapter is as follows. Section 2 describes neural spatial interaction modelling. The parameter estimation problem is defined in Section 3. Section 4 discusses current best practice of learning methods. Section 5 is devoted to Differential Evolution method and to Alopex. The comparison and conclusion is discussed in Section 6.

The Neural Network Approach to Spatial Interaction Modelling

The neural network model of spatial interactions can be understood as a particular type of input-output model. Given an input vector x, the network model produces an output vector $\tilde{y}$, say $\tilde{y} = g(x)$. The function g is given by a finite set of samples (the set of input and output vectors), say $S = \{(x^k, y^k)$ with $k = 1, \ldots K\}$, so that $g(x^k) = y^k$. The task is to find a continuous function approximating S. In real world application, K is generally small and the samples contain noise.

The Neural Spatial Interaction Model

In the unconstrained case of the spatial interaction that we consider here the objective is to approximate the parameter function $g: \mathfrak{R}^3 \to \mathfrak{R}$. In practice only bounded subsets of the spaces are considered. To approximate g, the feedforward neural network models with three input units, one hidden layer that contains H hidden units, and a single output unit Ω is considered. The three input units represent measures of origin propulsiveness, destination attractiveness and spatial separation. The output unit, denoted by $\tilde{y}$, represents the estimated flow from i to j. The neural network model for the unconstrained case of spatial interaction may be written in its general form as:

$$\left\{ \Omega; \mathfrak{R}^3 \to \mathfrak{R} \,\middle|\, \tilde{y} = \Omega(x, w) = \psi\left(\sum_{h=0}^{H} \gamma_h \, \phi_h\left(\sum_{n=0}^{3} \beta_{hn} \, x_n \right) \right), x \in \mathfrak{R}^3; \gamma_h, \beta_{hn} \in \mathfrak{R} \right\} \quad (1)$$

Vector $x = (x_0, x_1, x_2, x_3)$ is the input vector augmented with a bias signal x_0 that can be thought of as being generated by a dummy unit whose output is clamped at 1. Models $\Omega(x,w)$ may have any number of hidden units ($H = 1,2 ...$) with connections from hidden to the output unit represented by γ_h. The β_{hm} represent input-to-hidden connection weights. The symbol w denotes the vector of all the β_{hm} and γ_h network weights and biases. ϕ_h and ψ are arbitrarily differentiable, generally non-linear transfer functions of the hidden units and the output unit, respectively.

Based on the *universal approximation property*, proven by Hornik, Stinchcombe and White (1989) (the ability of single hidden layer feedforward networks with an arbitrary sigmoid transfer function to approximate any continuous function to any degree of accuracy, given sufficiently many hidden units), the neural spatial interaction models used by Fischer, Hlavackova-Schindler and Reismann (1999a and 1999b)

$$\Omega_L\left(x,w\right) = \sum_{h=0}^{H}\gamma_h\left(1+\exp\left(-\sum_{n=0}^{3}\beta_{hn}\,x_n\right)\right)^{-1} \tag{2}$$

with H arbitrarily large are capable of approximating any spatial interaction function which is continuous. Network models of type (2) are unfortunately often viewed as black boxes and lead to inappropriate applications. Failures in applications are often attributed to inadequate learning (training), inadequate numbers of hidden units, or a stochastic rather than a deterministic relation between input and target.

The Parameter Estimation Problem

Having the model structure for spatial interaction prediction in the form given by (2), the network training (or learning) can be viewed in an optimization context as the parameter estimation problem solved by least squares learning. Training, the process of determining optimal parameter values, can be formulated in terms of minimization of an appropriate error function (or cost function) E to measure the degree of approximation with respect to the actual setting of network weights. The most common error function is the squared-error function of the patterns over the finite set of training data, so that the parameter estimation problem may be defined as the following minimization problem:

$$\min_{w} E(w, S) = \min_{w} \sum_{(x^k,y^k)\in S}(\Omega_L(x^k, w) - y^k)^2, \tag{3}$$

where the minimization parameter is the weight vector w defining the search space. Many learning (training) methods have their origin in function minimization algorithms, which can be classified as local or global algorithms. Local minimization methods are fast, but usually converge to local minima. In contrast, global minimization algorithms have heuristic strategies to help escape from local minima, but for the price of slower algorithms.

Current Best Practice: Local Optimization Methods

The most common learning algorithm in feedforward networks is backpropagation of gradient descent errors (see, for example, Rumelhart, Hinton and Williams, 1986). It is an optimization method based on computing of gradient vectors of the error function guaranteeing solutions which are in general only local. Although many modifications and alternatives to this parameter estimation approach have been suggested in the neural network literature over the past years, the method itself can, in general, guarantee only locally optimal solutions. The solutions, which are globally optimal, can be achieved only with implementing the stochasticity into this learning approach (Fischer and Gopal, 1994).

The error function E is a function of the adaptive model parameters, i.e. network weights and biases. The derivatives of this function with respect to the model parameters can be obtained in a computationally efficient way using the backpropagation technique (see, for example, Fischer and Staufer, 1999, for more details on the equations of this technique). The minimization of continuous differentiable functions of many variables is a problem that has been widely studied, and many of the non-linear minimization algorithms available are directly applicable to the training of neural spatial interaction. The general scheme of these algorithms can be formulated as follows:

(i)   Choose an initial vector w in parameter space and set $\tau = 1$;

(ii) Determine a search direction $d(\tau)$ and a step size $\eta(\tau)$ so that
$$E(w(\tau) + \eta(\tau)) < E(w(\tau)), \ \tau = 1,2,\ldots; \tag{4}$$

(iii) Update the parameter vector
$$w(\tau + 1) = w(\tau) + \eta(\tau)d(\tau), \ \tau = 1,2,\ldots; \tag{5}$$

(iv) If $dE(w)/dw \neq 0$ then set $\tau = \tau + 1$ and go to (ii), else return $w(\tau + 1)$ as the desired minimum.

In this paper we refer to the Polak-Ribiere variant of the conjugate gradient procedure (Press et al., 1992), a commonly used local optimization method, which is used as a benchmark in next section. This algorithm computes the sequence of search directions as:

$$d(\tau) = -\nabla E(w(\tau)) + \beta(\tau)d(\tau - 1), \ \tau = 1,2,\ldots; \tag{6}$$

with

$$d(0) = -\nabla E(w(0)), \tag{7}$$

where $\beta(\tau)$ is a scalar parameter in the form

$$\beta(\tau) = \frac{\left[\nabla E(w(\tau)) - \nabla E(w(\tau-1))\right]^T \nabla E(w(\tau))}{\nabla E(w(\tau-1))^T \nabla E(w(\tau-1))} \text{ for } \tau = 1,2,... \tag{8}$$

$w(\tau - 1)^T$ is the transpose of $w(\tau - 1)$. The definition of β (8) guarantees that for the sequence of vectors $d(\tau)$ the condition $d(\tau - 1)^T \nabla E(w(\tau)) = 0$ holds. The parameter $\eta = \eta(\tau)$ is chosen to minimize:

$$E(w(\tau) + \eta(\tau)d(\tau)), \ \tau = 1,2,...; \tag{9}$$

in the τ-th iteration. This gives the automatic procedure for setting the step length, once the search direction $d(\tau)$ has been determined.

This and other local optimization methods tend to fail, when the surface is flat (i.e. gradient is close to zero), when the gradients of consecutive steps are in a large range, and when the surface is very rugged. When gradients vary greatly, the search may progress too slowly when the gradient is small and may overshoot where the gradient is large. When the error surface is rugged, a local search from a random starting point generally converges to a local minimum close to the initial point and a worse solution than the global minimum.

Global Optimization Methods

Stochastic (or probabilistic) search methods represent a large class of global methods. The simplest probabilistic algorithm uses restarts to bring a search out of local minima when a little improvement can be made locally. More advanced random search methods rely on probability to indicate whether the search should ascend from a local minimum, for example in simulated annealing (Metropolis et al., 1953), when it accepts uphill movements. Other stochastic search methods rely on probability to decide which intermediate points to utilize for new starting points, for example recombinations and mutations in evolutionary algorithms. Central to global search methods is a strategy which generates variations of parameter vectors. Once a variation is generated, a decision has to be made whether or not to accept the newly derived trial parameters. Standard direct search methods (with few exceptions such as simulated annealing) use the greedy criterion to make the decision. Under this criterion, a new parameter vector is accepted if and only if it reduces the value of the error function. Although this decision process converges relatively fast, it has the risk of entrappment in a local minimum. Some stochastic search algorithms like genetic algorithms and evolutionary strategies employ a multipoint search strategy, in order to escape from local minima. In the following we present two stochastic search methods which were successfully applied into spatial interaction modelling by Fischer, Hlavackova-Schindler and Reismann (1999a and 1999b).

Differential Evolution Method

The Differential Evolution Method (DEM) is a global optimization algorithm, suitable for optimizing real-valued, multimodal objective functions. DEM resembles to simulated annealing in employing a random (probabilistic) strategy. But one of the apparent differentiating features of DEM is its effective implementation of parallel multipoint search. DEM maintains a collection of samples from the search space rather than a single point. This collection of samples is called *population* of trial solutions. The initial population $P(0)$ of M d-dimensional parameter vectors w_m (0), $m = 0,...,$ M is chosen randomly to cover the entire parameter space. From the initial population, subsequent populations $P(t)$, $t = 1,2,...$ are computed by iterative application of mutation, crossover and selection operators according to a given schema (more details can be found in Fischer et al., 1999b). The mutation operator is applied to three randomly chosen, mutually different vectors w_m, and their indexes are also different from running index m. See the following schema:

Stage 1. Mutation For each population member $w_m(t)$, $m = 0, 1, ..., M - 1$, a perturbed vector $w_m(t + 1)$ is generated according to:

$$v_m(t + 1) = w_{\text{best}}(t) + \kappa[w_{r1}(t) - w_{r2}(t)] \tag{10}$$

with integer indexes r1,r2 randomly chosen from $\{0, 1, ..., M - 1\}$ and different from m and mutually different. For parameter κ, which is a real constant factor controlling the amplification of the differential variation $[w_{r1}(t) - w_{r2}(t)]$ and for that holds $0 < \kappa \leq 2$. The parameter $w_{\text{best}}(t)$ which is used to yield $v_m(t + 1)$ is the best parameter vector of population $P(t)$.

Stage 2. Crossover

$$u_m(t + 1) = [u_{0m}(t + 1), ..., u_{(d-1)m}(t + 1)] \tag{11}$$

where

$$\begin{aligned} u_{km}(t + 1) &= v_{km}(t + 1) && \text{for } k = <i>_d,..., <i + R - 1>_d \\ &= w_{km}(t) && \text{for all other } k \text{ in } [0, d - 1]. \end{aligned}$$

The brackets $< >_d$ denote the modulo function with modulus d. In other words, the sequence of R co-ordinates of vector $u(t + 1)$ is identical to the corresponding co-ordinates of vector $v(t + 1)$, while the other co-ordinates of $u(t + 1)$ are retained as the original values of $w(t)$. The starting index in (11) is a randomly chosen integer from $[0, d - 1]$. The integer R is from $[0, d]$ with probability $\Pr(R = b) = (CR)^b$, where $b > 0$ and CR is in $[0, 1]$ and is the crossover probability forming a control variable for the scheme. The random decision for both I and R are made new for each newly generated trial vector $u_m(t + 1)$. $CR = 1$ implies $u_m(t + 1) = v_m(t + 1)$.

Stage 3. The decision whether or not $u_m(t + 1)$ should become a member of $P(t + 1)$ is based on the greedy criterion. If

$$E[u_m(t + 1)] < E[w_m(t)] \tag{12}$$

then $w_m(t + 1)$ is replaced by $u_m(t + 1)$ otherwise the old value $w_m(t)$ is retained as $w_m(t + 1)$.

This method employs a very simple and straightforward strategy (the main search procedure can be written in less than 30 lines of C-code). It is also very easy to be used as it needs only a few control parameters that can be chosen from well-defined numerical intervals.

DEM successfully solves the parameter estimation problem of neural spatial interaction models. A benchmark comparison to backpropagation of conjugate gradients (for more details see Fischer, Hlavackova-Schindler and Reismann 1999a and 1999b) illustrates the superiority of DEM with respect to the benchmark in terms of in-sample and out-of-sample performance, but at the very high price of computational cost. DEM seems to be a more suitable training method than local gradient optimization method when the precision of the achieved solution is more important than the training time. When using non-linear optimization algorithms such as DEM, some choice must be made when to stop the training process. Possible choices are listed below:

(i) Stop after a fixed number of iterations. The problem with this approach is that it is difficult to know *a priori* how many iterations would be appropriate. But an approximate idea can be obtained from some preliminary tests.

(ii) Stop when the error function falls below some specified value. This criterion suffers from the problem that the *a priori* specified value may never be reached so a limit on iterations as in (i) is also required.

(iii) Stop when the relative change in error function falls below some *a priori* specified value. This may lead to premature termination if the error function decreases relatively slowly during some part of the training process.

(iv) Stop training when the error measured using an independent validation set starts to increase. This approach, called early stopping or cross-validation, may be used as part of a strategy to optimize the generalization performance of the network model (see Fischer and Gopal, 1994 for details).

In practice, some combination of the above strategies may be employed as part of a largely empirical process of parameter estimation. We have chosen the first termination criterion in the experiments that will be described in the next section.

Performance test results This section presents results of our experiments and the performance of the Differential Evolution Method to solve the parameter estimation problem (3) for the neural spatial interaction model (2) with three inputs, a single hidden layer with $H = 10$ hidden units and a single output unit. The output unit represents the intensity of telecommunication flows from one origin region to a destination region and the input units the three independent variables of the classical gravity model: the potential pool of telecommunication activities in the origin region, the potential draw of telecommunication activities in the destination region, and a factor representing the inhibiting effect of geographic separation from the origin to the destination region. The goal of this neural spatial interaction model is to exhibit good generalization performance, i.e. to make good predictions for new inputs. The spatial interaction modelling prediction accuracy (generalization measured in terms of out-of-sample performance) is generally more important than fast learning. The model performance is measured in this study by the *average relative variance ARV(S)* of a set S of patterns given by (Fischer and Gopal, 1994):

$$ARV(S) = \frac{\sum_{(x^k,y^k)\in S}(y^k - \Omega_L(x^k, w))^2}{\sum_{(x^k,y^k)\in S}(y^k - \bar{y})^2}$$

$$= \frac{1}{N_S}\frac{1}{\hat{\sigma}^2}\sum_{(x^k,y^k)\in S}(y^k - \Omega_L(x^k, w))^2$$

(13)

where y^k denotes the target value and $\bar{y}$ the average over the K desired values in S. The averaging, i.e. division by N_S, makes $ARV(S)$ independent of the size of the set S. Thus $ARV(S)$ provides a normalized mean squared error metric for assessing the in-sample and out-of-sample performance of trained neural spatial interaction models. $ARV(S) = 1$ if the estimate is equivalent to the mean of the data (i.e. $\Omega_L(x^k, w) = \bar{y}$). The division by the estimated variance $\hat{\sigma}^2$ of the data removes the dependence on the dynamic range of the data. In the following experiments, the ARV set {$ARV1$, $ARV2$} will refer to the average relative error corresponding to the {training set, test set}.

The experiments were conducted using Austrian telecommunication flow data (see Fischer and Gopal, 1994 for more details). The data set was constructed from three data sources: a (32, 32)-interregional telecommunication flow matrix, a (32, 32)-distance matrix, and gross regional products for the 32 telecommunication regions. It contains 992 4-tuples (x_1, x_2, x_3, y), where the first three components represent the input vector $x = (x_1, x_2, x_3)$ and the last component the target output of the neural spatial interaction model, i.e. the telecommunication intensity from one region of origin to another region of destination. Input and target output data were preprocessed to logarithmically transformed data scaled into [0, 1]. The telecommunication data stem from network measurements of carried telecommunication traffic in Austria in 1991, in terms of erlang, which is defined as the number of phone calls (including facsimile transmission) multiplied by the average length of the call (transfer) divided by the duration of measurement. This data set was randomly divided into two separate subsets: about two thirds of the data were used for parameter estimation only, and one third as test set for assessing the generalization performance. There was no overlapping of the two sets of data. In comparison to Fischer and Gopal (1994), the data utilized was updated to take some measurement errors into account. Consequently, the results of the experimental work described below cannot be directly compared to the previous results.

Figure 3.1 The Regional System for Modelling of Interregional Telecommunication Traffic in Austria

Before applying the Differential Evolution Method to the problem at hand, values for the DEM-parameters $\kappa \in [0, 2]$, $CR \in [0, 1]$ and M, the population size must be chosen. There is no way to *a priori* define useful combinations of values. In order to identify good settings, extensive computational tests with different combinations of values have been performed. Since all simulations have similar computational complexity, iterations to converge to the optimal $ARV2$ value (measuring out-of-sample performance) were used as a measure of learning time. Each experiment (i.e. a fixed combination of DEM parameter values) was repeated six times, the network model being initialized with a different set of random weights from [–0.3, 0.3] before each trial. To enable more accurate comparisons, the population of the parameter vectors was initialized with the same six sets of ($d = 51$) random weights for all experiments. All experiments were done on a Pentium PC 400 Mhz under Linux 2.0 using the egcs-1.0.3 C-compiler. In all experiments the algorithm did run for 7000 generations.

Table 3.1 presents the results of a first series of experiments illustrating the effects of the κ-parameter (0.7, 0.8, 0.9, 1.0, 1.1) that controls the amplification of differential evolution. The crossover parameter was set to 1.0 and the cardinality M of the population to $M = 1000$. In-sample (out-of-sample) performance is measured in terms of $ARV1$ ($ARV2$). There are some considerations which are worth making. First, there is strong evidence of the robustness of the algorithm (measured in terms of standard deviation) both with respect to the choice of the DEM-parameter κ and to the choice of the initial population of the parameter vectors. Second, $\kappa = 0.9$ leads to the best result in terms of the average out-of-sample performance ($ARV2 = 0.2280$).

Evolving Cities

Table 3.1 Performance of the Differential Evolution Method:
Different Parameter Settings with $M = 1000$, $CR = 1.0$ and Varying κ

Control Parameter κ	Trial	Iterations	ARV1		ARV2	
$\kappa = 0.7$	1	181	0.2137		0.2322	
	2	116	0.2195		0.2327	
	3	152	0.2080		0.2273	
	4	350	0.2106		0.2298	
	5	128	0.2122		0.2326	
	6	373	0.2042		0.2274	
	Average	217 ±156	0.2114	(0.0047)	0.2304	(0.0023)
$\kappa = 0.8$	1	2018	0.1988		0.2297	
	2	813	0.2128		0.2327	
	3	705	0.2047		0.2328	
	4	543	0.2080		0.2323	
	5	5474	0.1912		0.2363	
	6	440	0.2128		0.2305	
	Average	1666 ± 3809	0.2047	(0.0077)	0.2307	(0.0023)
$\kappa = 0.9$	1	1218	0.2152		0.2341	
	2	456	0.2183		0.2301	
	3	4590	0.1841		0.2162	
	4	622	0.2149		0.2335	
	5	1371	0.2111		0.2244	
	6	3328	0.1912		0.2294	
	Average	1931 ± 2659	0.2058	(0.0132)	0.2280	(0.0062)
$\kappa = 1.0$	1	250	0.2426		0.2531	
	2	207	0.2305		0.2360	
	3	236	0.2297		0.2378	
	4	507	0.2255		0.2384	
	5	111	0.2459		0.2621	
	6	597	0.2246		0.2364	
	Average	318 ± 279	0.2331	(0.0082)	0.2440	(0.0100)
$\kappa = 1.1$	1	2678	0.2121		0.2312	
	2	6089	0.2068		0.2235	
	3	390	0.2294		0.2326	
	4	4243	0.2174		0.2311	
	5	884	0.2227		0.2317	
	6	4846	0.2146		0.2326	
	Average	3188 ± 2901	0.2172	(0.0073)	0.2304	(0.0032)

Average: Performance values represent the mean (standard deviation in brackets) of six
simulations differing in the initial parameter values randomly chosen from [−0.3, 0.3];
Number of *Iterations* required to reach the parameter vector that provides the best out-of-
sample performance;
*ARV*1: In-sample performance measured in terms of relative average variances;
*ARV*2: Out-of-sample performance measured in terms of relative average variances.

The second series of experiments was carried out to analyze how in-sample and out-of-sample performance changes depending on the crossover parameter CR. The κ-parameter was set at value $\kappa = 0.9$ and $M = 1,000$. The best result (averaged over the six independent simulation runs) in terms of average in-sample and out-of-sample performance, was obtained with $CR = 1.0$ (0.2058 and 0.2280; respectively). The Differential Evolution algorithm generates stable performance over the six runs.

The third series of experiments involves variation of the cardinality M, with a range of $M = 50, 100, 200, 400,$ and 1000. The CR-parameter was set at value $CR = 1.0$ and κ at 0.9. Two observations are noteworthy here. First, larger populations of parameter vectors tend to provide better results, because a large population is more likely to contain representatives from a larger number of hyperplanes. Second, the computational cost of evolving large populations does not seem to be rewarded by a comparable out-of-sample improvement of the solutions obtained, for $M > 200$. In fact, for $M = 200$ we obtained an average $ARV1$ of 0.2136 and an average $ARV2$ of 0.2276 over the six runs. For $M = 1,000$ we obtained $ARV1 = 0.2058$ and $ARV2 = 0.2280$ averaged over the six trials.

The best settings obtained over six trial runs are presented in Table 3.2.

Table 3.2 Best DEM-Parameter Settings

DEM-Parameter	Value
M	200
κ	0.9
CR	1.0

For graphical presentation, $ARV1$ and $ARV2$ indices of the best solution obtained were plotted against learning time, measured in terms of the number of iterations (see Figure 3.2). Clearly, we would like to stop when the $ARV2$ curve arrives at its minimum (i.e. after 4,590 iterations), even though ($ARV1$ and) $ARV2$ decrease only very slowly after 3,000 iterations.

For comparison purposes, we implemented the Polak-Ribiere version of conjugate gradient error backpropagation as a benchmark. The runs were made using the batch mode of operation and letting the algorithm run six times. The results of the benchmark comparison are summarized in Table 3.3.

If out-of-sample performance is more important than fast learning, then DEM exhibits superiority. As can be seen by comparing the ARV-values, DEM leads to a statistically higher prediction performance in average. The average generalization performance, measured in terms of $ARV2$, is 0.2276 (DEM) and 0.2385 (backpropagation of conjugate gradients). DEM is rather stable over the different trials. If, however, the goal is to minimize learning time and a sacrifice in generalization accuracy is acceptable, then conjugate gradient error backpropagation is the method of choice. The benchmark procedure outperforms by far the DEM in terms of execution time.

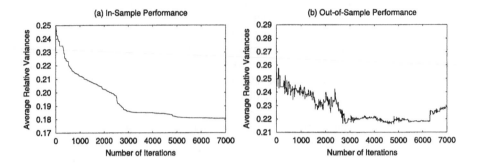

Figure 3.2   Performance of the Differential Evolution Algorithm with the Best Parameter Setting: $M = 1000$, $\kappa = 0.9$ and $CR = 1.0$ (run 3)
(a) In-sample performance; (b) Out-of-sample performance.

The Alopex Method

The method was originally introduced by Tzanakou and Harth in 1973. Consider a training data set $M = \{(x^k, y^k)$ where $k = 1, ..., K\}$ is generated by some function $g(x)$. Our objective is to find the parameter w solving (3).

Alopex is a correlation-based method for solving an optimization problem (3). The error function Q is minimized by means of weight changes, calculated for the n-th step ($n > 2$) of the iteration process in batch mode as follows:

$$w_k(n) = w_k(n-1) + \delta \ \text{sgn}(\varepsilon - p_k(n)) \tag{14}$$

where δ is the step size that has to be chosen *a priori* and ε a uniformly distributed random value with $\varepsilon \in [0,1]$. The probability of change of the parameter is calculated as:

$$p_k(n) = \left(1 + \exp\left(C_k(n)/T(n)\right)\right)^{-1} \tag{15}$$

with $C_k(n)$ given by the correlation

**Table 3.3 Benchmark Comparison of the Differential Evolution Method
($M = 200$, $\kappa = 0.9$, $CR = 1.0$) with Backpropagation of Conjugate
Gradients**

Method	Trial	ARV1		ARV2	
Differential	1	0.2068		0.2231	
Evolution Method	2	0.2182		0.2307	
$M = 200$	3	0.2087		0.2276	
$\kappa = 0.9$	4	0.2256		0.2287	
$CR = 1.0$	5	0.2128		0.2295	
	6	0.2095		0.2258	
	Average	0.2136	(0.0065)	0.2276	(0.0025)
Backpropagation	1	0.2148		0.2355	
of conjugate	2	0.2282		0.2385	
Gradients	3	0.2062		0.2256	
(Polak-Ribiere	4	0.2152		0.2357	
Method)	5	0.2140		0.2372	
	6	0.2423		0.2584	
	Average	0.2201	(0.0118)	0.2385	(0.0098)

Average: Performance values represent the mean (standard deviation in brackets) of six
simulations differing in the initial parameter values randomly chosen from $[-0.3, 0.3]$;
ARV1: In-sample performance measured in terms of relative average variances;
ARV2: Out-of-sample performance measured in terms of relative average variances.

$$C_k(n) = \left[w_k(n-1) - w_k(n-2) \right]\left[Q(x, y, w_k(n-1)) - Q(x, y, w_k(n-2)) \right]$$
$$= \left[\Delta w_k(n) \right]\left[\Delta Q(x, y, w_k(n)) \right] \tag{16}$$

The weight will be incremented in a given fixed magnitude δ, when $\Delta w_k > 0$,
and the opposite when it is less than zero. The sign of C_k indicates whether Q varies in the same way as w_k. If $C_k > 0$ both Q and w_k will be raised or lowered.
If $C_k < 0$, one will be lowered and the other one raised. If T is too small, the algorithm gets trapped into local minima of Q. Thus, the value of T for each iteration,
$T(n)$, is chosen using the following heuristic "annealing schedule":

$$T(n) = \begin{cases} \dfrac{\delta}{3HN} \displaystyle\sum_k \sum_{n'=n-N}^{n-1} |C_k(n')| & \text{if } n \text{ is a multiple of } N \\ T(n-1) & \text{otherwise} \end{cases} \tag{17}$$

where $3H$ denotes the number of weights. The annealing schedule controls the
randomness of the algorithm. When T is small, the probability of changing the pa-

rameters is around zero if C_k is negative and around one if C_k is positive. If T is large, then $p_k \cong 0.5$. This means that there is the same probability to increment or decrement the weights and that the direction of the steps is random. In other words, high values of T imply a random walk, while low values cause a better correlation guidance (see Bia, 2000). The effectiveness of Alopex in locating global minima and its speed of convergence critically depends on the balance of the size of the feedback term $\Delta w_k \Delta Q$ and the temperature T. If T is very large compared to $\Delta w_k \Delta Q$ the process does not converge. If T is too small, a premature convergence to a local minimum might occur.

The algorithm has three parameters: the initial temperature T, the number of iterations, N, over which the correlations are averaged for annealing, and the step size δ. The temperature T and the N-iterations cycles seem to be of secondary importance for the final performance of the algorithm. The initial temperature T may be set to a large value of about 1,000. This allows the algorithm to get an estimate of the average correlation in the first N iterations and reset it to an appropriate value according to Equation (14). N may be chosen between 10 and 100. In contrast to T and N, δ is a critical parameter that has to be selected with care. There is no way to *a priori* identify δ.

It has been observed that forceful training may not produce network models with adequate generalization ability, although the learning error achieved is small. The most common remedy for this problem is to monitor model performance during training to assure that further training improves generalization as well as reduces learning error. For this purpose an additional set of validation data, independent from the training data is used.

In a typical training phase, it is normal for the validation error to decrease. This trend may not be permanent, however. At some point the validation error usually reverses or its improvement is extremely slow. Then the training process should be stopped. In our implementation of the Alopex procedure, network training is stopped when $\kappa = 40,000$ consecutive iterations are unsuccessful. κ has been chosen so large at the expense of the greater training time, to ensure more reliable estimates. Of course, setting the number of unsuccessful iterations to 40,000 (or more) does not guarantee that there would be any successful steps ahead if training continued. At some stage a training algorithm may recover from some local attractor and accomplish further error minimization, but we require it should occur within a certain number of iterations. Obviously, when training is stopped, the final set of network weights does not correspond to the best result found. It is, therefore, necessary to store the parameter values in a separate array every time a successful training step is made. At the end of the training process the best set of parameter values is then recalled.

Alopex was tested on the same telecommunication data as in the case of DEM with respect to the method of backpropagation of conjugate gradients as a benchmark. Similarly, if out-of-sample performance is more important than fast learning, then Alopex exhibits superiority. As can be seen by comparing the *ARV*-values, DEM leads to a statistically higher prediction performance in average.

If the goal is to minimize learning time and a generalization accuracy is secondary, then conjugate gradient error backpropagation is a more appropriate method. The benchmark procedure outperforms Alopex in terms of execution time.

Model Estimation and the Overfitting Problem

Selection of the value for parameter δ in Alopex involves the trade-off between speed and accuracy. The approach adopted for this evaluation was stopped (cross-validation) training. The Alopex-parameters T and N were set to 1,000 and 10, respectively.

The training process depends on its starting point. The most common approach for Alopex application still uses random weight initialization to reduce fluctuation in evaluation.

The training process was stopped when $\kappa = 40,000$ consecutive iterations were unsuccessful. Extensive computational experiments with various $H-$ and $\delta-$ values have been performed on a DEC Alpha 375 Mhz. The best simulation results were achieved for the pair of $H = 16$ and $\delta = 0.0025$ for our particular application.

Typically, at the beginning of the training process, the validation error oscillates rapidly. Later, after about 5,000 iterations, the training process stabilizes and the changes in the validation error become smaller. Instead of a clear increasing trend in the validation error characterizing overfitting, it starts around 12,500 to wander around some constant value. This is caused by an increase of T in order to escape from shallow, local minima of the error surface. Later, the training process stabilizes and the changes in validation error become smaller. According to our termination criterion, training is stopped after 18,841 iterations. At this stopping point, P, the model is used for testing (prediction).

Conclusions and Outlook

This paper presented two global search methods, Differential Evolution Method and Alopex, that have been found suitable for application in spatial interaction modelling. Little is known about the behaviour of both global search procedures in real world applications. Both methods permit search over the whole parameter space, providing the possibility of escaping from local minima. They employ simple and straightforward strategies and successfully solve the parameter estimation problem of neural spatial interaction models. Both DEM and Alopex achieve better out of sample performance than the benchmark method of backpropagation of conjugate gradients, supposing that learning time is secondary. In case of primary learning time and secondary in and out-of-sample performance, the benchmark method is in both cases superior.

In the case of DEM, it needs only three control parameters that can be chosen from well defined numerical intervals. Alopex has three control parameters but it is much more difficult to set them. In our first comparison simulations, which we have recently started, Alopex seems to achieve the same in and out-of-sample performance in a shorter computing time than DEM, supposing that the control parameters are appropriately selected. However, the selection of appropriate parameters requires more testing simulations in the case of Alopex.

References

Bergkvist, E. (2000), "Forecasting Interregional Freight Flows by Gravity Models", *Jahrbuch für Regionalwissenschaft*, 20, 133-148.

Bia, A. (2000), "A Study of Possible Improvements to the Alopex Training Algorithm", *Proceedings of the VIth Brazilian Symposium on Neural Networks*, pp. 125-130, IEEE Computer Society Press.

Fischer, M.M. and Gopal, S. (1994), "Artificial Neural Networks: A New Approach to Modelling Interregional Telecommunication Flows", *Journal of Regional Science*, 34 (4), 503-527.

Fischer, M.M. and Leung, Y. (1998), "A Genetic-Algorithm Based Evolutionary Computational Neural Network for Modelling Spatial Interaction Data", *The Annals of Regional Science*, 32(3), 437-458.

Fischer, M.M., Hlavackova-Schindler and, K. Reismann, M. (1999a), "An Evolutionary Algorithm for Efficient Weight Training in Sigmoidal Neural Networks and Its Application to Spatial Interaction Modelling", *Proceedings of CIMCA'99*, pp. 54-59, IOS Press, The Netherlands.

Fischer, M.M., Hlavackova-Schindler, K. and Reismann, M. (1999b), "A Global Search Procedure for Parameter Estimation in Neural Spatial Interaction Modelling", *Papers in Regional Science*, 78, 119-134.

Fischer, M.M. and Reismann, M. (2000), "Evaluating Neural Spatial Interaction Modelling by Bootstrapping", Paper presented at the *6th World Congress of the Regional Science Association International*, Lugano, Switzerland, 16-20 May 2000 [published in *Networks and Spatial Economics*, 2 (3), pp. 255-268].

Fischer, M.M. and Staufer, P. (1999), "Optimization in an Error Backpropagation Neural Network Environment with a Performance Test on a Spectral Pattern Classification Problem", *Geographical Analysis*, 31, pp. 89-108.

Fotheringham, A.S. (1983), "A New Set of Spatial Interaction Models: The Theory of Competing Destinations", *Environment and Planning*, A 22, 527-549.

Harth, E. and Pandya, A.S. (1988), "Dynamics of ALOPEX Process: Application to Optimization Problems", in Ricciardi, L.M. (ed.), *Biomathematics and Related Computational Problems*, pp. 459-471, Kluwer, Dordrecht, Boston and London.

Hornik, K., Stinchcombe, M. and White, H. (1989), "Multilayer Feedforward Networks are Universal Approximators", *Neural Networks*, 2, 359-366.

Metropolis, N., Rosenbluth, A., Rosenbluth, M., Teller, A. and Teller, E. (1953), "Equation of State Calculations for Fast Computing Machines", *Journal of Chemical Physics*, Vol. 21, pp. 1087-1092.

Mozolin, M., Thill, J.-C. and Usery, E.L. (2000), "Trip Distribution Forecasting with Multiplayer Perceptron Neural Networks: A Critical Evaluation", *Transportation Research B*, 34, 53-73.

Openshaw, S. (1993), "Modelling Spatial Interaction Using a Neural Net", in Fischer, M.M. and Nijkamp, P. (eds.), *Geographic Information Systems, Spatial Modeling, and Policy Evaluation*, pp. 147-164, Springer, Berlin, Heidelberg and New York.

Openshaw, S. (1998), "Neural Network, Genetic, and Fuzzy Logic Models of Spatial Interaction", *Environment and Planning A*, 30, 1857-1872.

Press, W.H., Teukolsky, S.A., Vetterling, W.T. and Flannery, B.P. (1992), *Numerical Recipes in C: The Art of Scientific Computing*, Cambridge University Press, Cambridge.

Reggiani, A. and Tritapepe, T. (2000), "Neural Networks and Logit Models Applied to Commuters' Mobility in the Metropolitan Area of Milan", in Himanen, V., Nijkamp, P. and Reggiani, A. (eds.), *Neural Networks in Transport Applications*, pp. 111-129, Ashgate, Aldershot.

Rumelhart, D.E., Hinton, G.E. and Williams, R.J. (1986), "Learning Internal Representations by Error Propagation", in Rumelhart, D.E. and McClelland, J.L. (eds.), *Parallel Distributed Processing*, pp. 318- 362, MIT Press, Cambridge, Mass.

Storn, R. and Price K. (1996), "Minimizing the Real Functions of the ICEC'96 Contest by Differential Evolution", *IEEE Conference on Evolutionary Computation*, Nagoya, pp. 842-844.

Storn, R. and Price, K. (1997), "Differential Evolution – a Simple and Efficient Heuristic for Global Optimization Over Continuous Spaces", *Journal of Global Optimization*, 11, pp. 341-359.

Tzanakou, E. and Harth, E. (1973), "Determination of Visual Receptive Fields by Stochastic Methods", *Biophysical. Journal.*, 15, 42a.

Weigend, A.S., Rumelhart, D.E. and Huberman, B.A. (1991), "Back-Propagation, Weight-Elimination and Time Series Prediction", in Touretzki, D.S., Elman, J.L, Sejnowski, T.J. and Hinton, G.E. (eds.), *Connectionist Models: Proceedings of the 1990 Summer School*, pp. 105-116, Morgan Kaufmann Publishers, San Mateo, CA.

Chapter 4

Complexity in Sustainability: an Investigation of the Italian Urban System through Self-Reflexive Neural Networks

Lidia Diappi, Massimo Buscema and Michela Ottanà

Introduction

The notion of sustainable development developed by the most highly accredited international sources (Brundtland Report, 1987; World Conservation Union UN, 1991; ICLEI, 1993; Green Book on the Urban Environment, CEU, 1990) goes far beyond the concept of environmental protection, since it involves giving consideration to future generations and to the long-term health and integrity of the environment. It includes attention to the quality of life (and not only an increase in income), equity among people in the present (intra-generational equity), inter-generational equity (the inhabitants of the future deserve an environment with the same if not better quality than we enjoy today) as well as the social and ethical dimensions of human well-being. It also implies that any additional development should only occur if it does not exceed the load capacity of natural systems. Thus, it is evident that dealing with the difficulties of sustainable development involves solving new problems, and last but not least, the problem of effectively integrating urban policies within a multi-disciplinary context.

In fact, cities as a whole – in terms of their size, number of inhabitants and high levels of pro capita consumption – are among the entities with greatest responsibility for the current worldwide environmental crisis. But the city has, and historically has had, a major role in promoting human well-being and in offering a quality of life that is specifically related to urban values: a variety of lifestyles and social contacts, diversification of the job market, promotion of innovations, a variety of cultural options, the presence of rare and high-quality urban facilities.

Moreover the high density that characterizes cities can be used to provide more efficient environmental services (such as waste re-use and recycling, power and heating plants) and transport infrastructures, enabling a switch from cars to mass transit, so reducing the impact on the environment, and to promote more rational architectural and planning solutions that reduce natural resource depletion.

Only by considering urban capital as a *resource* capable of promoting human well-being is it possible to identify a more complex concept of sustainability, whose objective is based on a series of factors, with only some of them involving the "natural" environment.

This issue cannot therefore be addressed without involving the interactions between the *social system* (quality of life, social interaction, work, cultural and leisure opportunities), the *economic system* (level of wealth, diversification of the job market, efficiency of services and infrastructures, income and energy costs, investment opportunities) and the *physical-environmental system* (settlement morphology, climatic conditions, residential quality, parks and gardens, production technologies, energy consumption and disposal, communication technologies, road and transport networks).

The pre-conditions that are essential for the life and development of the city are only represented when there are positive interactions between the three subsystems. On the other hand, the undesirable effects of urban decay derive from negative interactions, which produce negative externalities.

The sustainability of development occurs at each territorial level with specific problematic connotations and requires adequate and specific policies. Thus, sustainability is by definition a *trans-scalar* objective.

Sustainability is an objective necessarily involving different space-time scales, but for which the urban scale expresses problems and opportunities where planning policies may play an important role.

The Italian urban system as a whole is in fact a complex and interconnected system where cities that are spatially differentiated carry out different and complementary functions. The regional identities, the cultural traditions of the inhabitants, the productive economic base and the historical and environmental assets cause interactions between the three subsystems to produce different and unpredictable results. Each city has its own problems and opportunities to utilize in a single and specific path towards sustainability.

The interactions among the above-mentioned systems (the social, the economic and the environmental) are complex and unpredictable and seem to present the opportunity for a new methodology of scientific investigation using Neural Networks. The aim of this study is to investigate the underlying relationships among the three sub-systems through a set of indicators of Italian cities, the 100 chief provincial towns, in order to verify if the underlying structure reproduces the heterogeneity of the real urban situation and allows subsets of Italian cities with similar sustainability assets or drawbacks to be identified.

The Data Base (DB), composed of 43 indicators for each city, was processed using Self-Reflexive Neural Networks (SRNN). These networks are a useful instrument for investigation and analogic questioning of the Data Base. Once the SRNN has learned the structure of weights from the DB, by querying the network with maximization or minimization of specific groups of attributes, it can read the related properties and rank the cities according to this urban profile.

In summary, based on all the various considerations, it is found that the city, along with its objective weaknesses and vulnerabilities, also has important positive factors which can be effectively implemented within a sustainable approach.

The Data Base

The definition of sustainability as a positive co-evolution between the three systems – social, economic and physical/environmental – leads to the methodology adopted. It is based on an analysis of urban conditions, using appropriate indicators selected to represent the problems and the sign of interactions (Table 4.1).

Table 4.1 The Indicators of Urban Sustainability

Externalities	*Social-environmental system*	*Social-economic system*	*Economic-environ. system*
positive	+Soc Env	+Soc Ec	+Ec Env
	1. Local cultural associations 2. Sporting event expenditure 3. Theatre and music expenditure 4. Movie expenditure 5. Health-care centres 6. Bookshops 7. Parks and gardens	16. Immigration 17. Bank deposits 18. Life insurance 19. Amount of pension 20. Per capita income 21. New companies 22. High-school students 23. Circulating vehicles (city centre excluded)	33. Separate waste collection 34. Unleaded gasoline 35. Public transport
negative	–Soc Env	–Soc Ec	–Ec Env
	8. Tumours 9. Divorces 10. Murders 11. Car thefts 12. House break-ins 13. Bank robberies 14. Fraud 15. Pick-pocketing and purse-snatchings	24. Dwelling prices 25. Protests 26. Bankruptcy declarations 27. Uncovered cheques 28. Mail waiting time 29. Telephone connection waiting time 30. Unemployment 31. Youth Unemployment 32. First pension waiting time	36. Fuel consumption 37. Water consumption 38. Domestic power consumption 39. Urban waste

- The first group of indicators is used to estimate how the quality of human life is supported by the functional-environmental structure, that offers local opportunities for social interaction, cultural and leisure activities, but also the risks of social and environmental degradation;
- the second group concerns the complex relationships between residence, work, professionalism, culture and income of the population;
- the third group is designed to measure the economic vitality of the city, the efficiency of the urban structure, the transformation and investment

opportunities to promote economic development, thus fostering social well-being; the negative externalities include the risks of economic stagnation, reduction of investments and degradation of buildings.

The interactions between variables should highlight associations of phenomena and different urban profiles. The question to be posed is the following: is it possible to evaluate urban sustainability in cities with different contexts, with major dissimilarities in terms of size, economic sectors, spatial structures, as well as dynamics of growth and decline? Since the cities differ in their institutional, historical, cultural and economic aspects, there is no uniform scale for understanding the potential for sustainability and the process of urban ranking is somewhat arbitrary. We would like to acquire insights into the underlying relationships among the indicators described above, trying to understand, within the Italian urban system, how the various ways in which each city appears are explained in terms of associations among attributes. To what extent is good economic performance linked to the quality of the environment? Is it possible to lead a comfortable life in a beautiful historical city that is poor in resources and business opportunities? How do good transport and mobility systems affect urban well-being?

Neural Networks as a Data Base Analogic Questioning Instrument

Over the last few years, artificial neural network models have generated increasing interest in urban and regional analyses (Fischer and Leung, 2001; Openshaw and Abrahart, 2000).

The idea of training the system to carry out operational capabilities independently, as an adaptive response to an information environment, is a fundamentally new approach to information processing. Openshaw (1992 and 1993), White (1989), Fischer and Gopal (1994) were pioneering scholars who realized the potential of Geocomputing in Regional Science. Recent contributions have pointed out the potential of some Auto-Associated Neural Networks when used as a data base analogic questioning instrument (McClelland, 1981; Rumelhart et al., 1986; Buscema, 1994a).

During the learning phase, these networks behave as normal pattern encoders, while during the recall phase they use specific algorithms which are different from the algorithms used during the learning phase. The algorithms allow the auto-associated neural networks to *adjust* their own answer in a certain number of steps, which is not pre-determined; moreover, during the *answer process*, they dynamically restructure their target. For this reason they have been called Self-Reflexive Neural Networks (Buscema, 1995).

Self-Reflexive Neural Networks

Self-Reflexive Neural Networks (SRNN) have been shown to be highly efficient in determining fuzzy similarities among different records in any data base (DB) and the relationship of gradual solidarity and gradual incompatibility among the different variables. Therefore, self-reflexive neural networks can be used as *prototypical* generators, as the means of discovering *ethnotypologies* and as simulators of *possible scenarios* in any data base.

Once the network has learned, it can be queried, and questions asked that we may define as:

- prototypical;
- virtual; and
- impossible.

The first question tries to identify the common relationships among variables which highlight one or more prototypes. By activating two or more properties from the DB the SRNN activates the subjects and the other connected properties which best represent those properties imposed externally. The second question searches a set of properties which are not found in any subject (city) of the DB. This does not mean that in the future it will not be possible to add other subjects to the DB that would have those same features. In some respects this is a more interesting and useful approach to querying a SRNN. In fact, we can envisage an imaginary city, which corresponds to some ideal targets (i.e. an ecological city with low pollution and high cultural facilities) and evaluate the related consequences. With the third question the network is queried about properties which cannot belong to any of the DB subjects at the same time. Nevertheless, according to the fuzzy set theory, it is possible to conceive of a subject that in some respects belongs to both types, as a fuzzy intersection of two incompatible sets of the classical set theory. This approach seems promising and may lead to insights about the relationships among urban assets while stressing the underlying common structure.

Recirculation Neural Networks (RCNN)

These networks are already known in the literature (Hinton and McClelland, 1988). The RCNN Model that we created consists of a 2-layer architecture, with three operating steps and is very distinctive. In fact, we must distinguish between *visible* and *hidden* input and output units as well as between *hypothetical* and *real* ones.

Recirculation Learning

We define the Input vector a_i^R as *Real Visible Input*. Starting from a_i^R it is possible to perform a *first step* to calculate a *Real Hidden Output* a_o^R. In a second step, retroacting from the Output to the Input, and starting from a_o^R, it is possible to calculate a *Hypothetical Visible Input*, a_i^I. In a third step, starting from a_i^I, it is possible to calculate a *Hypothetical Hidden Output* a_o^I.

Therefore, the signal in a RCNN is transferred in three steps

- t_1: Real Visible Input ($\underline{a_i^R}$)   Real Hidden Output ($\underline{a_o^R}$)

- t_2: Real Hidden Output ($\underline{a_o^R}$)   Hypothetical Visible Input ($\underline{a_i^I}$)

- t_3: Hypothetical Visible Input ($\underline{a_i^I}$)   Hypothetical Hidden Output ($\underline{a_o^I}$).

Learning occurs when the Hypothetical Visible Input (a_o^I) reproduces each Real Visible Input a_i^R; this means that the two hidden unit vectors, a_i^R and a_o^R, have created their own internal representation of the input vector a_i^R:

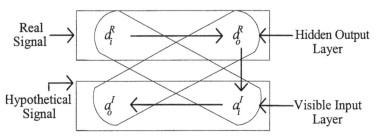

The weights matrix of a RCNN consists of *maximum gradient* connections between the Input and the Output layer. Therefore, if there are N Input Nodes a_i^R in a RCNN, the weights matrix W_{oi} will be made up of N^2 connections. The learning algorithm of the RCNN occurs in two steps; each time the signal is filtered by the Real Input (a_i^R) to the Hypothetical Output (a_o^I), two corrections are made on the same weights matrix: the first one considering the difference between the Real Input and the Hypothetical one, the second one calculating the difference between the Real and the Hypothetical Output. In this way, the RCNN converges after a very low number of cycles. The transferring equations of the signal are the following:

(1) $$a_o^R = f\left(\sum_i W_{oi} \cdot a_i^R + \theta_o\right) = f\left(Net_o^R\right) = \frac{1}{1 + Exp\left(-Net_o^R\right)} \; ;$$

(2) $$Net_i^I = \sum_o W_{io} \cdot a_o^R \; ;$$

(3) $$a_i^I = R \cdot a_i^R + (1 - R) \cdot Net_i^I \; ; \qquad 0 < R < 1$$

(4) $$Net_o^I = \sum_i W_{oi} \cdot a_i^I + \theta_o \; ;$$

(5) $$a_o^I = R \cdot a_o^R + (1 - R) \cdot \frac{1}{1 + Exp\left(-Net_o^I\right)} \; .$$

In our experimentation we have chosen $R = 0.75$.

The learning algorithm consists of two equations; each of them corrects the same W weights matrix:

(6) $\quad \Delta W_{io} = Rate \cdot a_o^R \cdot \left(a_i^R - a_i^I\right) ; \qquad 0 < 1.$

(7) $\quad \Delta W_{oi} = Rate \cdot a_i^I \cdot \left(a_o^R - a_o^I\right) ;$

(8) $\quad \Delta \theta_o = Rate \cdot \left(a_o^R - a_o^I\right) .$

The Recall Phase of the RCNN: the Re-entry

With regard to this we have developed a technique called the *Re-entry* (Buscema, 1994b).

We consider the answer of a network during the questioning phase as "*an information Input Re-entry process*" in output, for a number of steps independently decided by the same network, according to the type of input that the network is processing. We called this the *Re-entry* technique. This mechanism is used to state two important methodological concepts and creates a practical advantage. The first point of the method is the following: when reacting to a stimulus, the network not only has to handle the information internally, but it also has to *perceive* its own handling of the information. This means the information produced by the new input stimulus *must be allowed to circulate* internally, until such information has been integrated (deformed) with the previous information that the network has codified in its own weights. This *Re-entry* mechanism is internal to the Network and it is impossible to know how many re-entries a network will need in order to stabilize its own output answer for any input. The algorithm of any re-entry is very simple: it consists in "re-introducing" the output just generated by the network as a new input until the output which is generated each time stops changing:

WHILE

(9) $\quad (U_O(\text{n-1}) \neq U_O(\text{n}))$

DO

(10) $\quad U_i(\text{n+1}) = U_O(\text{n})$

where:

U_O $\quad$ = Output vector

U_i $\quad$ = Input vector

n $\quad$ = answering cycle

It is as if the actual output of the previous cycle is the target desired by the network. If this has not occurred, we carry on with the *forcing in* of the output obtained in the input of the following cycle. This simple mechanism allows the network *to process the interpretation* that it is providing to the external stimuli and to stabilize its own answer just when it has "digested" the external input through a re-evaluation of its own activity. The Re-entry configures a *meta activity* of the network, a *higher control* activity on its own activities. In this sense the name Re-entry is not a bad analogy with the concept of Re-entry drawn by Edelman in his Neural Groups Selection theory (Edelman, 1992). The second point of the method is perspective. With the re-entry it is possible to imagine a learning activity and an answering activity of the network that learns, evaluates, deforms and responds to the input stimuli that continuously activate it. There is also a practical advantage in using the re-entry when questioning a network: a network *forces its interpretation* against an unknown input as much as it can. This allows it to read the *Gestalt* of many stimuli against which those networks, which are not given the re-entry, confuse or banalize their answer.

In a Recirculation Neural Network the re-entry technique is particularly useful and simple: during the questioning phase the Real Input consists of the type of question that we want to ask the data base. Therefore, the Real Input vector is first transformed into Real Output and then into Hypothetical Input, through the transferring equations that were already described. At this point, we measure the distance between the two input vectors (Real and Hypothetical) and if this is greater than a certain tolerance value (close to zero) the Hypothetical Input values are *forced in* again in the Real Input for a second cycle. Also in this case the number of cycles which are necessary to stabilize the system is independently decided by the Recirculation Neural Network. During the learning phase the Recirculation Neural Network, through its own weights matrix, draws the *hypersurface* defined by all the variables present in the data base.

During the questioning phase, the re-entry used this hypersurface *to deform* the new input in the input vector which is nearest to those already defined by the weights matrix.

Therefore, the stabilization process of the Recirculation Neural Network occurs through a *minimization* of the internal energy of the network, starting from the perturbation that the network has undergone in the input. It is also possible, in this case, to adjust the records of the data base as an additional layer of the nodes of the Recirculation Neural Network during the questioning phase. This means that we create a new weights matrix, with the same technique described for the Constraint Satisfaction Neural Network, between the layer of the hypothetical input that represent the variable of the data base and the new layer of Nodes-Records.

The Ways of Questioning a Data Base

The Recirculation Neural Networks represent one interesting way to question a data base in an analogic manner. We could say that they function as a Structural Query Language with fuzzy borders. These networks can be used to create:

- *Dynamic simulations of scenarios*: how the entire data base would structure itself again if certain variables assumed specific values, in a stable or temporary way.

- *Associating process based on meaning*: what are the prototypical meanings of a group of variables in a specific data base and how a group of contradictory variables can work together.

Compared with other associative networks, such as Constraint Satisfaction Networks (McClelland and Rumelhart, 1988; Buscema, 1994c), these RCNN have a very different way of dealing with and trying to resolve these problems. The RCNN is a *co-operative* kind of neural network: all its units cooperate during the answering process to *minimize* the perturbation produced by the "question" asked of the data base. The answering process stabilizes on a value that is the result of a *complex negotiation* among its weights and its nodes to resolve a conflict and to maintain a *homeostasis*: this is its value but also its limit. Nevertheless, its sequential dynamics are still important and complex, since they are very similar to the associating dynamics of human memory.

Querying the Network: Some Experimental Results

After training and testing, the network learned the weights of the attributes of the Italian urban system from the 95 models (the cities). The dataset was randomly divided into two separate subsets:

- *a training set* (80%) used only for the training process;
- *a testing set* (20%) used only to verify the result of the network training performance.

The following parameter values were chosen for the training phase:

- N° of cycles: 10,000,000
- Delta Rate: 1
- Tolerance: 0.05
- Diagonal weights: <u>on</u>
- Variables were normalized.

The testing phase consisted in evaluating the real dataset of several cities compared with those produced by the network.

The query phase started from the three-way division of urban attributes (Table 4.1), by maximizing or minimizing the externalities in each group and asking the weights on the remaining attributes (Table 4.2 to Table 4.4). This approach is designed to understand the prototypical profile of cities with:

- high socio-environmental advantages;
- high socio-economic advantages;
- high economic-environmental advantages.

Table 4.2 Urban Profiles and Associated City Rankings
    Case a - activation of socio-environmental advantages and
    Case b - activation of socio-economic advantages

Case a				Item		Case b	
Bologna	0.73	1.00	+SocEnv	1) Local cultural associations	0.13	Roma	0.82
Roma	0.64	1.00		2) Sporting event expenditure	0.38	Milano	0.64
Trieste	0.60	1.00		3) Theatre and music expenditure	0.10	Bologna	0.20
Firenze	0.56	1.00		4) Movie expenditure	0.33	Firenze	0.16
Milano	0.42	1.00		5) Health-care centres	0.53	Trieste	0.14
Genova	0.42	1.00		6) Bookshops	0.14	Novara	0.10
Parma	0.38	1.00		7) Parks and gardens	0.32	Genova	0.09
Forlì	0.35	0.42	−SocEnv	8) Tumours	0.70	Torino	0.09
Piacenza	0.20	0.77		9) Divorces	0.69	Livorno	0.05
Verona	0.20	0.17		10) Murders	0.02	Venezia	0.05
Reggio E.	0.18	0.04		11) Car thefts	0.19	Verona	0.05
Modena	0.18	0.12		12) House break-ins	0.15	Ravenna	0.05
Torino	0.17	0.05		13) Bank robberies	0.12	Forlì	0.05
Pistoia	0.17	0.05		14) Frauds	0.89	Parma	0.04
Ravenna	0.16	0.79		15) Pick-pocketing and purse-snatchings	0.90	Piacenza	0.04
Livorno	0.16	0.91	+SocEc	16) Immigration	1.00	Varese	0.03
Ferrara	0.16	0.78		17) Per capita income	1.00	Modena	0.03
Lucca	0.14	0.88		18) Bank deposits	1.00	Bergamo	0.03
Siena	0.14	0.07		19) Life insurance	1.00	Brescia	0.02
Mantova	0.12	0.11		20) Amount of pension	1.00	Lucca	0.02
Vercelli	0.11	0.34		21) New companies	1.00	Cremona	0.02
Imperia	0.10	0.05		22) High school students	1.00	Ferrara	0.02
Venezia	0.10	0.03		23) Vehicles (city centre excluded)	1.00	Padova	0.02
Savona	0.10	0.25	−SocEc	24) Price of dwellings	0.73	Pistoia	0.02
Perugia	0.10	0.17		25) Protests	0.92	Siena	0.02
Arezzo	0.10	0.35		26) Bankruptcy declarations	0.94	La Spezia	0.02
Gorizia	0.10	0.04		27) Uncovered cheques	0.96	Savona	0.02
La Spezia	0.09	0.06		28) Unemployment rate	0.76	Pavia	0.02
Cremona	0.08	0.12		29) Youth unemployment	0.90	Aosta	0.02
Aosta	0.08	0.08		30) First pension waiting time	0.24	Alessandria	0.02
Udine	0.07	0.12		31) Mail waiting time	0.08	Arezzo	0.02
Grosseto	0.07	0.04		32) Telephone connection waiting time	0.32	Vicenza	0.02
M. Carrara	0.07	0.15	+EcEnv	33) Separate waste collection	0.08	Terni	0.02
Alessandria	0.06	0.04		34) Unleaded gasoline	0.34	Brescia	0.02
Pesaro	0.06	0.60		35) Public transport	0.07	Vercelli	0.01

Case a   **Case b**

Ancona	0.06	0.02		36) Fuel consumption	0.29	Como	0.01
Trento	0.06	**0.89**		37) Water consumption	0.32	Reggio E.	0.01
Alessandria	0.06	**0.60**		38) Domestic power consumption	0.20	Bari	0.01
Bolzano	0.05	0.44	**−EcEnv**	39) Urban waste	0.85	Trento	0.01
		0.16		40) Resident population	0.66		
		0.03		41) Density	0.96		
		0.12		42) Birth rate	0.94		
		0.81		43) Death rate	0.64		

A different meaning of the query leads to minimizing the negative externalities in each group. In this case the cities present:

- low socio-environmental drawbacks;
- low socio-economic drawbacks;
- low economic-environmental drawbacks.

On the other hand, by maximizing the negative externalities it is possible to evaluate the structure of cities with:

- high socio-environmental drawbacks;
- high socio-economic drawbacks;
- high economic-environmental drawbacks.

The Maximization of Socio-Environmental Quality

(Input: Indicators 1 to 7 = +1) (Table 4.2 - Case a)

High environmental quality and richness of social opportunities arise with an efficient and attractive socio-economic system (high income, bank deposits, immigration). If the economic system seems to favour social well-being, however, it produces undesirable social degradation. Crime increases and urban life tends to cause families to break up. Furthermore, negative externalities arise in the economic-environmental system, with an increase in natural resource consumption. The quality of the advantages considered does not seem to be linked to particular environmental or innovative management of the city. With regard to economic factors this type of city is efficient and has a low level of business risk. Large cities are the most representative elements of this group, such as Bologna, Roma, Trieste, Firenze, Milano, Genova and Parma.

The Rich and Economically Efficient City

(Input: var. 16 to 23 = +1) (Table 4.2 - Case b)

The mere presence of an efficient economic system does not necessarily lead to social well-being. Competition between firms makes it difficult to establish new companies and there is a high risk of bankruptcy and insolvency. There is no strong correlation between good instruments in the urban structure of the first group and/or the environmental properties of the third group. This sub-system basically interacts with itself. This prototype of city is based mainly on scale economies and on the local business sector and lacks urban spatial organization. The cities in this group are Roma, Milano and Bologna.

Cities that are Able to Efficiently Manage the Environment
(Input: var. 33 to 35 = +1)

The urban instruments for environmental protection imply that there is an environmentally sensitive attitude to urban management, which is mainly present in large cities. In fact many negative externalities arise within this context, related to business risk and crime, even though they co-exist with high income, savings and accumulated wealth. The cities in this group are: Milano, Bologna, Roma and Firenze. Reversing the logic of querying the data base, we can ask the network to determine the attributes that minimize the negative impacts.

Cities with Low Socio-Environmental Risks
(Input: var. 8 to 15 = –1) (Table 4.3 - Case c)

This type of questioning is designed to identify the socio-economic profile of cities with low crime, reduced health risks and family stability. While the preceding queries resulted in the emergence of big cities, this question leads to the appearance of medium-size cities. While the metropolis maximizes the qualities and performance generated by high urban benefits, the intermediate cities display a more agreeable and less aggressive social environment. High birth rates, high income and high consumption, a dynamic level of economic activity, even if not without risks, and a pleasant urban environment with availability of green areas and shopping facilities, are the main features of these cities, which are mainly located in the north-central part of Italy. This group and the following include mainly cities in the North and in the Centre of Italy (Figure 4.1).

Cities with Low Socio-Economic Risks
(Input: var. 24 to 32 = –1) (Table 4.3 - Case d)

Administrative efficiency, high employment rates, affordable housing and low business risk are all elements which do not, however, define a particularly good lifestyle, and probably refer to an elderly population, with high mortality and diseases, family break-ups, a fair level of urban amenities and consumption patterns tending more towards private than social life. The cities in this group include: Gorizia, Reggio Emilia, Trieste, Modena, Aosta, Parma, Bologna, Vercelli and Livorno.

Cities with High Economic-Environmental Risks
(Input: var. 36 to 39 = –1)

The urban profile emerging from this query confirms the description made in the third query: there is an innovative vision of environmental urban problems and an environmentally-compatible behaviour of the population, combined with an efficient transport system based on public transport and the presence of green areas. A difficult economic environment with a high business mortality rate and consequent unemployment for young people seems to show that the environmental policies were carried out in an attempt to solve increasing urban problems deriving from scale diseconomies.

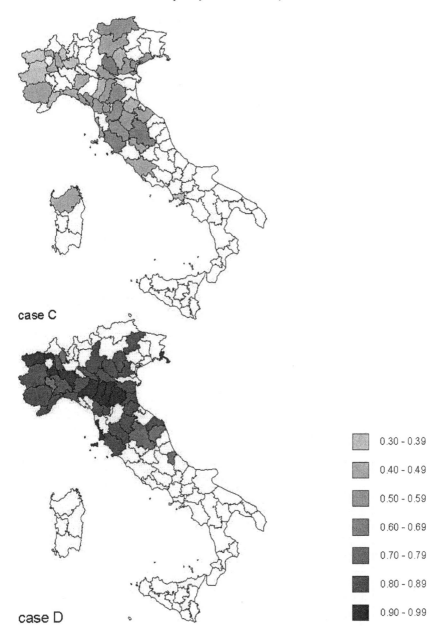

case C

case D

▫	0.30 - 0.39
▫	0.40 - 0.49
▫	0.50 - 0.59
▫	0.60 - 0.69
▪	0.70 - 0.79
▪	0.80 - 0.89
■	0.90 - 0.99

Figure 4.1   The Cities Obtained by Querying the Recirculation Neural Network to Minimize the Urban Risks
On the top: (Case c) low socio-environmental and, on the bottom (Case d) low socio-economic risks.

In this perspective the environmental approach seems to remedy rather than to promote a movement towards urban development. The cities in this group include: Bologna, Roma, Milano, Trieste, Venezia. Other interesting results may be achieved with an opposite query, asking the network what would happen if positive externalities are activated at –1.

Table 4.3 The Minimization of Negative Externalities in the Socio-Environmental System (Case c) and Socio-Economic System (Case d) and the Associated Ranking of Cities

	Case c				Case d	
Grosseto	0.57	0.29	+SocEnv	1) Local cultural associations	0.08	Gorizia 0.91
Perugia	0.56	0.02		2) Sporting event expenditure	0.24	Reggio E. 0.91
Verona	0.56	**0.80**		3) Theatre and music expenditure	0.02	Trieste 0.88
Bolzano	0.52	0.19		4) Movies expenditure	0.04	Modena 0.88
La Spezia	0.51	0.06		5) Health-care centres	**0.66**	Aosta 0.88
Firenze	0.50	**0.88**		6) Bookshops	**0.61**	Parma 0.88
Venezia	0.49	**0.83**		7) Parks and gardens	0.01	Bologna 0.87
Siena	0.48	–1.00	–SocEnv	8) Tumours	**0.75**	Vercelli 0.86
Bologna	0.47	–1.00		9) Divorces	**0.56**	Livorno 0.86
M. Carrara	0.45	–1.00		10) Murders	0.12	Pavia 0.85
Trento	0.44	–1.00		11) Car thefts	0.05	Ravenna 0.84
Pesaro	0.44	–1.00		12) House break-ins	0.15	Pistoia 0.84
Piacenza	0.44	–1.00		13) Bank robberies	0.05	Mantova 0.83
Mantova	0.44	–1.00		14) Frauds	0.03	Cremona 0.83
Novara	0.43	–1.00		15) Pick-pocketing and purse-snatchings	0.02	Piacenza 0.82
Piacenza	0.42	0.03	+SocEc	16) Immigration	0.01	Savona 0.82
Livorno	0.42	0.18		17) Per capita income	0.15	Ferrara 0.82
Trieste	0.41	**0.83**		18) Bank deposits	0.33	Forlì 0.81
Pistoia	0.41	0.00		19) Life insurance	0.13	Genova 0.81
Lucca	0.40	**0.82**		20) Amount of pension	**0.59**	Grosseto 0.81
Terni	0.40	**0.85**		21) New companies	**0.82**	Torino 0.81
Roma	0.39	0.06		22) High school students	0.05	Alessandria 0.81
Arezzo	0.38	0.01		23) Vehicles (city centre excluded)	0.23	Verona 0.80
Genova	0.38	0.16	–SocEc	24) Price of dwellings	–1.00	Novara 0.79
Vercelli	0.37	**0.55**		25) Protests	–1.00	Imperia 0.78
Cuneo	0.37	**0.91**		26) Bankruptcy declarations	–1.00	Brescia 0.78
Padova	0.36	0.00		27) Uncovered cheques	–1.00	Ancona 0.78
Modena	0.35	0.04		28) Unemployment rate	–1.00	Arezzo 0.78
Sassari	0.35	0.36		29) Youth unemployment	–1.00	Siena 0.77
Varese	0.34	**0.58**		30) First pension waiting time	–1.00	Cuneo 0.77
Vicenza	0.34	**0.79**		31) Mail waiting time	–1.00	Lucca 0.76
Milano	0.33	0.23		32) Telephone connection waiting time	–1.00	Vicenza 0.76

Case c   **Case d**

City				Variable		City	
Napoli	0.33	0.00	+EcEnv	33) Separate waste collection	0.04	Belluno	0.76
Reggio E.	0.33	**0.82**		34) Unleaded gasoline	0.06	Padova	0.75
Torino	0.32	**0.82**		35) Public transport	0.01	Asti	0.74
Napoli	0.32	0.01		36) Fuel consumption	0.02	Perugia	0.74
Forlì	0.31	0.33		37) Water consumption	0.05	Pescara	0.74
Savona	0.31	0.09		38) Domestic power consumption	**0.91**	Macerata	0.73
Aosta	0.31	0.36	−EcEnv	39) Urban waste	0.09	Varese	0.73
		0.05		40) Resident population	0.01		
		0.01		41) Density	0.00		
		0.78		42) Birth rate	0.18		
		0.06		43) Death rate	**0.65**		

Lack of Socio-Environmental Opportunities
(Input: var. 1 to 7 = −1) (Table 4.4 - Case e)
For the socio-environmental system, the poor quality of the environment is associated with high mortality and high incidence of fraud. New companies do not guarantee economic recovery; unemployment and the risk of bankruptcy are high. It should be noted (Figure 4.2) that most of the cities in this group belong to the south of Italy, such as: Caserta, Siracusa, Napoli, Trapani, Taranto, Palermo and Bari.

Lack of Socio-Economic Opportunities
(Input: var. 16 to 23 = −1) (Table 4.4 - Case f)
Only a few attributes are significantly linked to this bleak scenario of poor quality urban life: legal separations, murders and bankruptcies. This is sufficient to indicate a dramatic state of degradation. Cities of this group (Figure 4.2): Caltanisetta, Reggio Calabria, Napoli, Catanzaro, Catania, Enna and Palermo. It is worthwhile to note that, again, most cities in this group belong to the South.

Lack of Economic-Environmental Opportunities
(Input: var. 33 to 35 = −1)
The absence of environmental policies is linked to tumours, pollution and traffic, criminality, low local government efficiency, and high consumption. Again big cities, Roma, Napoli and Milano are the leading cities in this group.
It is worth noting that if we query the network by imposing a maximization of all three groups of negative externalities, Roma and Milano emerge as the worst towns. Particularly the second group, expressing socio-economic externalities, shows the evident diseconomies of scale where density is linked to mortality, diseases and criminality.

Table 4.4 Minimization of Urban Advantages in Socio-Environmental (Case e) and Socio-Economic (Case f) Systems and the Associated Ranking of Cities

Case e   Case f

City (Case e)			Group	Item	Value	City (Case f)	
Caserta	0.82	−1.00	+SocEnv	1) Local cultural associations	0.07	Caltanisetta	0.86
Siracusa	0.80	−1.00		2) Sporting event expenditure	0.02	Reggio Cal.	0.76
Napoli	0.77	−1.00		3) Theatre and music expenditure	0.01	Napoli	0.71
Trapani	0.75	−1.00		4) Movie expenditure	0.01	Catanzaro	0.69
Pordenone	0.75	−1.00		5) Fitness centres	0.03	Catania	0.66
Taranto	0.74	−1.00		6) Bookshops	**0.80**	Enna	0.64
Palermo	0.73	−1.00		7) Parks and gardens	0.35	Palermo	0.64
Bari	0.71	0.49	−SocEnv	8) Tumours	0.09	Siracusa	0.64
Rieti	0.71	0.18		9) Divorces	**0.85**	Brindisi	0.63
Bergamo	0.70	0.05		10) Murders	**0.98**	Cosenza	0.61
Enna	0.69	0.15		11) Car thefts	0.02	L'Aquila	0.60
Benevento	0.68	0.16		12) House break-ins	0.03	Potenza	0.59
Matera	0.67	0.01		13) Bank robberies	0.11	Lecce	0.55
Brindisi	0.67	**0.85**		14) Frauds	0.11	Sassari	0.55
Frosinone	0.67	0.01		15) Pick-pocketing and purse-snatchings	0.01	Nuoro	0.54
Latina	0.65	0.07	+SocEc	16) Immigration rate	−1.00	Trapani	0.54
Alessandria	0.65	0.24		17) Per capita income	−1.00	Salerno	0.53
Brescia	0.64	0.03		18) Bank deposits	−1.00	Caserta	0.52
Viterbo	0.64	0.01		19) Life insurance	−1.00	Bari	0.52
Salerno	0.64	0.39		20) Amount of pension	−1.00	Foggia	0.52
Gorizia	0.63	**0.77**		21) New companies	−1.00	Matera	0.51
Aosta	0.63	0.04		22) High school students	−1.00	Cagliari	0.51
Catanzaro	0.63	0.02		23) Vehicles (city centre excluded)	−1.00	M. Carrara	0.51
Varese	0.63	0.01	−SocEc	24) Price of dwellings	0.03	Taranto	0.51
Catanzaro	0.63	0.11		25) Protests	0.05	Roma	0.50
Catania	0.62	**0.89**		26) Bankruptcy declarations	**0.89**	Firenze	0.48
Rovigo	0.62	0.16		27) Uncovered cheques	0.01	Benevento	0.46
Avellino	0.62	**0.81**		28) Unemployment rate	0.10	Messina	0.46
Agrigento	0.61	0.25		29) Youth unemployment	0.07	Ferrara	0.46
Vicenza	0.61	0.14		30) First pension waiting time	0.15	Avellino	0.46
Campobasso	0.61	0.06		31) Mail waiting time	**0.67**	Udine	0.46
Oristano	0.61	0.16		32) Telephone connection waiting time	0.13	Aosta	0.45
Isernia	0.61	0.00	+EcEnv	33) Separate waste collection	0.00	Imperia	0.45
Treviso	0.60	0.02		34) Unleaded gasoline	0.03	Campobasso	0.43
Cagliari	0.60	0.00		35) Public transport	0.02	Trieste	0.42

Case e   **Case f**

Foggia	0.60	0.07		36) Fuel consumption	0.00	Latina	0.42
Cosenza	0.59	0.21		37) Water consumption	**0.54**	La Spezia	0.42
Lecce	0.59	0.13		38) Domestic power consumption	0.29	Ragusa	0.41
Ascoli P.	0.59	0.04	–EcEnv	39) Urban waste	0.11	Agrigento	0.41
		0.01		40) Resident population	0.00		
		0.06		41) Density	0.02		
		0.35		42) Birth rate	0.24		
		0.82		43) Death rate	0.34		

Concluding Remarks

A particularly interesting finding shown by the results is that the single set of relations among attributes of Italian cities, identified by the RCNN, is able to represent the patterns found in the different cities examined, though the cities differ significantly from each other.

The results also allow the effects of large urban size to be highlighted. It is a contradictory role since, while large cities provide greater opportunities for culture, social relations and leisure (group +SocEnv), the best opportunities for earning high incomes, education and fulfilling professional work (group +SocEc), as well as technologically efficient environmental management (group +EcEnv), yet they display the highest risks to health, safety, family stability (–SocEnv), and, from a socio-economic perspective, risks from business criminality, a high cost of living and high levels of social exclusion and unemployment.

From the results of the queries (Cases c-d) the high quality of life in medium-size cities is evident. Although they do not excel in terms of valuable urban amenities for culture, research and finance, they have fewer disadvantages for all the risk factors considered. They display greater social equity and cohesion (there is a significant absence of an underclass which is excluded from society and the labour force), and they can offer many services for people. In medium-size cities it is still possible to accumulate wealth and start up new companies and it is favoured by an environment with fewer business risks.

It should be noted, however, that the results of queries *c-d* in the groups of indicators EcEnv show little resolve to reducing environmental impact or managing the environment, which could perhaps be due to environmental emergencies being less serious in many of these cities, particularly in the north and centre of Italy.

The final questions, regarding urban profiles with lowest socio-environmental and socio-economic prospects (Cases e-f) clearly highlight the geographical location of the urban settlements identified in the queries. The most critical urban conditions are found in South Italy.

In these cities the lack of urban prospects is accompanied by a high level of widespread insecurity due to crime, poverty and social inequality, compounded by the inefficiency of public administration.

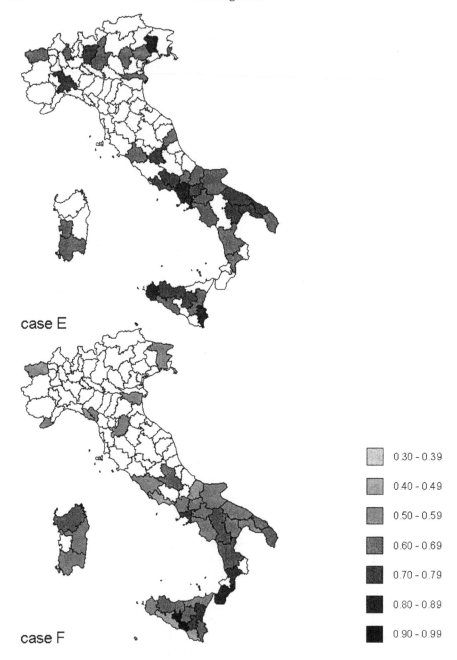

case E

case F

	0.30 - 0.39
	0.40 - 0.49
	0.50 - 0.59
	0.60 - 0.69
	0.70 - 0.79
	0.80 - 0.89
	0.90 - 0.99

**Figure 4.2   The Cities Obtained by Querying the Recirculation Neural
Network about the Minimization of Urban Opportunities**

Some remarks on the methodology: our simulations, that we queried to the network, indicated that the prototypical and virtual profiles are not copies of the representation of any particular city, but they simply indicated that the connections between those profiles and the other units in the system are such that activation of the unit will cause the pattern for the city to be reinstated on the property units. This is the reason why the results display some unexpected features when compared to urban realities.

References

Buscema, M. (1994a), "Constraint Satisfaction Networks", in M. Buscema, G. Didoné, M. Pandin, *Reti Neurali AutoRiflessive*, Quaderni di Ricerca, Armando Editore, Rome, n. 1.

Buscema, M. (1994b), *Squashing Theory*, Collana Semeion, Armando Editore, Rome.

Buscema, M. (1994c), *Constraint Satisfaction Neural Networks. Shell for Schemata Analysis*, Semeion Software n. 6, Rome, 1994.

Buscema, M. (1995), "Self-Reflexive Networks. Theory, Topology, Application", in *Quality & Quantity*, Kluwer Academic Publishers, The Netherlands, vol. 29 n. 4, November.

CEU-Commission of the European Union (1990), *Green Book on the Urban Environment*, Office of Official Publications of the European Union, Luxembourg.

Edelman, G.M (1992), *Bright Air, Brilliant Fire. On the Matter of the Mind*, Basic Books, USA.

Fischer, M.M., Gopal, S. (1994), "Artificial Neural Networks: a new approach to modeling Interregional Telecommunication flows", *Journal of Regional Science*, vol. 34(4), 503-527.

Fischer, M.M., Leung, Y. (2001), *GeoComputational Modelling - Techniques and Applications*, Springer Verlag, Berlin.

Hinton, G.E., McClelland, J.L. (1988), "Learning Representation by Recirculation", *Proceedings of IEEE Conference on Neural Information Processing Systems*, November.

ICLEI - International Council for Local Environmental Initiatives (1993), *The Local Agenda 21 Initiatives*, ICLEI Guidelines for Local and National Local Agenda 21 Campaign, Toronto.

McClelland, J.L. (1981), "Retrieving General and Specific Knowledge From Stored Knowledge of Specifics", in *Proceedings of the Third Annual Conference of the Cognitive Science Society*, Berkeley, CA.

McClelland, J.L., Rumelhart, D.E. (1988), *Explorations in Parallel Distributed Processing*, The MIT Press, Cambridge, Mass.

Openshaw, S. (1992), "Some Suggestions Concerning the Development of AI Tools for Spatial Modelling and Analysis in GIS", *Annals of Regional Science*, vol. 26, pp. 35-51.

Openshaw, S. (1993), "Modelling Spatial Interaction Using Neural Nets", in Fischer M., Nijkamp P. (eds), *GIS, Spatial Modelling and Policy Evaluation*, Springer-Verlag, Heidelberg, pp. 147-164.

Openshaw, S., Abrahart, R.J. (2000), *Geocomputation*, Taylor & Francis, London and New York.

Rumelhart, D.E., Smolensky, P., McClelland, J.L., and Hinton, G.E. (1986), "Schemata and Sequential Thought in PDP Model", in McClelland, J.L., Rumelhart, D.E. (eds.), *PDP, Exploration in the Microstructure of Cognition*, The MIT Press, Cambridge, MA, Vol. II°.

White, R. W. (1989), "The Artificial Intelligence of Urban Dynamics: Neural Net Modelling of Urban Structures", *Papers of the Regional Science Association* 67, pp. 43-53.

WCED-World Commission for Environment and Development (1987), *Brundt Land Report or Our Common Future.*

World Conservation Union (1991), *Caring for the Earth*, United Nations Environment Programme, World Wide Fund for Nature, IUNC, UNEP, WWF, Gland, CH.

PART II
LAND USE DYNAMICS THROUGH
ARTIFICIAL INTELLIGENCE TOOLS

Chapter 5

Knowledge Discovery and Data Mining to Investigate Urban and Territorial Evolution: Tools and Methodologies

Francesco Bonchi, Silvana Lombardo and Serena Pecori

Introduction

In the urban/ territorial planning process, the quality of the evaluation procedure is crucial. Quality increases, among other things, with knowledge of the dynamic behaviour of the spatial system for which decisions are required. The factors and relationships which influence this behaviour have been theorised, formalised and modelled since the birth of urban and territorial studies in many disciplines. Such theories and models (including the "dynamic revolution" of the 1980s) are based on an explicit formulation of the rules, relationships and forces which trigger actors' choices and then determine a city and territory's evolution. But, if we suppose that some of these rules and relations may now have changed in the new era of communications and globalisation, we need to develop a strongly targeted theoretical and operational field of study: knowledge building and management in the territorial planning process.

The study of *"Towns, polycentric development and urban-rural relations"* has been placed among the priority 1 measures in the ESPON 2006 Program of the European Community. This indicates the relevance of developing research work towards, on the one hand, better understanding and interpreting the evolution of urban organisation and growth and, on the other hand, towards investigating the relations between natural or agricultural land uses and urbanised areas. For this purpose it is necessary to select and implement innovative tools able to handle the huge amount of available data concerning territorial systems (statistical, economic, cartographic data and so on) in order to extract useful information from them.

In this context, we propose building cognitive systems (intelligent systems) which, on observing a given reality, are able to extract knowledge regarding the role played by urban/territorial factors and their relations in urban/territorial evolution and change.

We describe the goals and tools of the "knowledge builder and manager", and illustrate the aims in applying some of these tools to the investigation of the causes of land use change in a metropolitan context and in an urban-agricultural context.

On the basis of a survey on the state of the art in presently available tools, we selected some tools derived from Artificial Intelligence, and from the field of GIS through the elaboration of various types of available data (thematic maps, population density, transport infrastructures, productive settlements, maps of archaeological and historical heritage, etc.) we are able to extract and build knowledge directly from experimental data and also to represent the extracted knowledge very effectively and communicatively, in the form of sets of spatial transformation rules.

Large amounts of data are indeed available for analysing and simulating the evolution of urban and territorial systems: however, the value of this data mainly depends on our ability to exploit knowledge from them. To perform this task, innovative and efficient tools and methodologies can be found in the field of Data Mining and Knowledge Discovery in Database Process (the former being the core of the latter), a new technology which merges concepts and techniques from many different research areas, such as statistics, machine learning, etc.

While the first generation of studies and applications of data mining was mainly developed in fields not involving territorial considerations, in recent research a growing interest has emerged around the possibility of applying data mining techniques in order to extract useful knowledge from geographical data, using them as learning tools.

In this chapter we describe the structure of the data mining tools which are most suitable for applications in the field of urban and territorial planning, aimed at discovering the transformation rules driving the evolution of cities and the territories in analysis.

In particular, one of the tools most suitable for the aims of the work is classification: the classification-based methodology is described in detail, paying particular attention to the problems of database structure, parameter setting, pruning level, etc.

In Chapter 6 we describe the results of some experimental applications of knowledge discovery learning tools, coupled and integrated with GIS. It must be stressed that the GIS was used not only as a georeferenced archive and a quick information retrieval tool, but it was programmed in order to be integrated with the AI model and to produce additional geographic information.

We carried out two groups of experiments, connected to two different case studies:

- the effect of urban growth on the agricultural system of the Pisa urban area between 1978 and 1992;
- the evolution of land use in the metropolitan area of Rome between 1981 and 1991.

The results are illustrated in detail and evaluated.

Data Mining and Knowledge Discovery in Databases

In the past three decades, the development of database technologies has been so rapid and successful that nowadays almost every company and enterprise has stored huge quantities of data. However, whether the context is business, medicine, science, or government, the databases themselves are of little direct value. The value of storing huge volumes of data depends on our ability to extract the knowledge which is hidden in the databases and to exploit this knowledge in support of the decision-making process. This is the main goal of **Data Mining** and of the **Knowledge Discovery in Database** (KDD) process.

Many people treat the two terms, Data Mining and KDD, as synonymous. Alternatively, others view data mining simply as the core of KDD: we agree with this second view. In fact KDD is a process consisting of many steps, which enables the data analyst to progress from raw, inconsistent and noise data to interesting and actionable knowledge. Data Mining is just the main (but not the hardest or most time-consuming) step in this process. The KDD process consists of an interactive sequence of the following steps:

1. **Data Cleaning** (to remove noise and inconsistent data).
2. **Data Integration** (where multiple data sources may be combined).
3. **Data Selection** (where data relevant to the analysis task are retrieved from the database).
4. **Data Transformation** (where data are transformed or consolidated into forms appropriate for mining, for example by performing summary or aggregation operations).

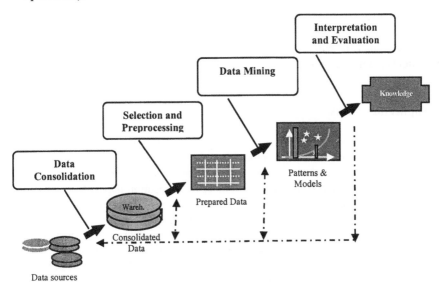

Figure 5.1 Steps in the KDD Process

5. **Data Mining** (an essential process where intelligent methods are applied in order to extract data patterns)
6. **Pattern Evaluation** (to identify the truly interesting patterns representing knowledge based on some interestingness measures)
7. **Knowledge Presentation** (where visualisation and knowledge representation techniques are used to present the mined knowledge to the user).

Figure 5.1 shows a summary of all the steps described.

KDD is a multi-disciplinary field which merges concepts and techniques from many different research areas, such as statistics, database technology, artificial intelligence, expert systems, machine learning, neural networks, pattern recognition, information retrieval, high-performance computing and data visualisation.

While each of these areas contributes in its specific ways, data mining focuses on the value that is added by creative combination of the contributing areas in order to produce innovative solutions to the data analysis task and to resolve the lacunae that each of them presents.

Expert systems, for instance, differ from discovery in databases in that the expert examples are usually of much higher quality than the "common" data stored in databases, and they usually cover only the most important cases. Furthermore, experts are available to confirm the validity and usefulness of the discovered patterns. As with database-management tools, the autonomy of discovery is lacking in these methods.

A statistical approach, although able to provide a solid theoretical foundation with regard to the problem of data analysis, is inadequate for many reasons: firstly, standard statistical methods are ill suited for the nominal and structured data types found in many databases; secondly, statistics are totally data driven, precluding the use of available domain knowledge, which is an important issue; thirdly the results of statistical analysis can be overwhelming and difficult to interpret; finally statistical methods require the guidance of the user to specify where and how to analyse data.

Application Fields

The KDD field is nowadays receiving growing attention and interest from the business world and research community.

In fact, over the past few years, research and development work in data mining has made great progress and a large number of application papers have appeared in the literature. Many successful applications have been reported in various sectors such as marketing, finance, banking, manufacturing, and telecommunications. Some examples of business applications include using data mining techniques both to analyse customer databases so that potential customers can be selected more precisely, and to analyse patterns of fraud (starting from historical data, models of fraudulent behaviour are built and used to identify similar instances).

In short, data mining systems typically help businesses to expose previously unrecognised patterns in their databases. These information "nuggets" are used to improve profits, enhance customer service, and ultimately achieve a competitive advantage.

Another typical field for data mining applications is market basket analysis. In this case, starting from such data as credit card transactions, discount coupons and so on, the principal aim is to build customer profiles (what types of customers buy what products) or to find clusters of "model" customers who share the same characteristics (interests, income level, spending habits, etc).

Applications are now being successfully developed in many other fields, such as sports, astronomy, internet web-surfing aids, text mining and so on: for this reason data mining is today considered a "hot technology" for the next decade.

In the last few years, some research has also emerged for applying data mining techniques to discover implicit knowledge in spatial databases.

In fact, with the present wide application of remote sensing technology and automatic data collection tools, a tremendous amount of spatial data has been collected and stored in databases.

Until now, statistical methods were the most common approach for analysing spatial data, but the assumption of statistical independence among the spatially-distributed data may cause problems as many data are interrelated, i.e. spatial objects are influenced by their neighbouring objects.

A spatial rule is a general description of a set of spatially-related data and is able to give the relation existing between different spatial attributes.

The principal aim of this data mining application to spatial data is to investigate the connections between the available information on territorial and urban systems and to find the relations driving both the physical and functional structure and the evolution of these systems.

In particular, by using selected mining algorithms, we aim to extract from data some sets of transformation rules which are able to give a measure of the influences existing between the various components (natural, anthropic, etc.) or the various localised activities of a certain territory.

Input Data

As we mentioned above, there is large amount of data concerning territorial and urban systems and, as one of the driving forces behind data mining tools is the emphasis on the analysis of observational data (for which the data set has not been collected to answer a particular question), we can use almost all our available information.

The initial data we adopted for our application are very heterogeneous, consisting in economic, statistical and cartographical data: in particular we mainly used thematic maps (land use maps, maps of archaeological and historical heritage, transport networks, etc.) and various kinds of census data (population density, information on productive settlements, etc.).

Before the mining phase, the primary data has to be converted into a format suitable for insertion into the algorithms. The most common mining algorithms require input data in the form of a relational table in which each line represents an elementary unit (i.e. an example).

To perform this conversion we chose to use a GIS software. Automated procedures have been constructed within GISs in order to perform various kinds of cartographic analysis (map overlays, neighbouring analysis, etc): in particular we used "map algebra" language functions (focal functions), specifically designed and very useful for geographic cell-based systems.

The general assumption of our experimental work is that the factors underlying urban change are:

1. the land use and the presence of various kinds of infrastructure in each elementary territorial cell;
2. the spatial relations of each cell with other cells, measured in terms of "strict adjacency" and "enlarged adjacency".

For each application a set of land use classes was defined, obtained by aggregating and homogenising the land use values corresponding to each map used for that application. The studied area was modelled using elementary cells (square or polygonal) and two land use values referring to two different time slices were assigned to each cell in order to study the evolution of the cell itself.

For each spatial entity there is a description (defined by means of alphanumeric attributes) of the state of the entity itself and a description of the states of the neighbouring entities. All the results were presented in the form of relational tables, using the previously quoted automated procedures within a GIS.

Figures 5.2 and 5.3 show the way in which the territory was modelled and the correspondence between cartographic and relational data (Table 5.1).

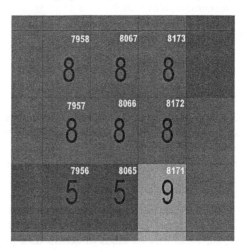

Figure 5.2 Adjacent

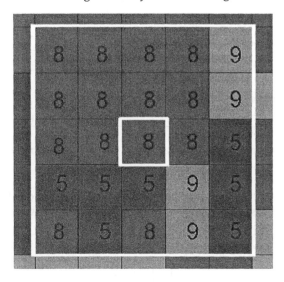

Figure 5.3 Neighbouring

Table 5.1 Report Table Corresponding to a Single Territorial Entity
(cell identified as 8066 in Figure 5.2)

Description of the "core" cell		Description of the land use of the adjacent cells									Description of the land use of the neighbouring cells									Other information
ID number	Land use	Land use 1	Land use 2	Land use 3	Land use 4	Land use 5	Land use 6	Land use 7	Land use 8	Land use 9	Land use 1	Land use 2	Land use 3	Land use 4	Land use 5	Land use 6	Land use 7	Land use 8	Land use 9	⋮
8066	8	0	0	0	0	2	0	0	5	1	0	0	0	0	7	0	0	13	4	...

Other information can be added related to the presence (in the cell and in the neighbouring cells) of roads, stations, railroads, archaeological and historical places and so on.

In this table each line represents an elementary territorial entity and each column an attribute useful for describing a characteristic of this entity. The values that each single attribute may assume can be continuous or discrete. In our applications, it was in many cases preferable to express each attribute by means of discrete quantitative values in order to more easily understand the information stored within the data set. In this case the conversion can be performed by defining a range of numerical values corresponding to a qualitative one. For instance, if we define:

For adjacent description:	0 = nothing (N) 1-2 = low (L) 3-4 = medium (M) > 4 = high (H)
For neighbouring description	0 = nothing (N) 1-5 = low (L) 5-10 = medium (M) > 10 = high (H)

the information contained in Table 5.1 can be put into the form reported in Table 5.2.

Table 5.2 Report Table Corresponding to a Single Territorial Entity (cell identified as 8066 in Figure 5.2) **with Discrete Values of Attributes**

Description of the "core" cell		Description of the land use of the adjacent cells									Description of the land use of the neighbouring cells									Other information
ID number	Land use	Land use 1	Land use 2	Land use 3	Land use 4	Land use 5	Land use 6	Land use 7	Land use 8	Land use 9	Land use 1	Land use 2	Land use 3	Land use 4	Land use 5	Land use 6	Land use 7	Land use 8	Land use 9	⋮
8066	8	N	N	N	N	L	N	N	H	L	N	N	N	N	M	N	N	H	L	......

Both of these relational tables (numerical and discrete) are in a form suitable for insertion into a mining algorithm.

Preliminary Comments on Tools and Methods for Knowledge Extraction

Two different approaches to knowledge extraction are highlighted.

- *Hypothesis Verification* is a top-down approach, which verifies predefined assertions about the data. The domain expert generates hypotheses, which are matched against the available data.
- *Knowledge Discovery* is a bottom-up approach, which starts from data and tries to induce some relevant features that are not known in advance. In this analysis, the data themselves suggest conjectures on their semantics.

When dealing with a specific case of analysis, both approaches are interleaved, switching from one to the other in different phases of the same project. In the literature, knowledge discovery is further characterised as either *directed* or *undirected*. In directed knowledge discovery, the goal of the process is to explain the value of some particular attribute in terms of others. Usually a particular attribute is selected, which is called the target, and the system is asked to estimate, classify, or predict the target attribute. In undirected knowledge discovery there is no target attribute, and the system is asked to identify patterns, or regularities, or relationships in the data that may be significant. A typical data mining tool for directed knowledge discovery is classification, whereas typical tools for undirected knowledge discovery are clustering and association rules. In this chapter, we refer to a process of directed knowledge discovery, based on classification techniques.

Classification

Classification is a daily human activity. We continually classify objects, people and situations. At its broadest, the term could cover any context in which some decision or forecast is made on the basis of currently available information, and a classification procedure is then some formal method for repeatedly making such judgments in new situations. Classification techniques are today successfully used in medicine, science, business and government.

In our context, classification is the process of finding a set of *models* (or functions) that describe and distinguish data classes or concepts, for the purpose of being able to use the model to predict the class of objects whose class label is unknown. The models are constructed by analysing database tuples described by attributes. Each tuple is assumed to belong to a predefined class, as determined by one of the attributes called the *class label attribute* (or target variable, or dependent attribute). The models describe this class label attribute on the basis of the other attributes (or *independent attributes*). The data tuples analysed are also referred to as samples, examples or objects, and are collectively referred to as a training set.

Since the class label of each training sample is provided, this kind of learning is also known as *supervised learning*, in that the analyst specifies to which classes each training sample belongs, thus the classification procedure is supervised by the human. It contrasts with *unsupervised learning* (as the clustering task) in which the objects are still grouped in classes, but the class label for each object is not known. Supervised learning corresponds to directed knowledge discovery and unsupervised learning corresponds to undirected knowledge discovery.

The derived model (also called classifier) may be represented by a set of classification (IF-THEN) rules, decision trees or neural networks. The decision tree method is the classification technique used in this paper. Such a choice is a natural one when predictive models are to be developed. In particular, decision trees are perceived as a consolidated tool with high explanatory capability, as the obtained classifiers can be readily expressed using rules, as we will show later. Simple, explanatory models are needed when, as in this case study, it is crucial to convince the user of the usefulness of the KDD approach. Neural networks can provide accurate predictions in the discrete and continuous domain: the problem is that the results are sets of mathematical formulas, that is, they are incomprehensible black boxes. Multiple regression formulas, which are the typical statistical model, are black boxes too. Some researchers have been developing rule extraction techniques from neural networks, but there are many unsolved problems in this field. Interpretability is the main reason for preferring decision trees to neural networks, but not the only one. The computation time involved in generating and using the model is a very important factor to consider when many experiments have to be conducted, and training a neural network is in general much more time consuming then inducing a decision tree. In addition, the predictive accuracy of decision trees, which is the ability of the model to correctly predict the class label of new previously unseen data, has proved to be no worse than that of neural networks.

We are aware that other classification tools may be adopted; however, the main focus of this research was the methodology needed to tailor the KDD process to the target application and to prove the usefulness of KDD for such an application.

Decision Trees

A decision tree is a flow-chart-like tree structure where:

- each internal node represents a test on an independent attribute;
- each branch represents an outcome of the test;
- each leaf node represents a class (a value of the target variable) or a class distribution.

In order to classify an unknown sample, the attributes value of the sample is tested against the decision tree, starting from the root node. The value of the leaf in which the sample falls is the class of the sample. If leaf nodes are labelled not with just one class, but with a class distribution, then this represents the probability distribution of the target variable for a sample falling in a leaf node.

In Figure 5.4 we have a decision tree to decide whether to play tennis or not. Nodes labelled with "yes" or "no" are the leaves of the tree, boxed nodes are internal nodes labelled with the test-attribute.

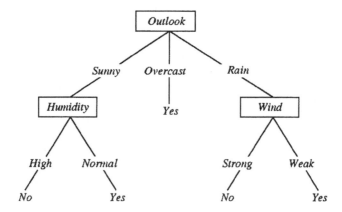

Figure 5.4 Decision Tree

Decision trees may be cumbersome, complex and inscrutable. This is due to the fact that a decision tree may have a very large size (a huge number of internal nodes) and that each internal node has its own specific context established by the outcomes of tests of parent nodes. It could therefore be very difficult to keep track of a continually changing context while scanning a large tree. This consideration seems to contradict our statement of the previous section about the interpretability of decision trees. This is not the case. The good news is that a decision tree can easily be converted to a set of classification (IF-THEN) rules which are very easy for a human to understand. One rule is created for each path from the root to a leaf node. Each attribute-value pair along a given path forms a conjunction in the antecedent rule ("IF" part). The leaf node holds the class prediction, forming the consequent rule ("THEN" part). For instance from the leftmost path of the tree in Figure 5.3 we can derive the following rule:

IF (Outlook = sunny) and (Humidity = high)
THEN PlayTennis = No

Many decision tree induction algorithms have been developed by the machine-learning community. In our experiments, we used C5.0, the most recently available version of the decision tree algorithm that J. Ross Quinlan has been evolving and refining for many years. C5.0 is an extension of the well-known C4.5 algorithm. The basic C4.5 algorithm is a greedy algorithm that constructs decision trees in a top-down recursive divide-and-conquer manner. The basic strategy is as follows.

1. The tree starts as a single node (the root node) containing all the training samples.
2. If the samples, are all of the same class, then the node becomes a leaf and is labelled with the class.
3. Otherwise the algorithm uses an entropy-based measure known as information gain as a heuristic for selecting the attribute that will best separate the samples into individual classes. This attribute becomes the "test" (or "decision" or "split") attribute at that node.
4. A branch is created for each known value (in the case of a discrete attribute) or for each generated interval (in the case of a continuous attribute), and the samples are partitioned accordingly.
5. The algorithm uses the same process recursively to form a decision tree for the sample at each partition. Once an attribute has occurred at a node, it will not be considered in any of the node's descendants.
6. The recursive partitioning stops when one of the following conditions holds:
    - all samples for a given node belong to the same class, or
    - the number of samples in the node is less than a threshold, which is given to the algorithm as an input parameter, or
    - there are no remaining attributes on which the sample may be further partitioned.

In the last two cases *majority voting* is employed: the node becomes a leaf and it is labelled with the class which forms a majority of the samples of the node. Alternatively, the class distribution of the node sample may be stored.

The criterion used to choose the split attribute is the main characteristic which differentiates one decision tree induction algorithm from another. The information gain measure used by C4.5 is an information-theoretical measure which selects the attribute which minimises the information needed to classify the samples in the resulting partitions (maximise entropy reduction), and reflects the least randomness or impurity in these partitions.

With regard to the data set we adopted for our applications, many relational tables have been built, with a different number of attributes used to describe each single cell.

This is because various classes of distance (and consequently of criteria for neighbouring cells) have been defined and tested, ranging from 500 to 2000 metres corresponding to the "importance" of each attribute.

For instance, after various trials performed using different values of neighbouring radiuses, we realised that the presence of a metro station influenced cells within a distance of about 500 metres, while the presence of a park or a railway access was felt at a greater distance (1000 or 2000 metres).

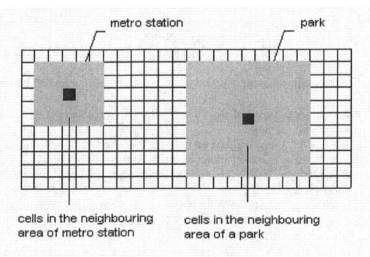

Figure 5.5 Neighbouring Radiuses Assigned to Various Attributes

For all the applications, the attribute corresponding to land use value at the second time slice was chosen as class label. In other words, a class value was assigned to each cell by adding a column to the report table, as in Table 5.3.

Table 5.3 Report Table Corresponding to a Single Territorial Entity Including Class Label

Description of the "core" cell		Description of the land use of the adjacent cells									Description of the land use of the neighbouring cells									Class label
ID number	Land use (time 1)	Land use 1	Land use 2	Land use 3	Land use 4	Land use 5	Land use 6	Land use 7	Land use 8	Land use 9	Land use 1	Land use 2	Land use 3	Land use 4	Land use 5	Land use 6	Land use 7	Land use 8	Land use 9	Land use (time 2)
8066	8	N	N	N	N	L	N	N	H	L	N	N	N	N	M	N	N	H	L	7

In such a way the extracted rules are in the form:

IF→ Description of cell and cell's neighbouring areas at the first date

THEN→ Land use at the second date

A classification task performed using a decision tree technique is more efficient if there are more numerically comparable examples corresponding to each class, while in our case the class distribution of examples was not at all homogeneous.

For instance, when applying the method to the "area of Pisa" the class distribution is as follows:

Table 5.4 Class Distribution for the "Area of Pisa"

Land use class	Number of examples (cells)	Distribution (%)
1) Continuous urbanisation	84	0.74%
2) Discontinuous urbanisation	707	6.25%
3) Productive settlement	190	1.68%
4) Crop land	6320	55.93%
5) Olive grove	226	2.00%
6) Vineyard	100	0.88%
7) Orchard	110	0.97%
8) Wood	2725	24.11%
9) Pasture land	468	4.14%
10) Beach	139	1.23%
11) River	226	2.00%

In this case, the mining algorithm simply ignores the classes with low values of X distribution (*yellow rows*) because it is not able to learn anything by observing such a small number of examples.

Various possible solutions have been tried:

1. Building a different distribution of the classes by aggregating the classes hav-
    ing a lower per cent distribution. For instance, instead of separately
    considering olive groves, vineyards and orchards we can aggregate the three
    classes in order to build a new class named, for example, "specialised cultiva-
    tion": the per cent distribution of the new class (0.97%+ 0.88%+ 2.00% =
    3.85%) will be large enough to be considered by the mining algorithm.
2. We can use a "'misclassification matrix" able to weight the classification error
    associated with different classes in a different way.
3. We can randomly eliminate some examples of the classes presenting a higher
    per cent distribution in order to make these classes comparable with the others:
    however, in our case this solution is often not appropriate, since the total num-
    ber of examples is not X high.
4. We can separately consider the examples corresponding to each class and
    build a classificator for each class.

Pruning Decision Trees

The recursive partitioning method of constructing decision trees described in the
previous section will continue to subdivide the set of training cases until some of
the stopping conditions described above are X met. The result is often an over-
complex decision tree in which many branches will reflect anomalies in the training data due to noise or outliers. This effect is called overfitting the training data.
The constructed tree learns too much the training data and thus reduces its generalisation capability. By generalisation we mean the capacity to correctly classify
new unseen data. There are basically two ways of avoiding this problem: stopping
the construction of the tree earlier or building the tree completely and then pruning
its less relevant branches.

The first approach, called early stopping or *pre-pruning*, looks the best way of
splitting a subset and if some statistical measure (such as information gain or chi
squared, etc.) falls below a pre-specified threshold, then further partitioning of the
given subset is halted and the actual node becomes a leaf.

The second approach, *post-pruning*, removes branches from a fully grown tree.
Moving bottom-up, for each internal node in the tree, a function calculates the expected error rate that would occur if the sub-tree rooted at that node were pruned. If
replacement of this sub-tree with a leaf would lead to a lower predicted error rate,
then the sub-tree is pruned accordingly.

Quinlan's C4.5 adopts the second approach. A specialised pruning algorithm is
invoked once the construction of the tree is finished. The severity of the pruning
algorithm is guided by a user-defined parameter called pruning severity level. This
parameter is an integer between 0 and 100. The higher is the value, the stronger is
the pruning (and the smaller is the resulting tree). The user can set this parameter
large to obtain smaller, more compact and more general results, or small to obtain

weaker pruning and thus larger results. If the user requests the result in form of decision rules, a further pruning is performed. First the tree is constructed, next it is pruned, then rules are extracted by the reduced tree. Finally the set of extracted rules is pruned itself to remove some useless or redundant conditions from the IF part of the rules. Using strong pruning when constructing decision rules results in a smaller set of rules with fewer conditions.

However, as already said, C4.5 also provides the opportunity to specify the minimum number of samples in a node. This can be seen as an early-stopping technique. Therefore pre-pruning and post-pruning can be interleaved for a combined approach.

In our applications we used various values of pruning for each data set, in order to obtain sets of rules characterised by various degrees of precision, that is more or less detailed.

In fact, if we increase the pruning level (in this case we cut the tree at a higher level) we obtain a lower number of attributes involved in each rule and consequently each rule involves a larger number of cases. On the other hand, if the pruning level is low, we obtain very detailed rules, each one related to a small number of cells.

Interpretation of Extracted Rules

A data mining tool is able to autonomously find all the patterns in a database, but these patterns could be too numerous and uninteresting. For this reason a data mining task should be an interactive and iterative process in which the user has to have a solid understanding of the domain in order to select the right subset of data (task-relevant ones), suitable classes of patterns and some good criteria for pattern interestingness measurements.

Once the rules have been extracted, we have to measure their interestingness. Interestingness measures and thresholds can be specified by the user in relation to his aim and various criteria may be used to decide whether some patterns are interesting or not.

Some authors support decisions on interestingness being based on subjective information provided by users, for instance:

- *Utility*: Although numerous pieces of information and patterns can be gleaned from any database, only those considered to be interesting and useful in some way are called knowledge. Naturally this is largely determined by the frame of reference, which can be either the scope of the system's knowledge or the scope of the user's knowledge.

  For example, a system might discover the following: If At-fault-accident = "Yes", Then Age > 16. To the system this piece of knowledge might be previously unknown and potentially useful; to a user trying to analyse insurance claim records, this pattern would be self-evident and not very useful.

- *Expressiveness:* The knowledge discovered should be precisely described and useful for certain applications. Discoveries must be represented in a form appropriate for the intended users. This may include natural language, formal logic or visual depictions of information. Sometimes, the discoveries from one process form the input for another process or program. In such cases, appropriate representation may include programming languages and declarative formalisms. While natural language is often desirable for human users, it is not always convenient for manipulation by discovery algorithms, hence logical representations are sometimes preferred. These are more natural for computation and can be translated into a natural language form. Common logic representations include production rules (e.g. If X, then Y), relational patterns (X < Y), decision trees (equivalent to ordered lists of rules), and semantic or causal networks. Each of these representations has certain advantages and some limitations. An appropriate choice for a discovery system depends on the application and the expected complexity of the problem and expertise of the human user.
- *Novelty:* If the rules are surprising in the light of human *a priori* knowledge regarding the domain.

Among the various methods using a subjective approach able to give a measure of interestingness, there is IAS (Interestingness Analysis System), a software product developed by some researchers at the University of Singapore. It is based on the fact that, as mentioned above, the interestingness of a rule depends on the user's existing knowledge about the domain and on his/her current interests.

IAS allows the user to specify his/her existing knowledge about the domain: the system then uses this knowledge to analyse the discovered rules according to three different degrees of preciseness, namely *general impressions, imprecise concepts, precise knowledge,* the first two types representing the user's vague feelings, the last one representing his/her precise knowledge of the domain. With respect to the user's specified knowledge the rules may conform, be partially unexpected and be completely unexpected.

Some other authors choose to look for objective measures.

- *Simplicity:* based on how easily the rules are understood, i.e. rule length, tree size.
- *Certainty:* Based on the values that assume the rule's support and confidence. There is a need to denote the degree of certainty the system or user should ascribe to a discovery. Certainty includes several factors, including the integrity of the data; the size of the sample on which the discovery was performed; and, possibly the degree of support from available domain knowledge. Without sufficient certainty, patterns may be termed as unjustified, and hence fail to be classified as knowledge.

Another approach to this problem proposes building a set of rules that together give good coverage of the search space. These researchers suggest a metric for the distance between two rules and use it to select the most heterogeneous set of rules that is possible, that is the one with the highest predictive power.

In our experiments we mainly used objective measures, so we chose the rules with the highest values of support and confidence. The thresholds were chosen, within a set of extracted rules, with regard to the numerical consistence of the examples contained in the class of each single rule.

We also tried to build a homogeneous set of rules by eliminating those rules too similar to others, in order to cover all the classes and cases but also to eliminate redundancy inside the set of results.

A subjective approach may also be used in our experiment, but the complexity of territorial systems makes it difficult to decide what is expected and what is not. For this reason our focus is mainly on trying to aggregate the extracted rules within a same set in order to obtain some more general information about the evolution of a certain territorial system. To do this we are considering the use of a clustering technique where the input data is the output set of rules obtained by using decision trees.

Chapter 6

Learning about Land Use Change in Rome and in Pisa Urban Areas

Francesco Bonchi, Silvana Lombardo, Serena Pecori and Alessandro Santucci

In this chapter we describe the results of some experimental applications of a knowledge discovery learning tool (decision trees, see previous chapter) aimed at discovering the relations and rules driving the evolution of some specific urban and territorial systems. We carried out two groups of experiments, connected to two different case-studies:

1. the effect of urban growth on the agricultural system of the "Pisa urban area" between 1978 and 1992;
2. the evolution of land use in the metropolitan area of Rome between 1981 and 1991.

For these applications, the territory was divided into elementary units whose size and shape depend on the disaggregation level and on the nature of available information. The input databases were prepared using both statistical (census data on population and economic activities) and geographical (land use, road network maps, etc) data, each referring to two different time sections. The information includes the initial and final state (land use) of each territorial unit and the quantitative and qualitative identification of the state of its neighbouring areas.

The experiments produced some sets of IF-THEN rules revealing some of the main transformation processes which took place in the studied areas in the considered time period. The results are illustrated in detail and evaluated.

Evolution of "Physical" Land Use: the Pisa Area

In the last few years there has been considerable debate about problems in the relations between city and country and the effects of urban growth on natural and agricultural areas.

For this application we chose the territory of the *Area Pisana*, Pisa and its environs, which includes the districts of Pisa, San Giuliano Terme, Vecchiano and Cascina. In particular, our aim is to investigate the effects produced by city growth on the structure and the working of agricultural systems. These effects involve both the environmental and the economic system; they also depend on the size of the city, on the kind of city growth (linear, diffuse, polycentric) and of the infrastructure system, on the morphology of the territory and on the "distance" of cultivation from the urban agglomerates.

The study of the described phenomena was performed by using and integrating two different tools: GISs and automatic learning tools.

During the first phase, the geographical georeferenced database of land uses, related to two different dates, was built by means of a GIS software.

Starting from information-based and conceptual methods and criteria, we are able to construct compatible surveys which were carried out in different time periods, from different sources and with different scales (land use regional maps, remote sensing maps and so on).

By means of spatial elaborations performed within the GIS software, the information coming from the various maps are put in the form of relational tables, where the elementary cells through which the territory was represented are reported in the rows, and the columns contain the attributes that give information about the description of each single cell. During the second phase, the table is fed as input data for the automatic learning tool, which is able to extract a set of land use transformation rules. During the third phase, we apply the extracted rules to the thematic map related to the first time section, and we verify, by means of the GIS tool, the reliability of these rules, by comparing the structure of the territorial system at the second time section with the one obtained by applying such rules.

Spatial Data Elaboration

By means of a GIS tool the primary data was converted into a format permitting subdivision of the territory into homogenous elementary units (cells 100x100 m): this representation enables conceptually correct and very quick spatial elaboration to be performed. After defining the shape and characteristics of each entity, it is then possible to select the local elements that are in the neighbouring area of every elementary cell.

We consider two types of "neighbouring area", namely:

- *adjacent*: Set of cells that shares at least an edge with the selected element;
- *neighbouring*: Set of all the cells that lie at a given distance from the selected "core" element.

This distance can be computed either starting from the edge or from the centre (defined from the average of the values of the spatial co-ordinates of vertexes that define the polygon itself) of the selected polygon. Moreover, we have identified some relevant infrastructures (roads, railroads, stations, etc.) that intersect each elementary territorial unit.

The results of these elaborations are put, by using some automated procedures, in the form of relational tables, in which, for each spatial entity, there is a description (defined by means of alphanumeric attributes) of the state of the cell and a description of the states of the neighbouring entities, previously described.

This table represents the input data for the automatic learning tools that enable the exploration of relationships between the elements of the studied area by generating a set of transformation rules. The link between a GIS and an automatic learning tool represents quite an innovation in the field of Geographical Information Systems. By now, in fact, GISs are eminently usable for the representation and recording of georeferenced information; in this research, by exploiting all the potentialities of these tools, we are able to make them useful for the development and the application of advanced artificial intelligence instruments.

The development and the building of a tool able to achieve the previous aim covers different phases:

- building of maps referred to different time slices;
- building of automated procedures within GIS in order to perform various kinds of building analysis such as map overlays, neighbouring analysis, etc.;
- building of automated report tables referred to cartographic analysis;
- implementation of an algorithm able to extract land transformation rules;
- building of thematic maps referred to the output data obtained in the previous phases.

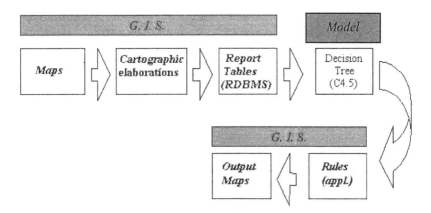

Figure 6.1 System Structure

During the first phase we built thematic maps of some areas of Tuscany (Italy) at two different time slices (1978 and 1992). The information contained in these maps concerned land uses, highways, railways, railway stations and so on.

The basic map for the analysis was for the year 1978 and was provided by the Tuscan Regional Authority. It is one of a series of maps at scale 1:25.000 indicating land uses of the whole of Tuscany. We georeferenced these maps and then we coded all the different land use values.

The basic map for the 1992 analysis was provided by the "Corine" project (*Coordination de l'Information sur l'Environment*), whose scale is 1:100.000.

One of the major problems in the second phase was the creation of a homogeneous code of land uses, because the basic maps come from different sources and have completely different land use codes. To solve this problem, we first grouped similar land uses and then we reclassified each land use by a new numerical code.

The resulting classes can be seen in Table 6.1:

Table 6.1 Class Distribution in the "Area of Pisa" Application

Land use class	Number of examples (cells)	Distribution (%)
1) Continuous urbanisation	84	0.74%
2) Discontinuous urbanisation	707	6.25%
3) Productive settlement	190	1.68%
4) Crop land	6320	55.93%
5) Olive grove	226	2.00%
6) Vineyard	100	0.88%
7) Orchard	110	0.97%
8) Wood	2725	24.11%
9) Pasture land	468	4.14%
10) Beach	139	1.23%
11) River	226	2.00%

Another problem was due to the different scale of the source maps: "Corine" is less detailed than the Tuscany map ("CTR"). We solved these problems by using reclassification methods and overlay mapping.

The results of this elaboration was an increase of the detail in the "Corine" map. In this phase of the work we transformed the shape of the vector data and we created regular grid data (called "vector grid") in order to obtain a homogeneous zoning of the territory. The land use code is given for each cell of the grid: if a cell matches different land uses, the code used is that in the predominant areal extension.

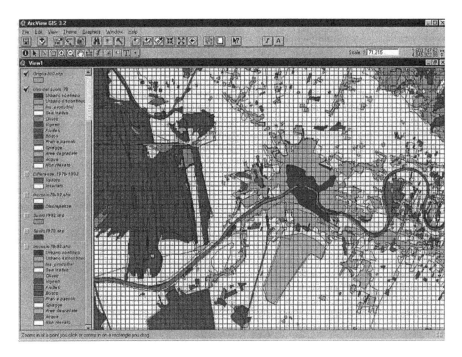

Figure 6.2 Map of the Study Area Subdivided in Cells

In the third phase, the results of these cartographic analyses were reported in relational tables (RDBMS) conceived to be learnt by the classification algorithm based on decision tree induction. This report table contains the identification number of the cell which generates the neighbouring cells, the land use code, the consistency of the neighbouring cells and the presence of road, railroad, stations, etc.

The contents of the fourth phase was explained in the previous chapter.

The Experiments

The report table created in the third phase was used as input for the automatic learning tool. Table 6.2 lists the attributes chosen for the description of the state of each cell, the state of its neighbouring cells and the classification target attribute (land use at 1992).

Table 6.2 Report Table

Attributes (IF)	
1. Land use 1978	14. Discontinuous urbanisation in the neighbouring cells
2. Continuous urbanisation in the adjacent cells	15. Productive settlements in the neighbouring cells
3. Discontinuous urbanisation in the adjacent cells	16. Crop land in the neighbouring cells
4. Productive settlement in the adjacent cells	17. Olive grove in the neighbouring cells
	18. Vineyard in the neighbouring cells
5. Crop land in the adjacent cells	19. Orchard in the neighbouring cells
6. Olive grove in the adjacent cells	20. Wood in the neighbouring cells
7. Vineyard in the adjacent cells	21. Pasture land in the neighbouring cells
8. Orchard in the adjacent cells	22. Beach in the neighbouring cells
9. Wood in the adjacent cells	23. River in the neighbouring cells
10. Pasture land in the adjacent cells	24. Presence of roads
11. Beach in the adjacent cells	25. Roads in the adjacent cells
12. River in the adjacent cells	26. Roads in the neighbouring cells
13. Continuous urbanisation in the neighbouring cells	
Class label (THEN)	
Land use 1992	

The extracted classification rules are an "IF ... THEN" statement, where "IF" describes both the observed state and the single rule to apply, while "THEN" assigns a code, that is to say a transition from one state to another state in different time slices. Then the extracted rules are applied to the thematic map related to the first temporal section and we verify, by means of the GIS tool, the reliability of these rules by comparing the structure of the territorial system at the second time section with the one obtained by applying such rules.

If the "reproduction" of the known data (1992 land use in our case) is satisfying, the experimented methodology can be used to estimate land use transformation in a changing environment and to build future scenarios.

Our automatic learning tool produced more than 100 land transformation rules. Later on we built a more aggregated explanatory level to express the extracted knowledge in a more concise and communicable way. The aforementioned aggregated interpretative level is, especially, of interest for the main aim of the present research, that is the understanding of urban influence on the agricultural system.

The results can be grouped according to four principal kinds of land transformations.

1)   Substitution of agricultural land uses with other activities:
    In areas that present a certain degree of urbanisation, with a high level of accessibility due to the strong presence of roads, the rural land uses tend to

disappear and to be replaced by productive activities (see small circle in Figures 6.3 and 6.4).

2) Substitution of agricultural land uses with other activities:

    In peripheral areas, like areas near to sea or rivers, with good infrastructure we observe that the agricultural land uses tend to be replaced by productive settlements (see small strip at bottom of Figures 6.3 and 6.4).

3) Specialisation of cultivation:

    In agricultural areas, the presence in the neighbouring areas of discontinuous urbanised settlements strongly affects the specialisation of the cultivation: inside the analysed territory, in many of the cells that present this property, we can observe the passage from crop land to orchards, while in some others pasture land uses tend to become cultivable areas (see big strip at centre of Figures 6.3 and 6.4).

4) De-specialisation of cultivation:

    It is possible to notice that inside some areas presenting a low degree of urbanisation we can verify the substitution of land use from pasturage to wood: such kind of rules are indicative of the abandonment of some agricultural and breeding activities (see big circle in Figures 6.3 and 6.4).

The selected rules are summarised in Table 6.3.

Table 6.3 Some Extracted Rules

In presence of (IF)	Substitution (THEN)
→Rare presence of discontinuous urban settlements →Presence in the neighbouring cells of all kinds of cultivations →Rare presence of sea and rivers	**From PASTURE to CROP LAND** (Substitution of cultivations)
→High degree of infrastructure facilities →Presence of discontinuous urban settlements in the neighbouring cells →Coastal areas or areas near to rivers	**From CROP LAND to PRODUCTIVE SETTLEMENTS** (Substitution of agricultural land uses)
→Low degree of infrastructure facilities →Rare presence of discontinuous urban settlements in the adjacent cells, high presence in the neighbouring cells →Presence of specialised cultivation in the neighbouring cells →High presence of non-specialised cultivation in the neighbouring cells	**From CROP LAND to ORCHARDS** (Specialisation of cultivation)
→Rare presence of discontinuous urban settlements	**From PASTURE to WOOD** (De-specialisation of cultivations)

Figure 6.3 Land Use Map of the Study Area in 1978

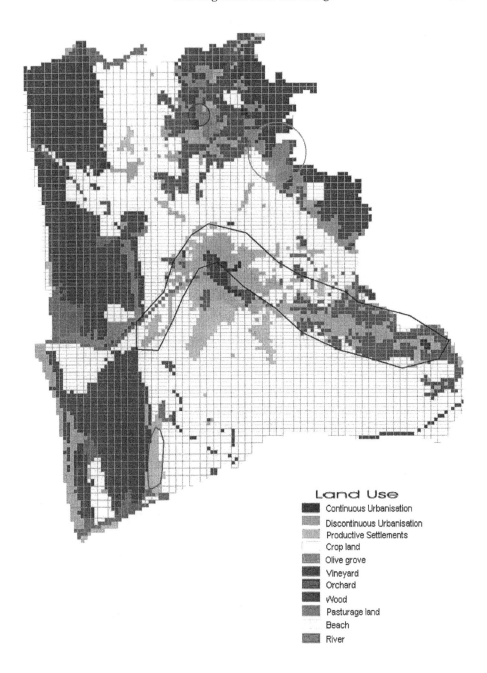

**Figure 6.4 Land Use Map of the Study Area in 1992 Obtained by Applying
the Extracted Rules**

Evolution of "Functional" Land Use: the Metropolitan Area of Rome

The first attempt to discover spatial transformation rules driving the evolution of the metropolitan area of Rome was developed in 1997-98 by Lombardo, Papini and Rabino, by using genetic algorithms for the learning process. The initial data base was made by 750 land use variables referring to 5600 census areas, derived from the 1981 and 1991 censuses. The variables were selected and grouped in land use classes following the criterion of homogeneity with respect to location behaviour.

The land uses adopted are described in Table 6.4 (see Figures 6.5 and 6.6):

Table 6.4 Classes in the Metropolitan Area of Rome

Land use classes	
Prevailing land uses	*Mixed land uses*
1) Empty (V)	8) Residential+ high tertiary(R-TS)
2) High-density residential (AR)	9) Residential + common tertiary (R-TI)
3) Low-density residential (BR)	10) Residential + industry (R-IN)
4) High tertiary (TS)	11) Residential + health services (R-SA)
5) Common tertiary (TI)	12) High tertiary + common tertiary (TS-TI)
6) Industry (IN)	13) High tertiary + industry (TS-IN)
7) Health services (SA)	14) Common tertiary + industry (TI-IN)
	15) Economic activity + health services (PR-SA)

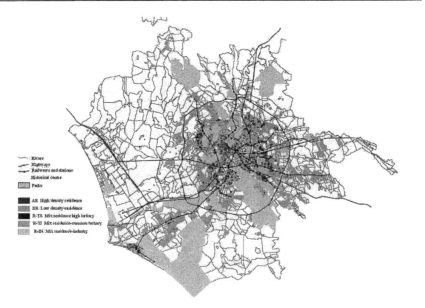

Figure 6.5 Residential and Mixed Land Uses

Figure 6.6 Economic Activity Land Uses

Moreover there are fixed characteristics ("attributes") of the cells: they do not change, but influence the evolution of the system. Therefore, they do not belong to the target map. They correspond to the presence in any cell of elements relevant for accessibility or characterising the whole surface of the cell. They are: 1) the presence of railway or underground stations; 2) the presence of access points to the motorway ring road; 3) parks and not transformable areas (by the Master Plan); 4) sea; 5) other municipalities; 6) adjacency to a cell which presents one of the 5 attributes listed above; 7) historic centre (see Table 6.5).

In order to study the same area by means of decision tree induction, we used the above described set of data, but we adopted a larger set of information for each cell, including the definition of various kinds of enlarged neighbouring areas (cells in a radius of 500, 1000 and 2000 metres).

The report table we adopted included the information described in Table 6.5.

Table 6.5 Report Table

Attributes (IF)
1.   Land use 1981
2.   Presence of Metro station:
3.   Metro stations in the adjacent cells
4.   Metro stations in the neighbouring cells (radius 500 metres) in adjacent cells
5.   Metro station in the neighbouring cells (radius 1000 metres)
6.   Presence of Highway access:
7.   Highway access in the adjacent cells
8.   Highway access in the neighbouring cells (radius 1000 metres)
9.   Presence of Historic centre:
10. Historic centre in the adjacent cells
11. Historic centre in the neighbouring cells (radius 500 metres)
12. Historic centre in the neighbouring cells (radius 1000 metres)
13. Park in the neighbouring cells (radius 1000 metres)
14. Park in the neighbouring cells (radius 2000 metres)
15. Sea in the neighbouring cells (radius 2000 metres)
16. Sea in the adjacent cells
17. Other municipalities in the adjacent cells
18. Other municipalities in the neighbouring cells (radius 2000 metres)
19. (V) in the adjacent cells (See codes in Table 6.4)
20. (AR) in the adjacent cells
21. (BR) in the adjacent cells
22. (TS) in the adjacent cells
23. (TI) in the adjacent cells
24. (IN) in the adjacent cells
25. (SA) in the adjacent cells
26. (R-TS) in the adjacent cells
27. (R-TI) in the adjacent cells
28. (R-IN) in the adjacent cells
29. (R-SA) in the adjacent cells
30. (TS-TI) in the adjacent cells
31. (TS-IN) in the adjacent cells
32. (TI-IN) in the adjacent cells
33. (PR-SA) in the adjacent cells
34. (V) in the neighbouring cells (radius 900 metres)
35. (AR) in the neighbouring cells (radius 900 metres)
36. (BR) in the neighbouring cells (radius 900 metres)
37. (TS) in the neighbouring cells (radius 900 metres)
38. (TI) in the neighbouring cells (radius 900 metres)
39. (IN) in the neighbouring cells (radius 900 metres)
40. (SA) in the neighbouring cells (radius 900 metres)
41. (R-TS) in the neighbouring cells (radius 900 metres)
42. (R-TI) in the neighbouring cells (radius 900 metres)
43. (R-IN) in the neighbouring cells (radius 900 metres)
44. (R-SA) in the neighbouring cells (radius 900 metres)
45. (TS-TI) in the neighbouring cells (radius 900 metres)
46. (TS-IN) in the neighbouring cells (radius 900 metres)
47. (TI-IN) in the neighbouring cells (radius 900 metres)
48. (PR-SA) in the neighbouring cells (radius 900 metres)
Class label (THEN)
Land use 1991

From the first experimental results we obtained some realistic information about the evolution processes taking place within the metropolitan area of Rome between 1981 and 1991. The most significant results are represented in the following tables.

Table 6.6 1981-1991 Residential Urbanisation
In the rules found, three types of evolution can be identified:

1 EXPANSION In presence of:	2 DENSIFICATION OF AREAS WITH GOOD ACCESSIBILITY In presence of:	3 URBANISATION OF AREAS WITH A GOOD ENVIRONMENTAL QUALITY In presence of:
- Empty cells in the enlarged neighbouring cells - High-density residential in the enlarged neighbouring cells - Services in the enlarged neighbouring cells	- Low-density residential inside a given radius - High-density residential in the neighbouring cells - Rail stations and/or metro stations in the radius	- High-density residential in the neighbouring cells - Some services located inside a given radius - Parks (adjacent in the radius)

We can observe that in each case high-density residential appear in proximity to already dense areas: it indicates a diffusion process driven by density, rather than the birth of new clusters. In the case of new expansion, there is the need for empty areas, with some access to services. Densification of course appears in low-density areas and is driven by accessibility to transport infrastructures. Dense residential urbanisation also appears in areas with good access to services and with good environmental quality.

Table 6.7 Location Choices of High Tertiary Activities
In the rules found, three main types of evolution can be identified:

1 GROWTH (from RTS, TSTI)	2 SUBSTITUTION		3 NEW LOCATIONS (from V)
	2a: *Centralisation and image effect*	2b: *Dragging and "quality" effect*	*Image effect and city effect*
- Available areas in the enlarged neighbouring cells - Demand from firms in the enlarged neighbouring cells	- Nearness to the historic centre - Adjacent to historic centre - Presence of metro stations in the neighbouring cells	- High tertiary in the enlarged neighbouring cells - Common tertiary in the enlarged neighbouring cells - Nearness to areas with good environmental context - Areas with good accessibility	- Presence of high-density residential - Nearness to historic centre - Nearness to parks

The evolution of high tertiary activities is a significant issue in a large metropolitan area which is the capital city. It has often been seen as "invading" the most valuable areas of the city. Indeed, we can see that high tertiary activities drove away other activities (2. Substitution) in areas with the best and more prestigious urban environment (historic centre and its surroundings), endowed with services and with good accessibility.

Table 6.8 Location Choices of Common Tertiary Activities

Also in this case, three main types of evolution can be identified:

1 *GROWTH* (from RTS, TSTI, TIND)		
1a: *Good potential demand basin*	**1b:** *Diffuse and mixed demand*	**1c:** *Dragging and image effect*
- Good accessibility in the enlarged neighbouring cells - Presence of high-density residential - Low urbanisation in the enlarged neighbouring cells - Areas with good environmental context	- Low-density residential in the enlarged neighbouring cells - Areas with demand from firms	- High tertiary in the enlarged neighbouring cells - Nearness to historic centre

2 SUBSTITUTION (from RIND, TSIND, IND, SA)		3 NEW LOCATIONS (from V)
2a: *Dragging effect and mixed demand*	**2b:** *Agglomeration and image effect*	*"Filling" of high quality areas*
- High tertiary in the enlarged neighbouring cells - Areas with population and firms' services	- High-density residential in the enlarged neighbouring cells - Presence of residential and tertiary in the area - Nearness to historic centre	- High-density residential in the enlarged neighbouring cells - Nearness to historic centre - Areas with good environmental context

The evolution of common tertiary activities – their growth, their replacement of other activities and their new location is driven by the presence of demand: high-density residential (1a, 2b, 3) or high tertiary (1c, 2a) and by the pulling effect of common tertiary activities themselves (2a, 2b). Moreover, we can deduce that in the first case they are mainly population services and in the second case they are mainly firms' services. Environmental quality (both urban and natural) exerts an attraction in many cases, but it is probably secondary to the preferences of demand.

Some Points of Reflection

At this point in the development of our research, some issues deserve some reflection: they concern methods, inputs and results.

As to methods, we must first of all recognise that understanding cognitive processes is a very demanding scientific challenge and the results obtained to date do not allow any method to be considered the most effective one.

A fundamental difficulty of all methods is connected to the problem of introducing specific knowledge regarding the considered cognitive domain.

In other words, we have to answer the following questions:

- What and how much do we already know? (*A priori* knowledge.)
- What and how much of our *a priori* knowledge do we want to feed into the cognitive system? (A great deal, if we hope to "discover" further knowledge; not much, if we have a poor *a priori* knowledge or we aim to "verify" our *a priori* knowledge.)
- How much and what kind of *a priori* knowledge can be "digested" by different techniques?

Then, some research issues emerged from the work carried out:

1) exploration of alternative learning mechanisms, in order to assess their performances and build synergies and/or integration between them;
2) investigation into the extent of dependence of the learning process on the *a priori* knowledge of the modeller, "embedded" in his/her choices concerning the urban system representation given to the learning tool. It is then necessary to make such knowledge explicit and represent it as a set of rules: to this end, Multicriteria Analysis can be used, as it is an efficient tool for analysing and structuring *a priori* knowledge.

As to inputs, the question, apart from involving the problem of *a priori* knowledge mentioned above, relates to a problem which (at least in Italy) has been frustrating research in our area since the 1960s: tools and models are always too advanced when compared to the detail, in space and time, of available data[1] and their comparability. It implies that the calibration and evaluation of methods, when applied to real situations, are very laborious and sometimes seriously compromised. The consequence is that some ideas often have to be left at a theoretical level (though sometimes beyond the purely theoretical) – and the operational level achieved can be of little support to the planning process.

---

[1] See for instance the problems we met with land use maps for different years, or the problems with the lack of traffic surveys in the 1970s.

References

Agrawal, R., Srikant, R. (1994), "Fast algorithms for mining association rules", in *Proceedings of the 20th International Conference on Very Large Databases*, Santiago, Chile.

Bayardo, R. J., Agrawal, R. (1999), "Mining the most interesting rules", in *Proceedings of the 5th ACM SIGKDD International Conference on Knowledge Discovery and Data Mining*.

Besussi, E., Cecchini, A. (1996), *Artificial Worlds and Urban Studies*, DAEST, Venice.

Breiman, L., Friedman, J., Olshen R., Stone C., (1984), *Classification and Regression Trees*, Wadsworth International Group.

Fayyad, U., Piatetsky-Shapiro, G., Smith, P., Uturusamy, R. (1996), *Advances in Knowledge Discovery and Data Mining*, AAAI/MIT Press.

Han, J., Kamber, M. (2000), *Data Mining: Concepts and Techniques*, Morgan Kaufmann.

Han, J., Koperski, K., Stefanovic, N. (1997), "GeoMiner: A System Prototype for Spatial Data Mining", *Proceedinga of the 1997 ACM-SIGMOD International Conference on Management of Data (SIGMOD'97)*, Tucson, Arizona, May 1997 (System prototype demonstration).

Hill, M.J., Aspinall, R.J. (eds) (2000), *Spatial Information for Land Use Management*, Gordon and Breach, Amsterdam.

Holland, J.H. (1975), *Adaptation in Natural and Artificial Systems*, University of Michigan Press, Ann Arbor.

Holland, J.H. (1986), "Escaping brittleness", in Michalski R.S. et al. (eds), *Machine Learning. An Artificial Intelligence Approach*, Morgan Kaufmann, pp. 592-623.

Holsheimer, M., Kersten, M., Mannila, H., Toivonen, H. (1995), "A perspective on databases and data mining", in *First International Conference on Knowledge Discovery and Data Mining (KDD '95)*, 150-155, Montreal, Canada, August 1995, AAAI Press.

Holsheimer, M., Siebes, A. (1994), "Data mining: The search for knowledge in databases", *CWI Technical Report CS-R9406*, Amsterdam.

Jantsch, E. (1980), *The Self-Organising Universe*, Pergamon Press, Oxford.

Kamber, M., Winstone, L., Gong, W., Cheng, S., Han, J. (1997), "Generalisation and decision tree induction: Efficient classification in data mining", in *Proceedings of International Workshop Research Issues on Data Engineering (RIDE '97)*, Birmingham, England.

Langton, C. (1989), "Artificial life", in C. Langton (ed), *Artificial Life*, Addison-Wesley, Reading, MA.

Liu, B., Hsu, W. (1996), "Post-Analysis of Learned Rules", *Proceedings of the Thirteenth National Conference on Artificial Intelligence (AAAI-'96)*, 4-8 August, Portland, Oregon, USA, pp. 828-834.

Liu, B., Hsu, W., Chen, S. (1997), "Discovering Conforming and Unexpected Classification Rules", *IJCAI-'97 Workshop on Intelligent Data Analysis in Medicine and Pharmacology (IDAMAP-'97)*, 23-29 August 1997, Nagoya, Japan.

Liu, B., Hsu, W., Ma, Y. (1998), "Integrating classification and association rule mining", in *Proceedings of the Fourth International Conference on Knowledge Discovery and Data Mining (KDD-'98)*, New York, USA.

Liu, B., Hsu, W., Ma, Y., Chen, S. (1999), "Mining interesting knowledge using DM II", in *ACM SIGKDD International Conference on Knowledge Discovery & Data Mining (KDD-'99)*, 15-18 August 1999, CA, USA.

Liu, B., Hsu, W., Mun, L., Lee, H. (1999), "Finding interesting patterns using user expectations", *IEEE Transactions on Knowledge and Data Engineering*, vol. 11, n. 6.

Lombardo, S. (1991), "Recenti sviluppi della modellistica urbana", in Bertuglia, C.S., La Bella, A. (a cura), *I sistemi urbani*, Angeli, Milano.

Lombardo, S. (1998), "Assessing uncertainty and complexity in urban systems", in Bertuglia, C.S., Bianchi, G., Mela, A. (eds.), *The City and its Sciences*, Physica Verlag, New York.

Lombardo, S., Papini, L., Rabino, G. (1998), "Learning urban cellular automata in a real world. The case study of Rome metropolitan area", in Bandini S., Serra R., Suggi Liverani F. (eds.), *Cellular Automata: Research Toward Industry*, Springer Verlag, Berlin.

Lombardo, S., Pecori, S. (2001), "Costruzione di sistemi cognitivi per la simulazione dell'evoluzione urbana: i L.U.C.A.", in Concilio, G., Monno, V. (eds.), *Atti della II Conferenza Nazionale INPUT2001*.

Lombardo, S., Rabino, G. (1999), "Learning in urban modelling", introductory speech to: *Quatriemes Rencontres de Theo Quant,* Besançon.

Mannila, H. (1997), "Methods and problem in Data Mining", in *Proceedings of International conference on Database Theory*, Delphy, Greece, January 1997, Afrati, F. and Kolaitis P. (eds.) Springer-Verlag.

Mannila, H. (2002), "Local and global methods in Data Mining: basic techniques and open problems", to appear in: *ICALP 2002, 29th International Colloquium on Automata, Languages and Programming*, Malaga, Spain, July 2002, Springer-Verlag.

Mitchell, T.M. (1997), *Machine Learning*, McGraw Hill.

Nicolis, G., Prigogine, I. (1977), *Self Organisation in Non-Equilibrium System*, Wiley, New York.

Piatetsky-Shapiro, G., Frawley, W.J. (1991), *Knowledge Discovery in Databases*, AAAI/MIT Press.

Quinlan, J. R. (1986), "Induction of decision trees", *Machine Learning*, 1, 81-106.

Quinlan, J. R. (1993), *C4.5: Program for Machine Learning*, Morgan Kauffmann.

Serra, R., Zanarini, G. (1994), *Sistemi complessi e processi cognitivi*, Edizioni Calderini, Bologna.

Chapter 7

The Identification and Simulation of the Urban Spatio-temporal Dynamic. The Case Study of Rome

Ferdinando Semboloni

Introduction

According to Tobler (1979), the identification problem can be formulated in the following way: "Given 20 pictures in order, of the board positions from a game of chess, determine the rules of chess". Unfortunately, there is a far more limited number of urban data available compared to the information that can be extracted from a game of chess. In fact some of the relevant characteristics of available data for urban analysis are:

- time series are limited and usually only a few temporal periods are available;
- the lag between two periods is too large in relation to the temporal causation of the urban phenomena.

Due to these characteristics of urban data, it is difficult to identify the system in order to apply a micro-simulation model. In some cases (Richards, Meyer and Packard, 1990; Mandelj, Grabec and Govekar, 2001) the identification problem has been approached by establishing a spatio-temporal function between the variable to forecast and the value of the other variables in the surrounding cells, in a set of previous periods. Lombardo, Papini and Rabino (1998) applied a method based on a genetic algorithm to the identification of the urban system of Rome.

The present method utilizes two sets of spatial data, related to two periods: initial and final. It is based on neural networks and simulated annealing and is an evolution of a previous method (Semboloni, 2000). In order to make up for the lack of a time series, the spatial interaction rules are calibrated first by using data of the initial period, and second by using the parameters previously estimated, in a dynamic model able to calculate the final state from the initial state through a set of iterations. The parameters of this model are further tuned by applying simulated annealing, which is an optimization technique based on statistical physics. In this way the difference between the simulated and observed data of the final period is minimized.

For these reasons the analysis has been divided into two correlated phases: static and dynamic. During the static analysis one focuses on the identification of spatial relations by using observed initial data. In turn, during the dynamic analysis one utilizes the spatial relations identified in the previous phase, in a dynamic model whose parameters are further calibrated by using simulated annealing. These aspects will be explained in the following sections.

Static Analysis

Let us suppose we have a set of N variables located in a two-dimensional space, for instance a grid of squared cells. In this spatial context the value $v_{h,i}$ of a variable h (h ranging 1-N) located in cell i is influenced by the value of the other variables located in the surrounding cells. To analyze these influences the neural network method has been utilized. In order to establish the input of the neural network, four annuli a^1, a^2, a^3, and a^4 surrounding each cell are considered.

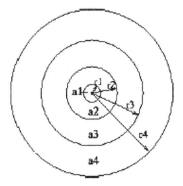

Figure 7.1   The Four Annuli a^1, a^2, a^3, and a^4 that Surround the Cell and the Corresponding Outer Radii r^1, r^2, r^3, and r^4

The centres of these annuli correspond to the centre of the cell, and the annuli are characterized by an inner and an outer radius. The inner radius r^{n-1} of the a^n annulus is the outer radius of the a^{n-1} annulus, as in Figure 7.1. The first annulus, a^1, has a fixed inner radius equal to zero. In other words the values of the variables located in the central cell are included in the calculation. In fact, to obtain the input for the neural network, a sum is made of variables located in cells and associated with a specific annulus. Normalization is achieved for the range $0 - 1$ by taking the sum of an annulus and dividing it by the maximum sum attained in all the other similar annuli:

$$A^n_{h,i} = \frac{\sum_{j \in a^n} v_{h,j}}{max_i \left(\sum_{j \in a^n} v_{h,j} \right)} \quad (1)$$

where $A_{h,i}^n$ is the normalized value resulting from the sum of variable v_h located in annulus a^n. These normalized values serve to relate the value of a variable located in the central cell with values of other variables located in the surrounding cells. Using this information, calculations can be made for the variables located in the central cell. By adopting this method, it is possible to define 4 x N input variables $X_{k,i}$ for the neural network; these are numbered from 1 to 4 x N by setting $X_{k,i} = A_{h,i}^n$ where $k = n + 4(h - 1)$. In addition the 4 x N + 1th input variable, the bias, is set equal -1.

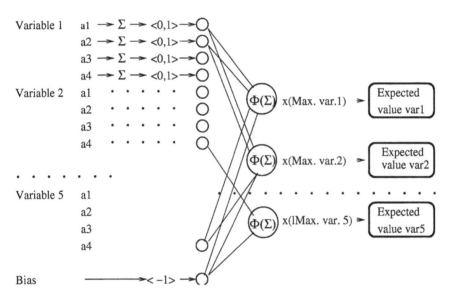

Figure 7.2 The Structure of the Neural Network. *N* has been supposed to equal 5 as in the following application.

For each variable, and in each cell, the expected value $y_{h,i}$, ranging from 0 to 1, is calculated by using the following equation:

$$y_{h,i} = \Phi\left(\sum_k W_{k,h} X_{k,i}\right) \quad (2)$$

where Φ is a sigmoid function and $W_{k,h}$ are the weights of the neural network (see Figure 7.2) calculated by using the back-propagation method. Some of the weights are constrained as being equal to zero if considered meaningless. In addition pruning is utilized in order to cut all the connections having a weight smaller than an established threshold. In other words it is supposed that each variable is attracted by the other variables located in the annuli surrounding the central cell.

When this attraction overcomes a threshold represented by the bias, it modifies the variable.

Thus, as demonstrated above, static analysis concerns the variation of variables in space. In contrast, the temporal variation of each variable in each cell is established by focusing on the dynamic of the system. This aspect is explained in the next section.

Dynamic Analysis

The dynamic analysis concerns the variation of the spatial distribution of the variables which is simulated by a model. However, because a city is influenced by outside factors, the total value of each variable in each period is constrained to some exogenously-established amount. In addition a share of the spatial variation in each cell is supposed to be exogenously determined, because not all the variations in spatial distribution can be explained by the interactions among variables.

The dynamic model is based on a recursive neural network, in which the calculated output is utilized as the input for the following period. Let us explain the method in depth, including some steps. First of all, the neural network previously estimated is utilized to calculate the desired normalized values $y_{h,i}$ (ranging $0 - 1$) of each variable h in each cell i, in the following way:

$$y_{h,i}(t) = f\left\{\Phi\left[\sum_k \alpha_{k,h} W_{k,h} X_{k,i}(t)\right]\right\} \quad (3)$$

where the $\alpha_{k,h}$ are a set of parameters estimated by using simulated annealing, and f is a function which truncates the lower tail of the values resulting from the neural network. In fact:

$$f\left\{\Phi\left[\sum_k \alpha_{k,h} W_{k,h} X_{k,i}\right]\right\} = \begin{cases} \Phi\left[\sum_k \alpha_{k,h} W_{k,h} X_{k,i}\right] & \text{if } \Phi\left[\sum_k \alpha_{k,h} W_{k,h} X_{k,i}\right] > \theta_h \\ 0 & \text{otherwise} \end{cases} \quad (4)$$

where the $0 < \theta_h < 1$ are a set of N parameters to be estimated by using simulated annealing. These parameters, as well as the $\alpha_{k,h}$ parameters, modify the neural network weights in order to obtain the best fit of the observed final data.

The $y_{h,i}$ values are de-normalized by using the total value of the variable in the period as in the following equation:

$$v_{h,i}^e(t) = \frac{y_{h,i}(t)}{\sum_i y_{h,i}(t)} V_h(t) \quad (5)$$

where $v_{h,i}^e$ is the expected real value of the variable h in cell i, $V_h(t)$ is the total value of the variable h in period t. This value is calculated with the following equation:

$$V_h(t) = V_h(1) + t \left[\frac{V_h(T) - V_h(1)}{T} - \frac{V_h^*(T) - V_h^*(1)}{T} \right] \quad (6)$$

where T is the total number of iterations, $V_h(1) = \sum_i v_{h,i}$ is the total value of the variable h over the initial observed period, and $V_h(T)$ is the same quantity over the final period. In turn $V_h^*(T) = \sum_i v_{h,i}^*(T)$ (1) is the total value of the exogenous share over the initial period obtained by the sum over the exogenous share of each cell, $v_{h,i}^*(1)$, and $V_h^*(T) = \sum_i v_{h,i}^*(T)$ is the corresponding value over the final period. The exogenous variation is subtracted from the total because it is added later to each cell. In fact, the value of a variable in a cell at time $t + 1$ depends on the value of the variable in the same cell in the previous period, the growth rate, the delay rate, and the exogenous variation in the cell, as in the following equation:

$$v_{h,i}(t+1) = g_h(t+1) \left[(1 - d_h) v_{h,i}(t) \right] + \Delta v_{h,i}^*(t+1) \quad (7)$$

where $g_h(t + 1) = V_h(t + 1)/V_h(t)$ is the growth rate, $\Delta v_{h,i}^*(t+1) = $ $= \left| v_{h,i}^*(T) - v_{h,i}^*(1) \right| / V_h(t)$ is the exogenous variation of the variable h in cell i, and $0 < d_h < 1$ is a delay rate.

In turn the values calculated at the end of each period are utilized as input for the next period, as in the following equation:

$$X_{k,i}(t + 1) = \Gamma[v_{h,i}(t + 1)] \quad (8)$$

where Γ is the spatial operator involving sums over annuli and normalization as explained in the previous section.

The main phases for the calibration of parameters are summarized in Figure 1.3. In essence through simulated annealing one estimates the values of parameters which result in the smallest difference between observed and calculated data. In this process the number of iterations, T, performed by the model is an important parameter which is chosen exogenously. It is established in relation to the supposed temporal causation lag, but also in relation to the computer time needed for a good estimation of parameters.

This method has been included in the SSI (Spatial System Identifier) package which has been designed for the application of the proposed method to urban analysis and simulation. The package includes other features such as a model of the land rent, and a road network, which have not been considered in the present study. The functioning of the package is explained in the appendix. In the following section the application of the method to the case study of Rome is shown.

Evolving Cities

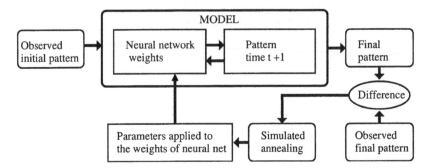

Figure 7.3   The Calibration of Parameters through Simulated Annealing

Application of the Method to the Case Study of Rome

Rome, the capital of Italy, is located in the centre of Italy near the Tyrrhenian sea. The number of inhabitants in 2001 was about 2,600,000. The data utilized in the present study were collected during the official Italian censuses of 1981 and 1991. The city territory is divided into about 5000 census areas and the data essentially covers population and activities. The city centre is situated in the historic city where the main administrative bodies are located. The expansion of the city occurred along the main radial roads which are intersected by a large motorway ring road, which is essentially the limit of the study area considered in the present chapter. The variables considered in each census area are:

1.   population;
2.   industrial employees;
3.   commercial employees, including retail, hotels, etc.;
4.   private service employees, including bank, insurance companies, etc.;
5.   public service employees, including administrative bodies, hospitals, schools, etc.

The values of these five variables in the study area in 1981 and in 1991 are shown in the Table 7.1. During this period the city was losing population and increasing service activities, as happened in many other cities.

Table 7.1 The Total Values of Variables in 1981 and in 1991

Variable	1981	1991
1 Population	2 085 187	1 841 170
2 Industry	114 136	101 284
3 Commerce	124 549	121 986
4 Private services	178 679	182 512
5 Public services	263 009	301 473

Before analyzing the spatial distribution, let us consider two basic features of the data. The first feature concerns the distribution of density in the census areas. This distribution shows a basic difference between activities (variables 2-5) and population. The activities density is distributed following a power law with a slope equal to about – 3 (Figure 7.4). In turn the distribution of population density is exponential (Figure 7.5).

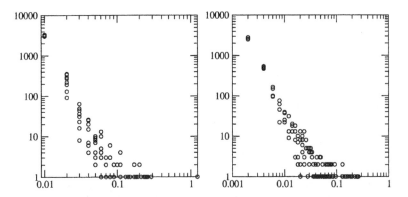

Figure 7.4 **The Distribution of the Densities Related to the Variables 2-5**
X axis: densities in census areas (ratio number of employees, surface of the census area in square metres). Y axis: frequency. Left side: densities of variables in 1981 and in 1991. Right side: absolute value of the variation of the density of each variable in the period 1981-1991. X and Y axis, logarithm scale.

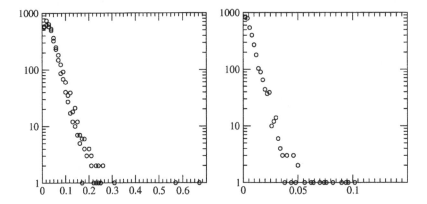

Figure 7.5 **The Distribution of the Densities Related to the Population**
X axis: densities in census areas (ratio number of inhabitants in the census area, surface of the census area in square metres). Y axis: frequency. Left side: density of population in 1981 and in 1991. Right side: absolute value of the variation of density of the population in the period 1981-1991. Y axis, logarithm scale.

The variations of the density of activities in the period 1981-1991 are also distributed as a power law. This result means that the city is essentially a stable object whose changes are normally of limited size, with a very small number of significant changes.

The second feature concerns the relation of density to the distance from the city centre. In this case the distribution is exponential for activities, while the distribution of population density follows the typical function $y = ade^{-\beta d}$ (y is the density and d the distance from the city centre) in which the exponential decay is combined with the negative effects in the vicinity of the city centre due to land rents, the scarcity of buildable land, etc (Figure 7.6).

The spatial distribution of data was determined by using the location of the census areas, measured by the co-ordinates of its centroid. In order to have a finer distribution, these data were spread over a grid of squared cells with a side of 250 metres, firstly by dividing the value of each variable located in the centroid of the census area among the nearest cells at a distance not more than 250 metres away (in other words the value was spread over the four bordering cells), and secondly by a partial smoothing. Using this method a distribution of variables on a squared grid of 100 x 100 cells was obtained, thus covering a surface of 625 km^2. By using this spatial distribution, the correlation coefficient between each couple of variables was calculated, as well as the correlation coefficient between the values in 1981 and 1991 of the same variable (see Table 7.2). The couples commerce-private services and population-commerce have the strongest correlations; in addition, population and commerce are the stablest variables, while the public services variable shows the highest variability (see Table 7.2, col. 6).

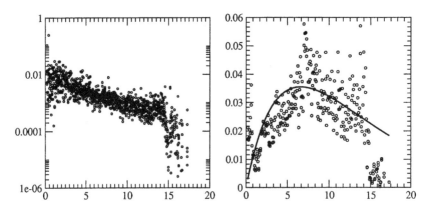

Figure 7.6 The Variation of Densities in Relation to the Distance from the City Centre

X axis: distance from the city centre in kilometres. Y axis: average density in census areas. Left side: Y axis, density of the variables 2-5 in 1981 and in 1991, logarithm scale. Right side: Y axis, population density in 1981 and in 1991; circles: densities in census areas, line: fit of the function $y = ade^{-\beta d}$ by using data for 1981.

Table 7.2 The Correlation Coefficient Between each Couple of Variables in 1981 (cols. 1-5), and of Each Variable Between 1981 and 1991 Data (col. 6)

Variable	1	2	3	4	5	81-91
1. Population	1.00	0.15	0.45	0.15	0.06	0.85
2. Industry	0.15	1.00	0.34	0.36	0.19	0.60
3. Commerce	0.45	0.34	1.00	0.53	0.38	0.77
4. Private services	0.15	0.36	0.53	1.00	0.36	0.59
5. Public services	0.06	0.19	0.38	0.36	1.00	0.54

Let us examine the spatial distribution of the five variables. As figure 7.7 shows, the population is star shaped, except for the central area which is mainly occupied by private services (Figure 7.10), and by commerce (Figure 7.9).

Industry (Figure 7.8) and public services (Figure 7.11) follow location strategies which are not necessarily connected with the spatial structure of the city. Public services in particular, mostly due to the role of Rome as a capital city, show a spatial behaviour which is a determinant for other activities, rather than being determined by them.

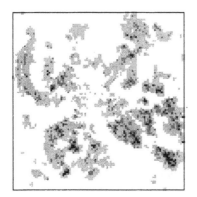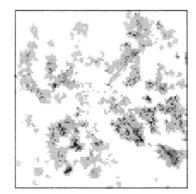

Figure 7.7   The Location of Population in 1981 and in 1991
The maximum value, represented in black is 2193.

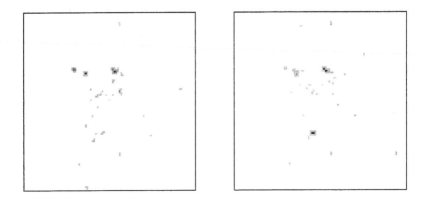

Figure 7.8   The Location of Industrial Employees in 1981 and in 1991
The maximum value, represented in black, is 1419.

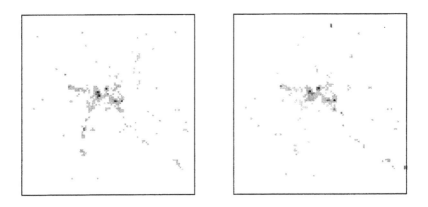

Figure 7.9   The Location of Commerce Employees in 1981 and in 1991
The maximum value, represented in black, is 772.

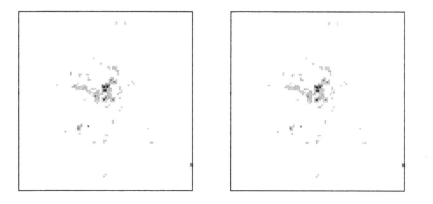

Figure 7.10   The Location of Private Service Employees in 1981 and in 1991
The maximum value, represented in black, is 1487.

The data distributed on the squared grid have been used for the calibration of the model, as is shown in the following section.

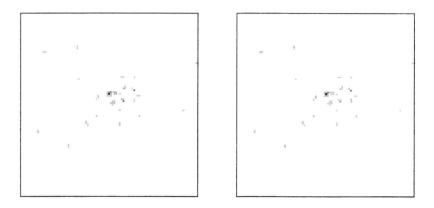

Figure 7.11   The Location of Public Service Employees in 1981 and in 1991
The maximum value, represented in black, is 5162.

Calibration of Parameters

The calibration phase includes the training of a neural network by using the data in the 1981 census. In this phase the radii of annuli are crucial parameters. These were established in the following way: the outer radius of the first annulus, r^1, was fixed equal to 250 metres. In other words the first annulus includes the central cell plus the four surrounding cells. The other inner and outer radii were established with the following formula: $r^n = 1.5\ r^{n-1}$. In this way radii grow exponentially up to a maximum of about 843 metres. Distance was calculated as a direct line. Obviously using the road network could increase the accuracy of the estimate, but the city of Rome has a well-connected road network and internal barriers are not so important.

The resulting parameters are shown in the first part of Table 7.3. Some of the weights were set to zero because they were considered meaningless. For instance, it is evident that the location of population is expected to have been influenced by industry but the converse was considered meaningless. On the other hand, causation between population and commerce is allowed in both directions. In other words something similar to urban economic base theory was applied. However, even if population is supposed to depend on all the other variables, the back-propagation method assigns a relevant value to the weight connecting the variable with the sum of the same variable in the first annulus. This feature means that the initial state plays an important role in the results obtained with the simulation model which was applied in the following phase. In fact, by using simulated annealing these parameters were modified as shown in the second part of Table 7.3.

The exogenous share v_h^* included in the simulation model, was considered only for activities (variables 2-5). It was established by using the average size of firms which was available from census data. In essence, when the average size in a census area exceeds 1000 the corresponding number of employees was considered as exogenous. In other words big firms are supposed to have a spatial behaviour which is not explained by the interactions with other activities or with the population. The resulting total quantity of employment considered as exogenous is about 11% of the total.

The delay rates (see equation 7) were estimated by using the correlation coefficients between data in 1981 and 1991, shown in Table 7.2, col.6. Basically, $d_h = 1 - r_h$, where r_h is the correlation coefficient (positive for all variables).

The number of iterations for each simulation was fixed at 10 (each iteration represents one year). This value was considered suitable both for forecasting purposes and for the computer time required for calculating simulated annealing which is limited to two or three days on a common PC.

Results

The results of the simulation are presented in the following Figures 7.12, 7.13, 7.14, 7.15, and 7.16. For each variable is shown the resulting spatial pattern to be compared with the corresponding pattern previously shown in Figures 7.7-7.11, and the graph of calculated values and observed values for each cell. As the figures show, the variable with best fit is the population, and the worst are the industrial and public service employees.

Table 7.3 The Weights Obtained by the Neural Network and the Simulated Annealing

Left side: the weights $W_{k,h}$ obtained by the training of the neural network. The sign "-" means that the corresponding weight has been constrained to zero. *Right side*: the weights modified by simulated annealing. Columns: inputs of the neural network. For each variable are considered four inputs related to the four annuli (see Figure 7.2 for comparison). Rows: output of the neural network. Last row: the threshold θ_h (equation 4) utilized for truncating the lower tail of the values resulting from neural network.

	Neural network					Simulated annealing				
	1	2	3	4	5	1	2	3	4	5
1	5.88	-	1.56	1.07	0	2.01	-	0.40	0.27	0
	0	-	0.78	0	0	0	-	0.20	0	0
	-	-	0	0	0	-	-	0	0	0
	-	-	0.13	0.57	0.95	-	-	0.03	0.14	0.24
2	0.35	3.90	0.71	1.62	1.50	0.09	4.21	0.18	0.41	0.55
	0.07	1.95	0.74	0.25	0.53	0.02	1.77	0.18	0.06	0.36
	0	-	-	0	-	0	-	-	0	-
	0.08	-	-	0.91	-	0.02	-	-	0.23	-
3	0	1.35	6.56	1.17	0	0	0.34	6.21	1.13	0
	0	0	0	0	0	0	0	0	0	0
	0	-	0	0	-	0	-	0	0	-
	0	-	-	0.04	-	0	-	-	0.02	-
4	0	0.71	0.71	4.18	1.46	0	0.18	0.09	1.85	0.40
	0	0.02	0.02	0.76	0.78	0	0.01	0	0.87	0.54
	0	-	0.64	-	-	0	-	0.16	-	-
	0	-	0	-	-	0	-	0	-	-
5	0.09	0	-	0.72	3.44	0.03	0	-	0.32	1.89
	0.11	1.36	0.76	0.69	2.70	0.03	0.34	1.15	1.46	2.94
	0.14	-	0	0	-	0.04	-	0	0	-
	0.21	-	-	1.22	-	0.04	-	-	0.31	-
Bias	3.48	5.01	4.59	5.12	5.59	0.05	4.70	3.97	4.91	5.88
θ_h						0.016	0.008	0.014	0.004	0.002

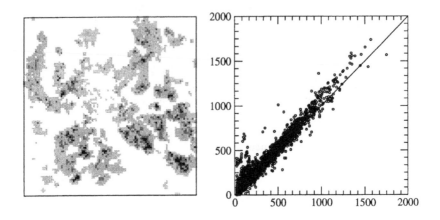

Figure 7.12 **Left Side**: the pattern of population calculated by the model on 1991 data, to be compared with Figure 7.7, right side.
Right Side: the fit of observed data. X axis, values calculated by the model, Y axis, observed values.

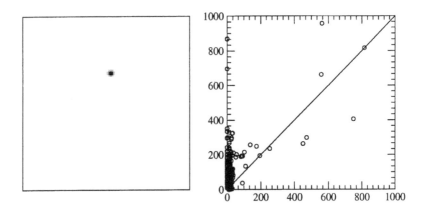

Figure 7.13 **Left Side**: the pattern of industrial employment calculated by the model on 1991 data, to be compared with Figure 7.8, right side.
Right Side: the fit of observed data. X axis, values calculated by the model, Y axis, observed values.

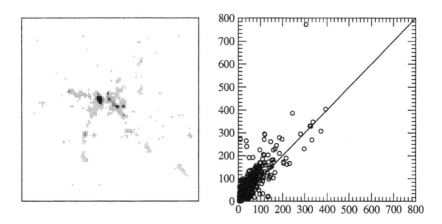

Figure 7.14 **Left Side**: the pattern of commerce employment calculated by the model on 1991 data, to be compared with Figure 7.9, right side. **Right Side**: the fit of observed data. X axis, values calculated by the model, Y axis, observed values.

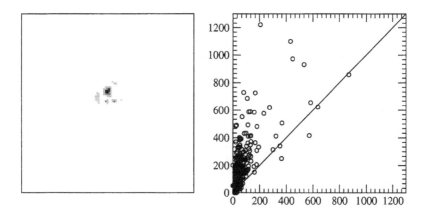

Figure 7.15 **Left Side**: the pattern of private service employment calculated by the model on 1991 data, to be compared with Figure 7.10, right side. **Right Side**: the fit of observed data. X axis, values calculated by the model, Y axis, observed values.

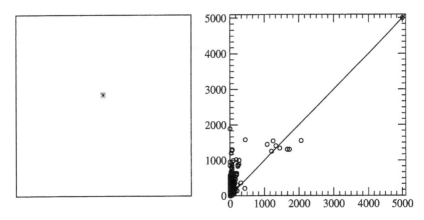

Figure 7.16 Left Side: the pattern of public service employment calculated by
the model on 1991 data, to be compared with Figure 7.11, right side.
Right Side: the fit of observed data. X axis, values calculated by the
model, Y axis, observed values.

In general terms the results show a good fit between calculated and observed
data. Obviously the result is closely dependent on the initial state. For this reason
the method is especially suitable for mature urban systems in which changes are
strongly related to the existing state.

Furthermore, the identification of the system depends on the theory one utilizes
to analyze the phenomenon. In fact the theory has an important role in reducing the
number of possible solutions, through the constraints applied to the neural network.

The utilization of this method for planning purposes consists in varying the
exogenous share of activities in some cells. This variation may represent the
expected result of some urban project whose probable effects one wishes to
simulate. In addition, as is shown in the appendix, the SSI package allows the
computation of distance by using a road network. In this case also, the effects of
the variation of the road network could be evaluated.

Conclusions

A method has been presented for identifying an urban system using available
census data. Three points should be emphasized. First, that identification is
possible even if the temporal series are limited, due to the spatial extension of
urban information. Second, that identification depends on the theoretical
hypothesis utilized for implementing the model. Third, that the interest in
identification is mainly due to the possibility of testing the functioning of the
model when some variables or some structural parameters are modified.

Acknowledgement

This research has been funded by MIUR (Italian Ministry of Education, University and Research) and is part of a research project concerning "Knowledge Engineering in the Planning Process" co-ordinated by Prof. Lidia Diappi, Polytechnic University of Milan. This research would not have been possible without the collaboration of Prof. Silvana Lombardo, Faculty of Engineering, University of Pisa who allowed me to utilize census data. Dott. Luisa Santini helped me in the utilization of data. Dott. Roberto Giannassi, Department of Systems and Computer Science, University of Florence, developed the software for the SSI package.

References

Lombardo, S., Papini, L., Rabino, G. (1998), "Learning Urban Cellular Automata in a Real World. The case study of Rome metropolitan area", in Bandini, S., Serra, R., Suggi-Liverani, F. (eds.), *Cellular Automata: Research Toward Industry*,. Springer Verlag, Berlin, pp. 165–184.

Mandelj, S., Grabec, I, Govekar, E. (2001), "Statistical Approach to Modelling of Spatiotemporal Dynamics", *International Journal of Bifurcation and Chaos*, 11, pp. 2731–2738.

Richards, C., Meyer, T.P, Packard, N.H. (1990), "Extracting Cellular Automaton Rules Directly from Experimental Data", *Phisica D*, 45, pp. 189–202.

Semboloni, F. (2000), "Identification and Simulation of an Urban Spatio-temporal Dynamic. An Approach Based on a Neural Network and Coupled Map Lattices", in *The 6th RSAI World Congress 2000. Regional Science in a Small World*, Lugano, Switzerland, pp. 1–19.

Tobler, W.R. (1979), "Cellular Geography", in Gale, S; Olsson, G. (eds.), *Philosophy in Geography*, D Reidel, Dordrecht, pp. 379–386.

Appendix

An Overview of SSI Handbook

Roberto Gianassi

Introduction

SSI (Spatial System Identifier) is a program conceived for the identification of urban spatial systems. It is based on a spatial neural network and on simulated annealing. Input data are limited to the spatial distribution over two periods of the following variables: population, industrial employment, commerce employment, private service employment, and public service employment.

Preparing the Execution

The files necessary are the following:

- input data file: a file containing the input variables;
- distances data file: a file containing a description of a road network (optional);
- simulation data file: a file containing a description of a road network to be used during simulation (optional).

Usage

In this section the use of the application and the setting of parameters are explained. At the start the user goes to the **Project files and directory settings** panel under the **Main configuration** shutter. The user sets up the working directory of the project (a directory in which the application will record all files) and the following files:

- **input data file**: a file containing the input variables;
- **distances file**: a file containing a description of a road network;
- **zeroes file**: a file containing null back-propagation network weights;
- **back-propagation network file**: a file containing back-propagation network weights;

- **simulated annealing network file**: a file containing simulated annealing network weights;
- **simulation distances file**: a file containing a description of a road network to be used during simulation.

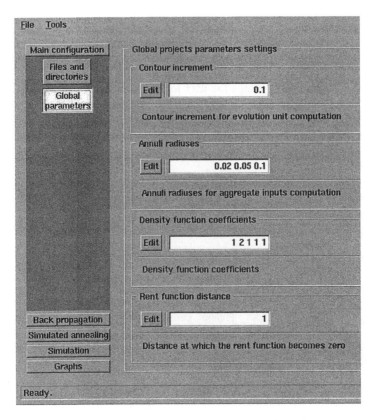

Figure 7.17   A Snapshot from the Global Parameters Panel

By clicking on the **Global parameters** shutter (Figure 7.17) the user may set up the global parameters of the projects. These are:

- **contour increment**: points are distributed in a 2-dimensional space; the application calculates the smallest rectangular area in which all the points are located and then calculates the maximum edge of this rectangle;
- **radius of annuli**: a list of the radii of annuli;
- **density function coefficients**: a list of coefficients associated with the density function;

- **rent function distance**: distance at which the rent function becomes equal to 0.01 assuming an exponential decay;
- **road coefficient**: a coefficient >1 which weights the distance traveled outside the road network.

Back-propagation

In this section parameters accessible from the **Back-propagation** shutter will be shown. In the **Neural networks weights** (Figure 7.18) two buttons are available. The **Null weights** button brings the user to the network weights matrix in which he/she can set the desired weight equal to zero. The **View weights** button is used to see the actual back-propagation weights. In the **Back-propagation parameters** the user sets the parameters affecting the back-propagation phase of the elaboration.

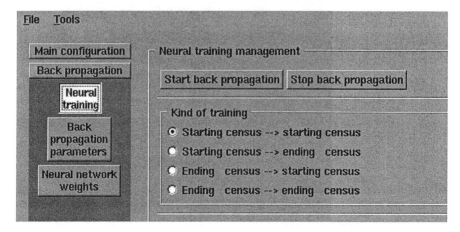

Figure 7.18   A Snapshot from the Back-propagation Panel

These parameters are:

- **momentum**;
- **learning rate**;
- **max initial weights**: the maximum value at which weights will be initialized.

In order to start back-propagation one clicks on the **Neural training** panel. In the training box the user specifies which data will be used in the training as input and as output.

Simulated Annealing

In this section the parameters available from the **Simulated annealing** shutter are shown. In the **Simulated annealing parameters** panel the user sets parameters affecting the simulated annealing phase of the elaboration. These parameters are:

- **sub-iterations**: the number of sub-iterations between initial and final census;
- **starting temperature**;
- **thermal attenuation**;
- **max iterations**: maximum number of iterations with a constant temperature;
- **min successes**: number of successes that must be hit to continue with the simulated annealing;
- **max successes**: number of successes that must be hit to decrease temperature;
- **weights variation**: per cent variation of weights calculated with back-propagation.

In order to start simulated annealing the user clicks on the **Simulated annealing panel**.

Simulation

In the **Simulation** panel the user sets up two parameters:

- **steps**: the number of sub-iterations of the simulation;
- **totals**: total variables values at last sub-iteration step.

Graphs

In the **Graphs parameter** panel the user sets up the following parameters:

- **canvas dimensions**: the canvas dimension for graphics;
- **correction**: a correction factor to better visualize low values;
- **grid dimension**: grid dimension (in pixels) in which values will be approximated;

In the **Graphs** panel the user sets up the following parameters:

- **variable**: number of the variable to be rendered;
- **census**: census code to be rendered; 0 means the initial census, 1 is the final census, 2 is related to the values obtained with simulation.

Chapter 8

Land Use Dynamics: a Stochastic Forecasting Model Based on SOM Neural Nets Knowledge

Lidia Diappi and Paola Bolchi

Introduction

The recent tendency of settlement patterns to sprawl is a central issue for all policies endeavouring to adopt sustainable approaches. It is surprising that there have been few efforts attempting to predict future urbanisation patterns even in the case of a "no action" scenario. The question was partly addressed by the integrated models of land use and transportation developed in the 1970s and 1980s. Recent applications of these models (Putman, 1979), models developed by the school of Dortmund (Wegener, 1998), TRANUS (De la Barra, 1989) and the very recent URBAN SIM model (Noth, Borning and Waddell, 2003), just to mention a few examples, indicate that there is still lively interest being shown by experts, planners and politicians to find out more about the future functional and spatial patterns of cities and regions. A principal objective of these models is to produce spatial patterns which are in accordance with theoretical principles.

This vast amount of scientific work has some common features:

- an assumption that the complexity of urban systems can be limited to some key measurable variables: population and dwellings, employment, economic activities, and space mainly assumed in terms of distance and available area;
- a formalisation in equations that is derived from a well-established theoretical basis (spatial interaction, principles of hierarchy, economic base theory, random utility theory, etc.);
- an economic efficiency criterion guides the choices of populations and activities;
- an aggregate scale of description and representation (a meso-scale) applies, which generates a defined transformation scenario for categories or classes.

In recent years new territorial problems and renewed epistemological needs have resulted in significant innovations to models of land use.

Environmental issues – brought to notice by the question of sustainable development, particularly in cities – have focused attention on the consumption of non-renewable resources, with consumption of land being a top priority.

Non-urbanised land, no longer considered a residual space or passive support, becomes a crucial asset and an important ecological and amenity resource, but is being steadily encroached upon by the pressure of dispersed urbanisation. However, if suitable settlement models could be identified, dispersed urbanisation could be compatible with the requirements of sustainability.

On an epistemological level, dissatisfaction with the results achieved so far using earlier models to capture the actual dynamics of land use has prompted growing interest in alternative approaches and the emergence of a new paradigm based on developments in Artificial Intelligence (AI), which is able to examine the structure of data, discover significant relationships and to extrapolate them to construct scenarios in complex situations marked by self-organisation and uncertainty.

In traditional modelling, the model is derived from theory in a top-down process, whereas the AI approaches reverse the order and construct knowledge endogenously through a bottom-up process. They start from data and the transformation rules – or more exactly, the transition from one state to another – are only discovered *a posteriori*. These approaches adopt distributed architecture such as Cellular Automata (CA), Neural Networks (NN) and Multi-Agent Systems (MAS), which process data occurring at the level of individual interactions on the micro-scale. Among these approaches, neural networks have proved to be a very effective and reliable tool since, via a learning phase, they can quantify and model complex data and behaviours. Neural networks have already been widely used as a method for classifying fuzzy data and as statistical estimators, but have only recently been applied in planning for land use forecasting. The LTM model (Pijanowski, Brown, Manik, Shellito, 2002) uses NNs applied to GIS to learn how factors such as roads, motorways and the local road system, recreational facilities, and agricultural settlements can influence urbanisation patterns, assessing their effects and effectiveness at different scales.

The authors of this chapter have already tested a model for forecasting land use which was based on a supervised neural network applied to a database containing information organised according to a cellular automata method. This assumed that the change in land use in a certain part of the territory was a function of land use in the neighbouring cells at the previous temporal threshold (Diappi, Bolchi, Franzini, 2001). However, the experiment was limited by the type of supervised neural network used and the results were not very satisfactory. In the present work we wished to follow a different approach which used the NN's ability to identify transition rules and, on this basis, to predict the spatial patterns of urbanisation via a stochastic simulation where the rules were translated into transition probabilities.

Methodology

The aim of the methodological approach chosen was to identify the transition rules from the information describing land use patterns at two temporal thresholds. The databases used referred to the southern area of the province of Milan described by main types of use and was subdivided into cells in a square grid.

The neural network method, and in particular, the SOM method, enables the typologies of transitions from an initial state at time t to the subsequent state at time $t + 1$ to be identified.

The type of information found in typical cellular automata hypotheses was used – what influences the transformation of one portion of the territory from one land use to another is a function of the initial state of the cell (and therefore of its land use) and of the state of neighbouring cells, i.e. of the surroundings at the initial timepoint. The logic of spatial localisation according to CA is therefore "local"; for example, a subject will decide to build his or her dwelling in a particular place on the basis of its proximity to other dwellings, services and roads. But in the classical form of territorial modelling based on CA (Cecchini and Rizzi, 2003; White, Engelen and Uljee, 1993), the rules are formulated *a priori* and exogenously. The resulting transformation mechanisms are necessarily oversimplified and the scenarios presented do not adequately reflect complex realities.

In this article, while we accept the "local" logic underlying CA and therefore use the same input information, our transformation rules are discovered *a posteriori*, by exploring the relations between the initial states of the cell and its neighbours, and the final state of each individual cell.

If the data is processed using SOM networks, which basically classify the data, some transformation typologies or classes emerge, which group all the individual cells according to similarities in their dynamic behaviour.

In particular, for each class, the SOM NN identifies a prototype, called a codebook, which represents the dynamic behaviour of that group of cells and expresses a "transition rule" which contains the "average" initial state of cells and neighbourhood and the expected "average" final state.

The rules, which are tested according to appropriate procedures, are the fundamental instrument used, and are applied to the most recent temporal threshold, and the pattern of future urbanisation.

So, starting at an initial state that is changed at time $t + 1$, the cells, that in the meantime have obviously also changed, are allocated to the SOM classes based on their similarity to the prototype *only for the initial state*.

At this point the easiest solution would consist in simply applying the use predicted by the class rule to each cell. But as mentioned, the codebook expresses an average transition behaviour, from which the cells of the group deviate to variable extents.

It therefore seemed preferable to build a simulation model, based on a Monte Carlo procedure, where the change in use is extracted from within a probability distribution calibrated from transformations that actually occurred for the cells of the group in the previous time period. The whole procedure is depicted in Figure 8.1.

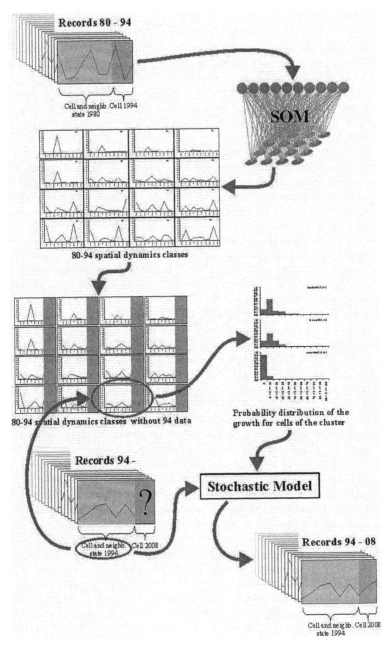

Figure 8.1 The Procedure Used. The SOM classes produce knowledge about the distribution of growth for each land use in each class. The probability distribution obtained feeds the stochastic model which produces the forecasted growth of each cell.

The Case Study and The Data

The area under study covered the territory extending in a semi-circle round the south of Milan, but excluding the city of Milan itself, containing a large amount of agricultural land and protected Natural Park areas (Parco del Ticino, Parco Sud). The area is being increasingly eroded by urbanisation caused by an exodus from Milan and by the creation of shopping centres and industrial developments. The objective of examining not only the amount, but also the form of future probable patterns of development, clearly meets the objective of assessing future patterns in the context of sustainability objectives.

The model uses a basic grid of cells with a side of 500 metres, for a total of 2703 cells. The land uses considered, residential, commercial, industrial and open land, are expressed as a percentage of the total cell area. Only two temporal thresholds were considered: 1980 and 1994.

The following information was provided to the neural network:

- land uses of cell i at time t (1980)
- land uses of neighbouring cells at time t
- average distance from roads at time t
- land uses of cell i at time $t + 1$ (1994)

In summary, the record contains seven data (on the cell and neighbourhood) related to the initial state and three data (only on the cell) related to the final state.

Artificial Neural Networks

Neural networks are powerful instruments which use the learning approach of an artificial intelligence machine to quantify and model complex patterns and behaviours. In recent years ANN models have generated increasing interest in the field of urban and regional analysis. The idea of training a system to independently develop cognitive abilities, such as adaptive responses to a set of information, is a fundamentally new approach to processing information. Openshaw (1993), and Fischer and Gopal (1994) were the first to appreciate the potential of neurocomputation applied to regional sciences.

There are two distinct phases in the operation of an Artificial Neural Network (ANN): the learning or *training phase,* when the network learns the rules (and thus defines the intensity of the connection or weights) starting from "examples", and the *querying phase*, when the network processes the input data using the learned rules. Between the two phases usually a *test phase* should verify the network's learning performances.

The ANN dynamic varies according to the *learning rules* adopted, which in turn depend on the objective of the network and thus on the type of output the network is required to learn to generate. The learning dynamic of networks is usually divided into two classes: *supervised networks* and *unsupervised networks*.

If the vectors of experimental data for which the network has to identify the connections are defined as "models", then (Hech-Nielsen, 1990; Buscema, 1994):

- *supervised networks* assume predefined targets to which every model in the network has to conform. These are output targets decided by the external environment and are not deduced by the input vector or any part of it.
- *monitored networks* are networks whose ideal targets are predefined for each input model, but each target is taken by the input vector of the network, or part of it.
- *autopoietic networks* are networks whose targets are formed dynamically during the learning phase and cannot therefore be defined *a priori*. They are networks that stabilise on the basis of the statistical regularities of their input models.

Most of the applications of NNs in the field of regional studies have used supervised networks (Griguolo, in this book; Fischer and Gopal, 1994; Fischer, 1997) and monitored networks (Buscema, Diappi, Ottanà, 1998). Some work has recently appeared using autopoietic, or self-organising, neural networks (Diappi, Bolchi, Franzini, 2001) such as SOM NNs, which belong to the more general set of "mapping networks", i.e. networks able to identify a mathematical interpolating function from a set of data.

To verify the ability of NNs to identify connections, records are first used to train the network, and then, deprived of the output variables, resubmitted to the network for the scenario phase. This makes it possible to calculate the error based on the number of cells which are "wrong" when compared with the output proposed to the network when being trained.

SOM Networks (Self-Organising Maps)

Some of the properties of SOM networks (Kohonen, 1995) are summarised here, since a detailed description of the obtained results is presented in a previous article (Diappi et al., 2002).

The functioning of SOM is directed towards this goal: creating a bidimensional map of the characteristics of the Input pattern, in a way that the present order among the Inputs is also kept in the map. The essential information pertinent to the considered problem is processed in order to reconstruct a map of the problem's fundamental features.

The architecture of the SOM is constituted by the Input layer (IL) and the Kohonen layer (KL), which maps Inputs of N-dimensional space in an ordered bidimensional space. There is no loss of information in this mapping, because the information is codified in the connection values between the Input vector and the node in the KL, which, by activating itself, reacts to the Input vector.

One of the NN SOM characteristics is that they self-organise the clusters of the Input and therefore they learn without supervision. The KL is an adaptive units layer, which gradually (during the training) transforms itself in a spatially ordered map of "features detectors" (Ritter, 1995). The competitive mechanism, in correspondence of an Input vector, brings both the activation of some nodes and the inhibition of some others.

The process of activation of Kohonen nodes is of *Winner takes all* (WTA) type. Each Input vector actives the most similar KL node (the winner unit), which is able to react and change itself in order to be spatially nearer to the Input vectors of his group. The winner Kohonen Node is called codebook and represents the prototypical features of the group.

Usually, instead of activating only one winner unit, (with the inhibition of all the others), scientists prefer to activate a region of KL nodes, where the decreasing distance from the winner unit means increasing similarity.

The only, but most sensitive, exogenous decision is selecting the number of classes desired, which obviously involves balancing the need to produce differentiated classes against the need to have significant class sizes. In the present study, a process of trial and error led to 16 classes being chosen. One objection, which needs to be immediately answered, is what advantage there is between this instrument and other well-known statistical methods, such as multivariate statistical analysis, which meet the same statistical objective of identifying classes of similar phenomena. The ability of NNs to gather nonlinear relations, unlike the above-mentioned methods, means that NNs are often used as an alternative or as a complement to them. Many studies have compared the effectiveness of approaches based on statistical estimates with those using NNs, for example when calibrating models. The range of different results obtained shows that they are instruments that operate with different logics and they measure different relations but they converge in indicating the "best fit" of some models compared to others if the choice is presented.

After analysing the study data, classification of records showed there is a spatial logic. Cells belonging to the same class are positioned contiguously or in consistent positions relative to urbanised areas: for example at the edge of the urban centre or along the main transport routes.

The results are summarised in Figure 8.2, where the profiles and codebooks of each group are shown, and in Figure 8.3 where the spatial map of cells according to their class is shown.

Figure 8.2 shows diagrams of the codebooks of an individual cluster superimposed on the profiles of cells belonging to it and the prototypical properties of the group; while the set of profiles of individual cells, through their deviations or agreement with the codebook, enables the distinguishing variables and the influences on the classification to be assessed.

The 16 groups of Figure 8.2 are each shown in a diagram with the x axis representing state variables (in order from the origin: land use of cell in 1980, proximity to roads and land use of neighbourhood in 1980, land use of cell in 1994). The y axis shows the degree of activation of individual variables. The envelope of all the records in the group is shown in grey, around the codebook in a dotted line.

As can be seen, the first row shows cells of open land which remain so at the second temporal threshold; they are mainly agricultural areas. However, on moving to the right, proximity to roads increases and the "probability of future urbanisation" arises.

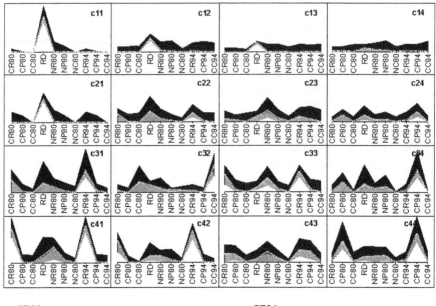

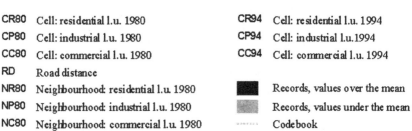

CR80	Cell: residential l.u. 1980	CR94	Cell: residential l.u. 1994
CP80	Cell: industrial l.u. 1980	CP94	Cell: industrial l.u.1994
CC80	Cell: commercial l.u. 1980	CC94	Cell: commercial l.u. 1994
RD	Road distance		
NR80	Neighbourhood: residential l.u. 1980		Records, values over the mean
NP80	Neighbourhood: industrial l.u. 1980		Records, values under the mean
NC80	Neighbourhood: commercial l.u. 1980		Codebook

Figure 8.2 The Classes of Records Produced by the SOM Neural Networks
The prototypical profile (dotted line) is the Codebook.

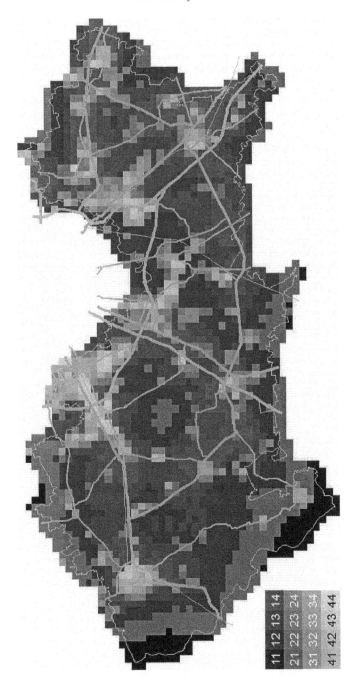

Figure 8.3 The Spatial Distribution of the Cells According to the SOM Classes

Going vertically down the first class C11, increasing proximity to roads and an increase in residential use over the considered time period can be seen. More precisely, transformations of agricultural areas to residential use occur in C12, of already partially urbanised areas in C13 or of areas already residential in 1980 in C14.

In the last row, C44 shows an increase in industrial development in areas which were already industrialised in 1980. In this case too, the final column gradually takes account of modifications towards the end use, which only emerges as a final state in classes C34 and C44.

From the description of the possible land use dynamics identified by the SOM, "transition rules" can be extracted which can be used as input for a model forecasting subsequent urbanisation.

As mentioned, a spatial logic to transformations also emerges. The map in Figure 8.3 shows spatial classification of cells according to their class. It can be seen how new residential settlements tend to favour expansion outwards from urban centres and proximity to roads while industrial development appears to have a tendency to cluster together.

In general it can be seen that cells of the same transition class are also spatially contiguous, thus confirming the validity of the method being tested.

The Probabilistic Model

We now face the problem of how to apply the discovered transition rules in the form of a dynamic model. The dynamic could be formalised as a stochastic process using transition probabilities between initial and final states that can be extracted by the codebooks identified by SOMs. The codebook in fact perfectly describes the average profile, both of the initial state and the final state.

However, this would result in an excessively oversimplified procedure; as mentioned above, these are average values and the real transitions occurring in the period deviate from them considerably. In fact the transformations in each class can be better described by a probability distribution of land use activations rather than a single average value.

It seemed preferable therefore to adopt a simulation procedure using probability distributions to allocate the land uses to the various cells. The initial state is therefore 1994 and the temporal threshold for the forecast, assuming the same time lag, will be 2008, the final state of the system.

The procedure adopted is as follows:

- from the SOM classification, for each group, growth probability distributions are extracted for the three land uses on the base of the observed frequencies of land use changes in the period;
- since the initial state of the system is now 1994, the records are updated with the present land use information for each cell and its neighbourhood (seven fields);

- the new records are assigned to the SOM classes previously discovered, on the basis of similarity to the "initial state" part of the codebooks;
- to assign a final state to each cell, a Monte Carlo procedure is used, by which a percentage of growth for each land use is drawn out;
- the model is tested using the 1980-1994 data to check its reliability;
- the model is implemented; and
- the results are evaluated by different criteria and indexes.

Results

The difficulties in interpreting results obtained from models are well known, particularly when neural networks are used, since their "black box" nature makes "objective" validation of results difficult to achieve. It is therefore appropriate to rely on qualitative evaluation to check whether the results achieved make sense and are consistent.

Various approaches have been followed in this work to adequately evaluate the results. Some are based on the aggregate area data for different land uses, others use SOM classes repeated at different temporal thresholds to analyse changes of class and position of cells, and other approaches use statistical indicators of compactness and dispersion to evaluate trends in spatial patterns.

Probability of Change

Before analysing the final results, it is worth making a few comments on the probability distributions obtained from evaluating the groups of SOM networks. Figure 8.4 show probability distributions of growth for all SOM groups. The x axis shows the percentage area activated in the considered time period (1980-1994) relative to the total area of the cell and the vertical axis shows the different probabilities. For the residential dynamic, it can be seen that the main increases occurred for classes C31 and C22 (extra-urban areas of residential settlement), C41 and C42 (urban areas of residential settlement), followed by C32 (extra-urban commercial areas). These classes of cells are in fact the ones producing greatest residential increases. The other groups display probabilities mainly below 10%.

The analogous distributions for industrial use display greatest increases in classes C34 (industrial areas near to roads) and C44 (infilling of existing industrial areas far from roads) and, to a lesser extent, in C24 (non-urbanised areas); increases for other classes are negligible (below 10%).

For commercial uses the main increases are concentrated in class C32 (extra-urban commercial areas).

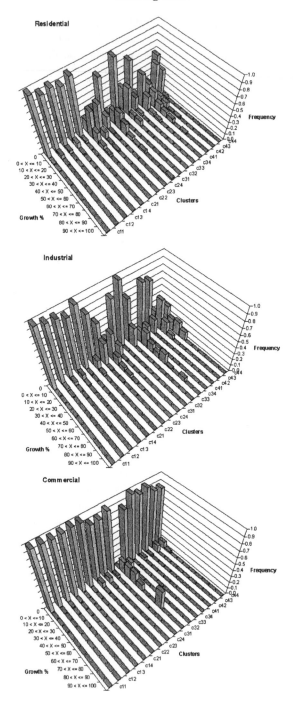

Figure 8.4 The Probability Distribution of Growth for Each Land Use

The Land Use Dynamics

Figures 8.5, 8.6 and 8.7 show the final results of the model for the three land uses. Before commenting in detail the spatial pattern obtained, a first examination of the results focuses on a comparison between total areas dedicated to the three land uses estimated for 2008 and the historical data of 1980 and 1994.

Table 8.1 The Land Use Surfaces

	Residential	Industrial	Commercial	total
1980	33.86	15.72	1.86	*51.44*
1994	47.04	24.56	3.34	*74.94*
2008	63.31	35.85	6.15	*105.31*
increase 80-94	13.18	8.84	1.48	*23.50*
increase 94-08	16.27	11.29	2.82	*30.37*
incr % 80-94	38.9%	56.3%	79.4%	*45.7%*
incr % 94-08	34.6%	46.0%	84.4%	*40.5%*

For residential and industrial uses, the increase would basically appear to continue, though at a reduced rate. Commercial use would grow at a constant rate.

The statistical distribution for the size of new urbanised areas according to function is shown in Figure 8.8. The x axis shows the percentage of growth and the y axis the number of cases. For all three functions the average lot sizes appear to be larger in the first period than the second.

The Change in Urbanisation Dynamic via SOM Classes

Since application of the model also required reclassifying the SOM of cells based on the initial state in 1994, another interesting comparison is to examine the number of cells present in each class at the two temporal thresholds (calibration and forecast).

It can be seen in Figure 8.9 how all the classes have decreased relative to non-urbanised land (C12-C14), with the exception of class C11, which represents permanently green areas; this result is predictable since part of the new urbanisation has obviously occupied unbuilt areas. The analysis of the intermediate classes (C21-C34) is more interesting, with an alternating tendency to increase and decrease being evident. Class 23, with a clear increase, is an exception and corresponds to transitions from pure residential to commercial/residential areas. The last four classes, which can be defined as zones of mixed residential/industrial use, from the more central, mainly residential ones (C41), to the more outlying ones of mainly industrial development (C44), all increase significantly.

If we consider the dynamics of cells and their neighbours between the three temporal thresholds 1980, 1994 and 2008 and analyse which SOM classes they belong to for each period, it is possible to evaluate the class changes that have occurred in the period. In the first period of time the principal transitions are of cells at the edges of inhabited centres or nuclei of new urbanisation mainly along road axes.

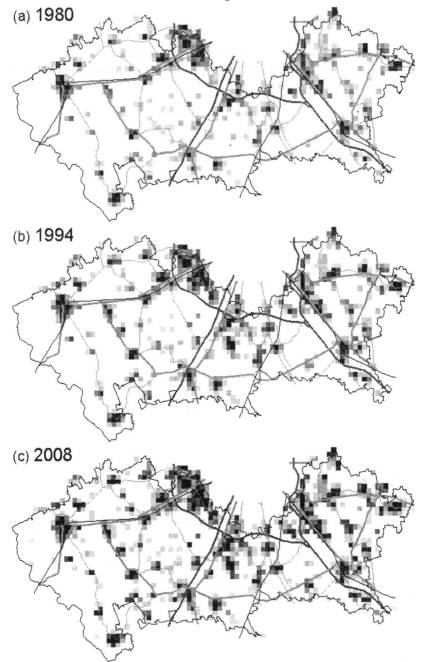

(a) 1980

(b) 1994

(c) 2008

Figure 8.5 Residence Dynamics. (*a*) and (*b*) observed state of the System in 1980 and 1994; (*c*) forecasted state of the System in 2008.

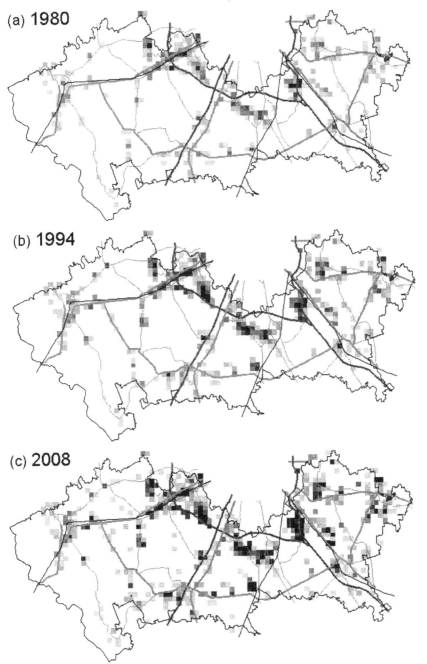

Figure 8.6 Industrial Dynamics. *(a)* and *(b)* observed state of the System in 1980 and 1994; *(c)* forecasted state of the System in 2008.

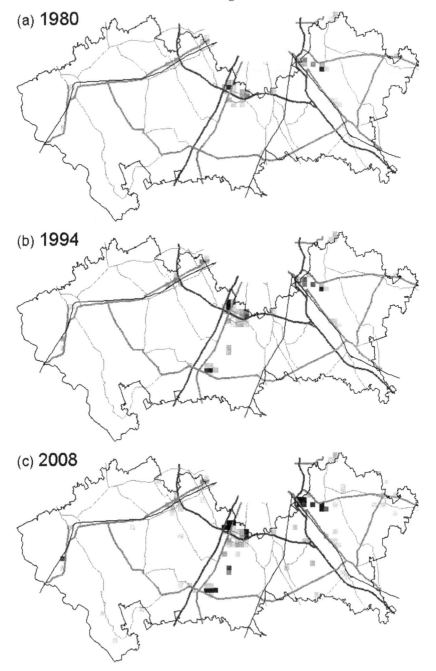

Figure 8.7 Commerce Dynamics. (*a*) and (*b*) observed state of the System in 1980 and 1994; (*c*) forecasted state of the System in 2008.

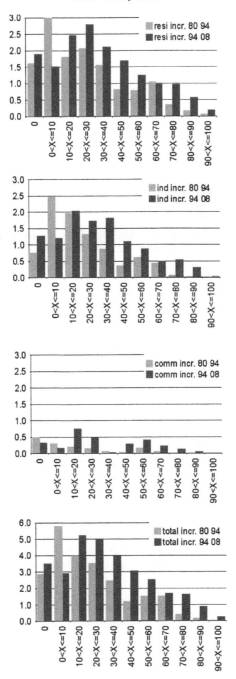

Figure 8.8 The Growth Distributions in the Two Periods: 1980-1994 and 1994-2008

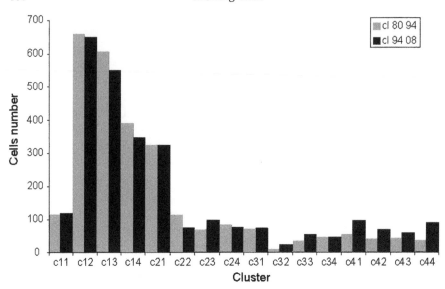

**Figure 8.9 The Number of Cells Present in Each SOM Class in the Two
Periods: 1980-1994 and 1994-2008**

Between 1994 and 2008, however, transitions are mainly of cells located further away from historic centres and situated around the nuclei which emerged in the previous period.

The Degree of Compactness

A significant help in interpreting the results obtained so far may be provided by applying an index of compactness for the historical thresholds 1980, 1994 and 2008, applying it first to the entire urbanised area and then just to the newly urbanised areas of the two periods.

The indicator used (Xuan Thinh, Arlt, Heber et al., 2002) measures the spatial configuration of urban functions applied to a grid of cells and expressing the area dedicated to different uses as a percentage.

For each pair of cells i and j ($i = 1(1)$ N $- 1, j = i + 1(1)$ i) with respective areas Z_i and Z_j, attraction is calculated using an inverse square relationship analogous to the law of gravitation:

$$A(i, j) = \frac{1}{C} \frac{Z_i Z_j}{d^2(i, j)}$$

where $d^2(i, j)$ is the Euclidean distance between the centres of the cells i and j and C (100 m^2) is a proportionality factor to make the term $A(i, j)$ dimensionless. The degree of compactness is defined as the mean value of the gravitational matrix:

$$T = \frac{\sum A(i,j)}{\dfrac{N(N-1)}{2}}$$

where N is the total number of urbanised cells. T is a measure of centrality for the spatial interaction between aggregate areas. If urban structures are more extensively dispersed and dot-like, then the interaction between urban aggregates is weaker. Conversely, as the compactness of urban structures increases then T will be larger.

The index, applied to the whole existing built area at the three temporal thresholds, shows (Figure 8.10) increasing compactness in all uses, particularly commercial, and highlights how new urbanisation processes fill areas and aggregate to old centres. When the same index is applied just to new construction in the two periods, there is a decrease, indicating that the settlement models are more dispersed. This second index is not very significant however since the position of new urbanisation clearly depends on pre-existing structures and not on the functions created in the same period.

The Degree of Dispersion

Assuming as centroids the main historical centres of the area (Abbiategrasso, Binasco Melegnano, Rozzano, Paullo, San Giuliano, San Donato, Trezzano) and tracing circles of variable radius, but sufficient to include both the urbanised area and the surrounding agricultural area (Figure 8.11), the following index was calculated for each use:

$$\frac{\sum_i S_i d_{ic}^2}{\sum_i S_i}$$

where S_i is the built area and d_{ic} is the distance from the centroid. The indexes applied to the total built area at the three thresholds show varying behaviour (Figure 8.12). For residential use, dispersion generally increases slightly in Abbiategrasso, Binasco and San Donato, decreases in Paullo and Trezzano and is stable in Rozzano. When the index is applied to increases occurring in the period it shows that dispersion decreases everywhere, except for San Donato, San Giuliano and Binasco.

Industrial settlements show settlement models similar to the residential ones, with some variability. Total dispersion is again stable or increases slightly, but Melegnano and Trezzano go against the trend, as is more evident in the diagram of just the increases occurring in the two periods.

The location of commercial functions is difficult to interpret since just a few large centres are involved and they are unlikely to display a common trend. Nonetheless, in this case too, when the index is applied to existing structures it seems to indicate greater dispersion, i.e. new extra-urban locations, but the increase diagrams do not support this hypothesis.

In short, this does not appear to show that most new settlements result in greater dispersion and hence greater use of land.

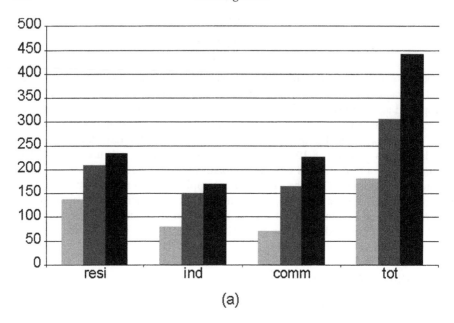

(a)

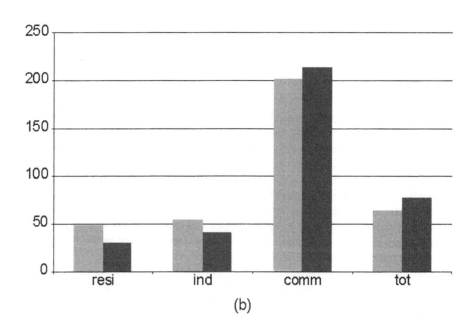

(b)

Figure 8.10 The Index of Compactness. (a) Of the whole urbanized area and (b) Only of the new settlements.

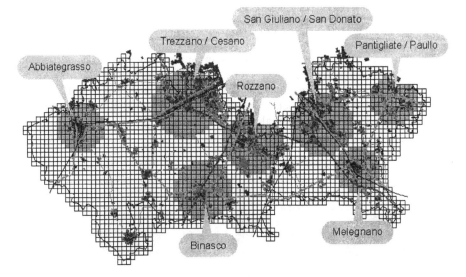

Figure 8.11 The Historical Centres and the Circular Areas Considered to Measure the Index of Dispersion

The Ratio Perimeter/Area

A further measure of compactness/dispersion is given by the simple ratio perimeter/area of urbanised cells, an index which indicates the degree of separation of urban agglomerates. The diagram of the existing situation at the three historic temporal thresholds shows a decrease of intermediate data and hence evidence of growth (Figure 8.13). This would seem to confirm the hypothesis that in the period 1980-1994 new settlements occurred via a process of infilling of existing urban areas and in the subsequent period there was a process of peri-urban urbanisation away from historic centres. This hypothesis is confirmed by the trends shown in the increase diagram.

In summary, some distinct trends can be seen to emerge in the dynamic of the area under consideration:

- While the process certainly involves encroachment on agricultural areas surrounding urban centres, it is not a process of uncontrolled diffusion of settlements over the territory. New urbanisation appears to form and consolidate in fairly compact fashion around urban nuclei, as is indicated by the indexes of compactness. The two phases – the calibrated and the simulated – show an initial period where urbanisation occurs in nuclei external to the inhabited area with settlement extending in large lot sizes and a second phase where infilling occurs with smaller size lots.
- The index of dispersion around historic centres is not inconsistent with this interpretation because the new nuclei which are established outside the centres

along roads, while they are compact, nonetheless increase the value of the index of dispersion, which increases with the square of the distance of
settlements from the centroid.

• There is a high functional mix in new urbanised areas, which bring together
  residential, industrial and commercial uses. The choice of residential location
  seems to be more focused on a search for privacy and proximity to services
  and workplace than the social contacts and environmental quality generally offered by exclusively residential zones.

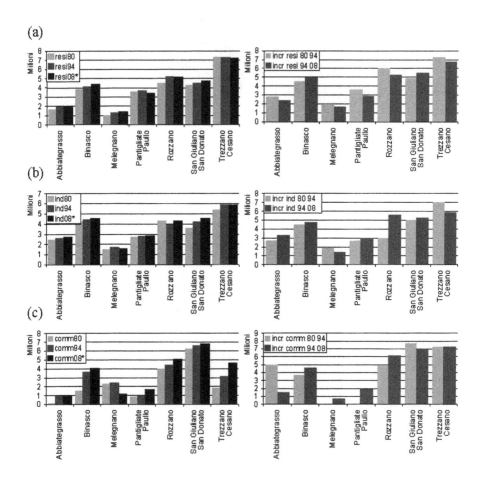

Figure 8.12 The Index of Dispersion. (*a*) for residence; (*b*) for industry; (*c*) for
            commerce.

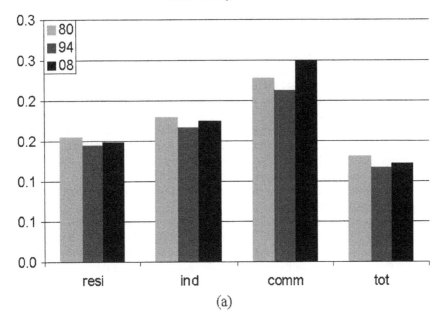

(a)

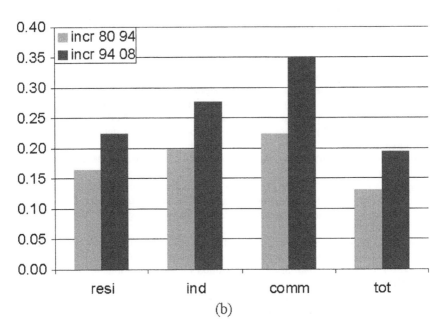

(b)

Figure 8.13 The Perimeter/Area Ratio. (*a*)for residential (left), industrial (centre), commercial (right) settlements at the three thresholds and (*b*) the
Index applied only to the new settlements built in the two periods:
1980-1994 and 1994-2008.

Concluding Remarks

The method presented here aimed to combine the significant investigative power of NN in organising knowledge with a stochastic simulation model able to produce urbanisation scenarios based on rules learned by NNs.

The NNs showed they were able to capture the fundamental characteristics of urbanisation, identifying fuzzy typologies in the spatial dynamic. These were then used as "rules" of change and entered into the stochastic simulation model.

It was then decided to adopt an "eclectic" approach, combining methods of geocomputation, with knowledge being built from the bottom up, and traditional "top-down" methods which apply explicitly-defined rules.

The benefits of this are that rules are transparent and it is therefore easier to interpret and evaluate the results.

In the context of understanding the phenomenon of "urbanisation", it is important to have discovered that the spontaneous process follows a logic of expansion around urbanised nuclei and road axes and does not appear to exhibit undifferentiated diffusion, contrary to the concerns expressed in much of the literature.

References

Buscema, M. (1994), "Constraint Satisfaction Networks", in Buscema, M., Didoné, G., Pandin, M., *Reti Neurali Autoriflessive, Quaderni di Ricerca*, 1, Armando Editore, Roma.

Buscema, M., Diappi, L., Ottanà, M. (1998), "A Neural Network Investigation on the Crucial Assets of Urban Sustainability", *Substance Use and Misuse*, Special Issue on Artificial Neural Networks and Social Systems, 33, pp. 793-817.

Cecchini, A., Rizzi, P. (2003), "Perché gli automi cellulari sono uno strumento utile della scatola di attrezzi per il governo del territorio dell'urbanista del nuovo millennio", in Lombardo, S. (ed.), *Ingegneria del territorio e ingegneria della conoscenza,* Alinea, Firenze.

De la Barra, T. (1989), *Integrated Land Use and Transportation Modelling*, Cambridge University Press.

Diappi, L., Bolchi, P., Franzini, L. (2001), "Urban Dynamics: Behavioural Rules of Land Use change in the South Metropolitan Area of Milan through Neural Networks SOM", *41st European Regional Science Association Congress*, Zagreb, 29 August-1 September 2001, CD-ROM.

Diappi, L., Buscema, M., Bolchi, P., Franzini, L. (2002), "The Urban Sprawl Dynamics: Does a Neural Network Understand the Spatial Logic Better than a Cellular Automata?", *42nd European Regional Science Association Congress*, Dortmund, 27-31 August, CD-ROM.

Fischer, M. (1997), "Computational Neural Networks: a new Paradigm for Spatial Analysis", *Environment and Planning A.*, 29, pp. 1873-1891.

Fischer, M., Gopal, S. (1994), "Artificial Neural Networks: a new Approach to Modeling Interregional Telecommunication flows", *Journal of Regional Science*, 34 (4), pp. 503-527.

Fischer, M.M., Leung, Y. (eds) (2001), *Geocomputational Modelling*, Springer Verlag, Berlin, Heidelberg.

Griguolo, S. (2004), "Neural Classifiers for Land Cover Recognition: Merging Radiometric and Ancillary Information", in this book.

Hecht-Nielsen, R. (1990), *Neurocomputing*, Addison-Wesley, Reading, Mass.

Kohonen, T. (1995), *Self-Organizing Maps*, Springer Verlag, Berlin, Heidelberg.

Kosko, B. (1992), *Neural Networks and Fuzzy Systems: a Dynamical System Approach to Machine Intelligence*, Prentice Hall, Englewood Cliffs, NJ, USA.

Noth, M., Borning, A., Waddell, P. (2003), "An extensible modular architecture for simulating urban development, transportation, and environmental impacts", *Computers, Environment and Urban Systems*, 27, pp. 181-203.

Openshaw, S. (1993), "Modelling spatial interaction using neural net", in Fischer M., Nijkamp P. (eds.), *GIS, Spatial Modelling and Policy Evaluation*, Springer Verlag, Heidelberg, pp. 147-164.

Openshaw, S. (1998), "Neural Networks, Genetic and Fuzzy Logic Models of Spatial Interaction", *Environment and Planning A*, 30, pp. 1857-1872.

Openshaw, S., Abrahart, R.J. (2000), *Geocomputation*, Taylor & Francis, London and New York.

Pijanowski, B.C., Brown, D.G., Manik, G. and Shellito B. (2002), "Using Neural Nets and GIS to Forecast Land Use Changes: A Land Transformations Model", *Computer Environment and Urban Systems*, 26 (6), pp. 553-575.

Putman, S.H. (1979), *Urban Residential Location Models*, Martinus Nijhoff Publishing.

Ritter, H. (1995), "Self-organising Feature maps: Kohonen maps", in Arbib, M. A. (ed.) *The Handbook of Brain Theory and Neural Networks*, A Bradford book, The MIT Press, Cambridge, Massachusetts and London, Great Britain.

Wegener, M. (1998), "Applied models of urban land use, transport and environment, state of the art and future developments", in Lundqvist, L., Mattson, L.G., Kim, T. J. (eds.) *Network Infrastructure and the Urban Environment: Recent Advances in Land Use/Transportation Modelling.*, Springer Verlag, Berlin, Heidelberg, New York, pp. 245-267.

White, R., Engelen, G. (2000), "High-resolution integrated modelling of the spatial dynamics of urban and regional systems", *Computers, Environment and Urban Systems*, 24, pp. 383-400.

White, R., Engelen, G., Uljee, I. (1993), "Cellular automata modelling of fractal urban land use patterns: forecasting change for planning applications", in *Eight European Colloquium on Theoretical and Quantitative Geography*, CD ROM Budapest.

Xuan Thinh, N., Arlt, G., Heber, B., Hennersdorf, J., Lehmann, I. (2002), "Evaluation of urban land-use structures with view to sustainable development", *Environmental Impact Assessment Review*, 22, pp. 475-492.

PART III
MULTI-AGENT SYSTEMS:
INTERACTIONS AMONG ACTORS
AND THEIR BEHAVIOURS

Chapter 9

Multi-agent Simulations for Traffic in Regional Planning

Kai Nagel and Bryan Raney

Introduction

The negative impact of traffic, such as noise, chemical emissions, accidents, or waste of time in congestion, is largely recognized as a problem. On the other hand, simple solutions are not possible: traffic is connected too much to the economic performance of a region and to the personal preferences of individuals living in the region. In addition, decisions on regional development, such as on infrastructure or on zoning laws, have a slow reaction time and a long life time: a freeway system or a train system takes a significant amount of time to build, and they will last for many decades.

In order to make such decisions, people make predictions about the future, and how the future would look with or without that change. Such predictions can be done in one's head or on a piece of paper. During the last century, the use of mathematical equations has been added to the set of possible methods. Finally, the computer has introduced a powerful new technology into the field of quantitative predictions.

Quantitative predictions are typically based on simulations. In simulations, a simplified version of the real world is constructed, and that simplified version of the real world is used to evaluate and compare different scenarios. A good solution is found via trial-and-error, that is, several solutions are constructed by humans and submitted to the simulation for evaluation. This is in contrast to direct optimization, where the solutions are also constructed by the algorithm. In consequence, simulation and optimization are related but not the same: an optimization needs to evaluate the quality of each option, and a simulation is a realistic but computationally expensive method to do that.

One can differentiate between the following simulation techniques:

- **Microscopic particle methods**. The simulation follows each particle individually through the system. The time evolution of the particles is often described by differential equations which are coupled via the interactive forces. For computer implementations, one treats each particle individually, but time is discretized into time steps of duration Δt. The differential equations are recovered in the limit $\Delta t \rightarrow 0$.

- **Field methods**. Often, the description of a system via a description of each individual particle is analytically or computationally ineffective. In such cases, one can employ field methods, where the fields represent quantities which are aggregated or averaged over many particles, such as density, velocity, or temperature. The time evolution of the fields is typically described by partial differential equations. For computer implementations, both time and space are discretized by Δt and Δx. The differential equations are recovered for the limit $\Delta t, \Delta x \rightarrow 0$.

- **Cellular automata (CA) methods**. In CA methods, space, time, and state space are coarse-grained discretized. The most important of those may be the coarse-graining of the state space, often down to just two states per cell. This can be seen as the simplest form of a strong non-linearity, as opposed to systems based on continuous equations, where the first approximation is normally linear. CA methods gain spatial resolution by giving up state space resolution. In consequence, they are particularly good at simulating complex geometries, such as fluid flow through porous media (e.g. Sahimi, 1993). In addition, they are often extremely useful when the goal is not so much a quantitative prediction but rather the understanding of mechanisms.

- **Intelligent agent methods**. Physical particles are normally described by a small number of state variables, such as position $\bar{x}$ and velocity $\bar{v}$. For complicated particles, such as humans, but also viruses or even for adaptive traffic lights, this is not appropriate and particles with more internal complexity need to be employed. The internal dynamics of such particles are often described by rules rather than by continuous equations. If a simulation is composed of many such agents, it are often called a *multi-agent simulation (MAS)*.

There are also hybrid forms of the above, such as what is also called *particle methods* but refers to quasi-particles which are computational aggregates of many physical particles and which is in consequence a hybrid between particle and field methods (Gingold and Monaghan, 1977), or *lattice Boltzmann methods* (McNamara and Zanetti, 1988), which are related to CA but allow a continuum of states in each cell.

Rule-based multi-agent simulations run well on current desktop PCs and they can be distributed on parallel computers of the type "networks of coupled PCs". Since such simulations do *not* run efficiently on traditional supercomputers (e.g. Cray), the jump in computational capability over the last decade has been much larger for multi-agent simulations than for, say, computational fluid-dynamics, which also runs well on traditional supercomputers. In practical terms, one is now able to run agent-based simulations of large metropolitan regions with more than 10 million travelers. These simulations are even fast enough to run them many times in sequence, which is necessary to emulate the dynamics of human learning, for example in reaction to congestion.

In consequence, these computational techniques are now far enough advanced to tackle problems of regional size, and to capture aspects which go beyond transportation alone. For example, as we will see later, it is possible to encode a different land use or maybe even just a different zoning system into the simulation and see how the whole system reacts. System reaction does not only include changes in traffic patterns and resulting emissions, but also how individual inhabitants change how they spend their days and weeks, which allows one to access individual satisfaction levels, coupled to demographic data.

This introductory chapter will in some detail describe how a multi-agent simulation for transportation planning is designed. It will then describe the current implementation status of such a simulation for "all of Switzerland", and related computational performance. This is followed by a discussion of possible extensions for applications in land use and regional planning. The chapter is concluded by a summary.

Simulation Modules

Traffic simulations for transportation planning typically consist of the following modules (Figure 9.1):

- **Population generation.** Demographic data is disaggregated so that one obtains individual households and individual household members, with certain characteristics, such as a street address, car ownership, or household income.
- **Activities generation.** For each individual, a set of activities (be-at-home, shopping, work, etc.) and activity locations for a day is generated.
- **Mode and route choice.** For each individual, the modes of transportation are selected and routes are generated that connect activities at different locations.
- **Traffic micro-simulation.** Up to here, all individuals have made *plans* about their behavior. The traffic micro-simulation executes all those plans simultaneously. In particular, one obtains the result of *interactions* between the plans – for example congestion.
- **Feedback.** In addition, such an approach needs to make the modules consistent with each other. For example, plans depend on congestion, but congestion depends on plans. A widely accepted method to resolve this is systematic relaxation – that is, make preliminary plans, run the traffic micro-simulation, adapt the plans, run the traffic micro-simulation again, etc., until consistency between modules is reached. The method is somewhat similar to the Frank-Wolfe algorithm in static assignment, or in more general terms to a standard relaxation technique in numerical analysis.

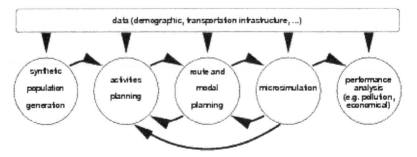

Figure 9.1 Some Modules of an Agent-based Transportation Simulation

This modularization has in fact been used for a long time; the main difference is that it is now feasible to make all modules completely microscopic, i.e. each traveler is individually represented in all modules.

Population Generation

In this module, demographic data is converted into individual households, populated by individual members. The input is spatially resolved census data. The output is synthetic individuals, with demographic characteristics such as age, gender, and income, and these individuals are grouped into households, with individual addresses, and additional characteristics such as car ownership. Such a population is a stochastic realization of the census data. In other words, the synthetic population does *not* correspond to the real world population. However, taking a census from the synthetic population would, within statistical errors, reproduce the original census data.

Many methods are possible to achieve these results. A typical problem is that census information only gives the so-called marginals for each census tract. For example, the number of males/females and the number of people below/above certain income levels is given, but one lacks the information how many females/males fall into a certain income category. Such information is often available for a microcensus, which is much more detailed in terms of such correlations, but which is only available for a small fraction of the population, and which is aggregated over larger geographical areas. In such situations, a typical solution is to use the correlation structure provided by the micro-census to provide the missing correlation structure for the census tracts (e.g. Beckman et al., 1996).

Activities Generation

In order to generate demand for transportation, one method is to generate complete daily or weekly activity patterns. The input is the synthetic population, plus information about land use such as the number and characteristics of workplaces, shopping options, etc. at all locations inside the area under consideration. In addition, behavioural data is needed, such as the sensitivity of people to distance. The output is complete activity plans for each member of the population, including starting and ending times and activity location. An example of a daily activity plan would be:

- "Be-at-home" on H-Street from the start of the simulation until 7:30am.
- Work on W-Street for 8 hours after arrival.
- Go shopping on S-Street for 1/2 hours.
- Pick up child at kindergarten on K-Street.
- Return home and stay there until the end of the simulation.

Again, many methods are possible to generate such activity plans. The only methods that seem to be operational at this point in time are discrete choice methods, which are based on randomutility theory (e.g. Ben-Akiva and Lerman, 1985; Bowman, 1998). The behavioural model behind these theories is that people attempt to pick the alternative with the highest utility, but either for psychological reasons or because of unobservable influences there is a random component in this. In the simplest version, called multinomial logit (MNL), the probability to select option i is

$$p(i) = \frac{e^{\beta U(i)}}{\sum_j e^{\beta U(i)}}$$

$U(i)$ is typically additive in its components, for example

$$U(i) = \alpha_0(i) + \alpha_1 T_{travel}(i) + \alpha_2 I \tag{1}$$

where $\alpha_0(i)$ is the basic utility of the given option, $T_{travel}(i)$ is the travel time to get there, and I is the income of the individual under consideration. α_1 and α_2 are conversion constants; β characterizes the amount of randomness.

One of the challenges is to find the α_i, which generate the sensitivities. For example, if in the above case $\alpha_0(i)$ is strongly positive but α_1 is strongly negative, then the individual is faced with a highly attractive option i but highly discouraging travel. In this situation, if the travel is short, then the option has a high probability of being accepted; if the travel is long, then it has a low probability of being accepted. A related challenge is to find a good composition of the sum Eq. (1): the individual terms need to be selected such that the α_i are different from zero on a statistically significant level. This means that finding the correct model and the corresponding constants is difficult; once those numbers are known, their insertion into an agent-based simulation model is fairly straightforward.

Models based on utility theory assume, at least in principle, that the human actor computes the utility for each option, and then carefully weighs their utilities. Given the combinatorial number of options that a dayplan can contain, this quickly leads to uncomputable situations. In addition, options are often not statistically independent, one instance of which is the famous "red bus, blue bus" problem: assume that a traveler is faced with the choice between taking the car, taking a red bus leaving from location X at time T, or taking a blue bus leaving from exactly the same location at the same time with exactly the same service characteristics. Further assume that the probability for each individual option is 1/3, that is, there is a 2/3 probability that the traveler takes a bus and a 1/3 probability that the traveler takes the car. Now assume that the red bus is removed from the set of options. In this case, the multinomial logit predicts that now the probability of taking the car increases to 1/2. Intuitively, one would have expected that selection between bus and car does not depend on the number of colours which are available for choice.

More advanced versions of the theory, such as probit, are necessary to resolve such issues; alternatively, the choice process can be nested, i.e. first making the choice between car and bus and only then choosing the colour of the bus if more than one colour is available. Nesting is subject to judgments on the side of the modeler.

Other aspects are: people typically choose only between options that they know, and that depends on their past experience ("mental maps") (e.g.Weinmann, in preparation); options have intricate interdependences that cannot be nested but make the model uncomputable when they are not nested (e.g. the decision who picks up the child may depend on car availability, which in turn may depend on the activity plan of another household member); the different activities are scheduled at different preplanning times (Doherty and Axhausen, 1998) which contradicts the assumption that individuals select between all possible alternatives simultaneously.

A completely different approach is to use methods from the field of Complex Systems, such as a Genetic Algorithm (GA) (Holland, 1992), to generate activity plans. A GA is a search method which is population-based, meaning that the solution algorithm considers a large number of possible solution instances simultaneously. Progress is made via crossover, mutation, and selection: crossover means that two solution instances are used in a meaningful way to generate a third solution instance. Mutation means that a solution instance is randomly modified. Selection means that bad solution instances are removed in order to save computer time. We have indeed implemented a prototype version of such a GA (Charypar, 2002), but calibration/validation are unresolved issues.

Mode Choice and Routing

Travelers/vehicles need to compute the sequence of links that they are taking through the network. A typical way to obtain such paths is to use a shortest path Dijkstra algorithm. This algorithm uses as input the individual link travel times plus the starting and ending point of a trip, and generates as output the fastest path.

It is relatively straightforward to make the costs (link travel times) time dependent, meaning that the algorithm can include the effect that congestion is time dependent: trips starting at one time of the day will encounter different delay patterns than trips starting at another time of the day. Link travel times are obtained from the micro-simulation, and the router finds the fastest route based on that information. Apart from relatively small and essential technical details, the implementation of such an algorithm is straightforward (Jacob et al., 1999). It is possible to include public transportation into the routing (Barrett et al., 2000).

The above algorithms generate routes which are optimal under the assumptions. It is, somewhat surprisingly, rather difficult to generate plausible alternatives that are not optimal. For example, consider an algorithm which systematically generates 2nd-best, 3rd-best, etc. paths. It turns out that from these paths, only very few of them are true innovations, and most are minor (and implausible) modifications of already existing solutions (Kelly and Nagel, 1998). This is consistent with studies which attempt to find plausible but potentially non-optimal solutions via heuristics (Park and Rilett, 1997). Other approaches are based on some kind of learning dynamics, for example collecting *all* fastest paths over learning iterations of a traffic simulation (Ben-Akiva, 2001), or based on mental maps which reflect which parts of a street network are known to a traveler (Unger, 1998, 2002; Weinmann, in preparation).

Traffic Simulation

Within the framework described so far, travelers have generated individual plans, but very little interaction between different people was considered. In fact, we are not aware of any implemented method which considers traveler interaction during plans generation, but it is clear that there is considerable interaction on the household level (who does the shopping? who gets the car?), and interaction exists for example for the co-ordination of car sharing. The most important interaction occurs because of constraints in the physical system when the plans are executed: cars are caught in congestion, buses are full and thus loading/unloading lets them fall behind schedule (leading to the famous "bunching" of buses [O'Loan et al., 1998]), or pedestrian facilities are crowded.

It is the task of the traffic simulation to realistically model all these effects. In consequence, a requirement for a traffic simulation to fit into the framework described here is that the travelers in the simulation follow individual plans. Only very few traffic simulations fulfill this requirement. Additional requirements, as we will see below, are that it generates output suitable for agent learning (usually easy to fulfill), and that it is computationally fast enough (often not fulfilled).

Apart from these requirements, the precise method used for the traffic simulation does not matter. In fact, models ranging from rather simple to rather complex are in use or under development. On the "complex" side, one wants a model that includes aspects such as street/intersection layout, signal plans, public transit and its interaction with car traffic, or crowding in pedestrian facilities. One of the most advanced models here which also includes the above-mentioned aspects of plans following and computational speed is the traffic simulation of TRANSIMS (transims.tsasa.lanl.gov, www.transims.net); it uses parallel computing to obtain good computational speed in spite of the realism and many implementation details. A complex simulation can generate realistic looking output, possibly embedded in a photorealistic visualization. This is a considerable advantage when dealing with the non-scientific public; and clearly, interaction with the general public should be of prime importance for research that deals with public systems.

On the "simple" side, it is important to be clear about the question that one wants to answer. For example, the volume-based link travel time function for static assignment is a perfectly acceptable "traffic simulation". It is however difficult to use when the situation is time dependent: a delay of a traveler on one link changes the time when (s)he is on the next link, which changes the delays on that next link, which influences other travelers, which influences further links, etc. The volume-based link travel time function is finally impossible to use when one considers spatial (also called physical) queues important, which means that a traffic volume above link capacity causes queuing, which will eventually reach the upstream end of the link and then spill back across intersections.

Time-dependent traffic simulations with emphasis on those aspects but not much else are for example DYNAMIT (its.mit.org; see also dynamictrafficassignment.org), DYNASMART (www.dynasmart.com; see also dynamictrafficassignment.org), NET-CELL (Cayford et al., 1997), or the queue simulation (Gawron, 1998). Out of these, the first two still contain a considerable amount of complexity, the usefulness of which should be tested. The last one has been used to systematically push computational limits (Cetin and Nagel, 2003). An advantage of all these simulations is that they run based on data that is typically available from public agencies, such as link capacity, or the free speed of a link.

There is sometimes discussion if microscopic traffic models are necessary in an agent-based framework. In our view this seems more a view of semantics than of content. It is (again in our view) clear that traffic simulations in an agent-based framework need to be able to execute individual plans, and to report back individual plans' performance. If this is achieved via a truly microscopic traffic dynamics, or rather via a dynamics where vehicles are moved according to aggregated speed calculations or as packets, is of considerably less importance.

Feedback

Basic Day-to-day Replanning. As mentioned above, plans (such as routes) and congestion need to be made consistent. This is achieved via a relaxation technique (Kaufman et al., 1991; Nagel, 1994/95; Bottom, 2000):

- The system generates some set of initial plans.
- The traffic simulation is run with these plans.
- A fraction of the population obtains new plans, which are calculated based on information from the last run of the traffic simulation.
- The traffic simulation is run again with the new plans.
- Etc.

This cycle is run for 50 times; earlier investigations have shown that this is more than enough to reach relaxation (Rickert, 1998).

Agent Database. A problem with basic day-to-day replanning is that it relies on the assumption that the replanning under Item 3 generates plans which are truly better than the previous ones. This cannot always be guaranteed, for example because the replanner is based on incomplete information. Incompleteness of information is typical; for example, the time-dependent link travel times are aggregated into time bins before they are used by the router. Such aggregation is nearly always necessary to reduce computational complexity and also to correctly model real world behavior.

In this situation, it is beneficial to have the agents remember more than one plan ("strategy"), to collect scores for the different plans, and to select between the different plans according to their scores. This is what the agent database does. This approach separates the learning problem into sub-problems:

- **Plans selection.** At each iteration, each agent selects which of its several plans will be used for that particular iteration. A good option is again a multinomial logit model,

$$p_i = \frac{e^{\beta U_i}}{\sum_j e^{\beta U_i}}$$

  where p_i is the probability of option i, and U_i is the utility (score) of option i. β is a free parameter, which can either be obtained from the estimation of a survey, or it can be regarded as a computational parameter where for $\beta \to 0$ one approaches random choice, and for $\beta \to \infty$ the agent will always select the best option.

- **Plans evaluation.** The agents need to obtain values for the U_i. This is achieved by forcing them to execute each option at least once; further exploration is given by the selection of the β parameter, as discussed above.

- **Plans generation.** The remaining question is how initial and additional plans are generated. This is where additional modules such as route or activity generation modules as discussed earlier come into play. Since it makes sense to evaluate new plans right away in the next iteration, new plans should only be given to a relatively small fraction of the population in each iteration. A value of 10% works well in practice.

More information can be found in Raney and Nagel (2003).

Within-day Replanning. The above discussion assumes that routes are fixed during the traffic simulation and can only be changed between iterations. However, many adaptations of behaviour occur while travelers are already on their way (e.g. Axhausen, 1990; Doherty and Axhausen, 1998). It is possible to add within-day replanning to a traffic simulation (e.g. Axhausen, 1990; Esser, 1998; Rickert, 1998). The main challenge is to avoid implementing a monolithic software package in which the functionalities cannot be separated. It is desirable to have, say, activity generation, route planning, learning, and traffic simulation all separated, so that they can be implemented by different groups, and so that modules can be exchanged.

One approach to this, which also has the advantage of being efficient for parallel computing, is to have the different functionalities in totally separated modules, and using messages for the exchange of information (e.g. Gloor, 2001). Implementations of this are in their early stages; at the current point in time the possible conceptual and/or computational problems are unknown.

Relaxation vs. Learning. The feedback mechanism, in particular when considered in conjunction with within-day replanning, has similarities to human learning: options are generated, evaluated, and selected. On the other hand, feedback also looks like a standard relaxation technique, known from numerical analysis. The difference is in where one puts the emphasis: for human learning, one would strive towards a psychologically faithful implementation, while for relaxation, the goal is to reduce the number of iterations. This implies a difference in the interpretation of the results: for human learning, a goal could be to predict the correct dynamics for each day after a major change of the system, for example the opening of a new public transit line. For relaxation, the assumption is that once humans are at the relaxed result, they will stay there, and the computation does not need to calculate *how* they get there. The latter resembles a Nash Equilibrium in (evolutionary) game theory; see, e.g., Hofbauer and Sigmund (1998) in particular for dynamic and evolutionary aspects. However, the relaxed result in our simulations does not strictly correspond to a Nash equilibrium, for example because agents do not use statistically valid estimators for expected values, and because the simulation keeps introducing new strategies in each iteration. A comparison between the theory and the simulation would be interesting but is made difficult by the fact that our simulations typically run for fifty iterations while the theory usually assumes a steady-state interpretation (Cascetta and Cantarella, 1991; Bottom, 2000).

On the other hand, what our simulations can do that was impossible with traditional theories is to explore the whole range from computational relaxation to psychologically correct learning. In particular, one could explore the consequences of path-dependent partial knowledge (Weinmann, in preparation), or of threshold-based behaviour.

A Practical Case

As a practical case, let us look at a project whose ultimate goal is the 24-hour simulation of all traffic in Switzerland for a regular weekday. The project operates by building up the necessary modules one by one, and by systematically testing if they operate according to their specifications. A strong emphasis of the project is on parallel and distributed computing, which is the enabling technology for really large scale scenarios. Our target speed-up, by which the distributed system should be faster than the 1-CPU version, is at least a factor of ten, since only with such speed-ups does the return on the programming overhead make sense.

As of now (summer 2002), the operational modules are: traffic simulation, router, and feedback (based on an agent database). These are the modules which were used for the following results. The simulation is a queue simulation as described in *Traffic Simulation* section. The router is a time-dependent fastest path router as described in *Mode Choice and Routing* section. As of now, only cars are considered. The feedback mechanism uses the agent database as described in *Feedback* section. As utility U_i in the strategy selection we use $U_i = -T_i$, where T_i is the travel time of that particular option. β was set heuristically to $1/(360 \text{ sec})$ which results in a fraction of about 10% non-optimal users. The input data consists of two parts: the street network, and the demand. The street network will be described next. Demand will be described together with the studies and the results.

The Street Network

The street network that is used was originally developed for the Swiss regional planning authority (Bundesamt f"ur Raumentwicklung), and covered Switzerland. It was extended with the major European transit corridors for a railway-related study (Vrtic et al., 1999). The network has the fairly typical number of 10,564 nodes and 28,624 links. Also fairly typical, the major attributes on these links are type, length, speed, and capacity. As pointed out above, this is enough information for the queue simulation.

Validation of Router and Feedback ("Gotthard" Scenario)

In order to test our set-up, we generated a set of 50,000 trips going to the same destination. Having all trips going to the same destination allows us to check the plausibility of the feedback since all traffic jams on all used routes to the destination should dissolve in parallel. In this scenario, we simulate the traffic resulting from 50,000 vehicles which start between 6am and 7am all over Switzerland and which all go to Lugano, which is in the Ticino, the Italian-speaking part of Switzerland south of the Alps. In order for the vehicles to get there, most of them have to cross the Alps. There are not many ways to do this, resulting in traffic jams, most notably in the corridor leading toward the Gotthard pass. This scenario has some resemblance to real world vacation traffic in Switzerland.

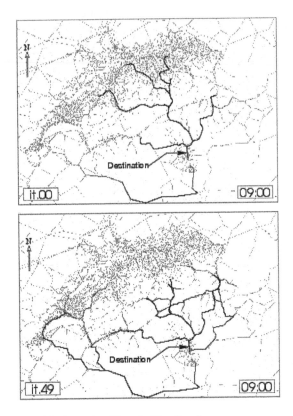

Figure 9.2 Example of Relaxation Due to Feedback
TOP: Iteration 0 at 9:00 – all travelers assume the network is empty.
BOTTOM: Iteration 49 at 9:00 – travelers take more varied routes to
try to avoid one another.

Figure 9.2 shows an example of how the feedback mechanism works in the Gotthard scenario. The figure shows two "snapshots" of the vehicle locations within the queuebased micro-simulation at 9:00 AM. The first image in the figure is a snapshot of the initial (zero) iteration of the simulation, and the second is the simulation after 50 iterations via the agent database feedback system described above.

Initially the travelers choose routes without any knowledge of other traffic, so they all use the fastest links, and tend to select very similar routes, which compose a subset of available routes. However, by driving on the same links, they cause congestion and those links become slower than the next-fastest links which were not selected. Thus, alternate routes which were marginally slower than the fastest route become, in hindsight, preferred to the routes taken. By allowing some travelers (in the next iteration) to select new routes using the new information about the network, and others to choose previously tried routes, we allow them to learn about the demand on the network caused by one another.

After 50 iterations between the route selection and the micro-simulation, the travelers have learned what everyone else is doing, and have chosen routes accordingly. Now a more complete set of the available routes is chosen, and overall the travelers arrive at their destination earlier than in the initial iteration. Comparing the usage of the roads, one can see that in the 49th iteration, the queues are shorter overall, and at the same time in the simulation, travelers are, on average, closer to their destination.

The "Switzerland" Scenario

Our starting point for demand generation for the full Switzerland scenario is 24-hour origin-destination matrices from the Swiss regional planning authority (Bundesamt f"ur Raumentwicklung). Eventually, we intend to move on to activity-based demand generation.

The original 24-hour matrix is converted into 24 one-hour matrices using a three step heuristic. The first step employs departure time probabilities by population size of origin zone, population size of destination zone and network distance. These are calculated using the 1994 Swiss National Travel Survey (Bundesamt f"ur Statistik und Dienst f"ur Gesamtverkehrsfragen, 1996). The resulting 24 initial matrices are then calibrated against available hourly counts using the OD-matrix estimation module of one of the macroscopic assignment environments used at the IVT (VISUM; see www.ptv.de). Hourly counts are available from the counting stations on the national motorway system. Finally, the hourly matrices are rescaled so that the totals over 24 hours match the original 24 hours matrix. An hourly static assignment of the matrices shows that the patterns of congestion over time are realistic and consistent with the known patterns.

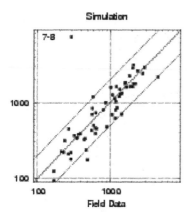

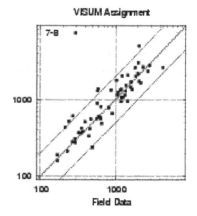

Figure 9.3 (a) Simulation vs. Field Data. The x-axis shows the hourly counts from the field data; the y-axis shows throughput on the corresponding link from the simulation. "7-8" refers to the corresponding hour during the morning rush hour.
(b) Assignment vs. Field Data. The x-axis is the same as (a); the y-axis shows the volume obtained from the static assignment model.

These hourly matrices are then disaggregated into individual trips. That is, we generate individual trips such that summing up the trips would again result in the given OD matrix. The starting time for each trip is randomly selected between the starting and the ending time of the validity of the OD matrix.

The OD matrices assume traffic analysis zones (TAZs) while in our simulations trips start on links. We convert traffic analysis zones to links by the following heuristic:

- The geographic location of the zone is found via the geographical co-ordinate of its centroid given by the data base.
- A circle with radius 3 km is drawn around the centroid.
- Each link starting within this circle is now a possible starting link for the trips. One of these links is randomly selected and the trip start or end is assigned.

This leads to a list of approximately 5 million trips, or about 1 million trips between 6am and 9am. All results in the following refer to the latter. Since the origin-destination matrices are given on an hourly basis, these trips reflect the daily dynamics. Intra-zonal trips are not included in those matrices, as by tradition.

Figure 9.3(a) shows a comparison between the simulation output and field data taken at counting stations throughout Switzerland (Bundesamt f ¨ur Strassen, 2000). The dotted lines outline a region where the simulation data falls within 50% and 200% of the field data. Figure 9.3(b) shows a comparison between the traffic volumes obtained by IVT using static assignment against the same field data. Visually one would conclude that the simulation results are as good as – or better than – the static assignment results. Table 9.1 confirms this quantitatively. Mean absolute bias is $\langle q_{sim} - q_{field} \rangle$, mean absolute error is $\langle |q_{sim} - q_{field}| \rangle$, mean relative bias is $(\langle q_{sim} - q_{field} \rangle)/q_{field}$, mean relative error is $\langle |q_{sim} - q_{field}| \rangle / q_{field}$, where $\langle . \rangle$ means that the values are averaged over all links where field results are available.

Table 9.1 Bias and Error of Simulation and Assignment Results Compared to Field Data

	Simulation	Assignment
Mean Abs. Bias:	−65	+99
Mean Abs. Error	263	309
Mean Rel. Bias:	−5.3%	+16%
Mean Rel. Error:	25%	30%

For example, the "mean relative bias" numbers mean that the simulation underestimates flows by about 11%, whereas the hourly assignment overestimates them by 5%. The average relative error between the field measurement and the simulation is 29%, between the hourly assignment and reality 37%. These numbers confirm that the simulation result is at least as good as the hourly assignment result; also, the simulation results are better than what we obtained with a recent (somewhat similar) simulation study in Portland, Oregon (Esser and Nagel, 2001); conversely, the assignment values in Portland were better than the ones obtained here. Further information can be found in Raney et al. (2003).

A curious aspect of this result is that the hourly OD matrices were calibrated against the counts using the static assignment model. In other words, they were modified in order to make the assignment match the counts as much as possible. These OD matrices were then fed into the simulation, without further adaptation. It is surprising that even under these conditions, which seem very advantageous for the static assignment, the simulation generates a smaller mean error.

Computational Issues

A metropolitan region can consist of 10 million or more inhabitants which causes considerable demands on computational performance. This is made worse by the relaxation iterations. And in contrast to simulations in the natural sciences, traffic particles (= travelers, vehicles) have internal intelligence. As pointed out in the introduction, this internal intelligence translates into rule-based code, which does not run well on traditional supercomputers (e.g. Cray) but runs well on modern workstation architectures. This makes traffic simulations ideally suited for clusters of PCs, also called Beowulf clusters. We use domain decomposition, that is, each CPU obtains a patch ("domain") of the geographical region. Information and vehicles between the domains are exchanged via message passing using MPI (Message Passing Interface, www-unix.mcs.anl.gov/mpi).

Figure 9.4 shows some computational performance results, for the "Switzerland" simulation. The plot shows two quantities:

- **Speed-Up** (the lower set of points). Speed-up $S(p)$ is defined as the ratio between the computing time on one CPU and the computing time on p CPUs:

$$S = \frac{T(1)}{T(p)}$$

Ideally, the speed-up would be p, but in reality inefficiencies reduce the speed-up.

- **Real time ratio** (the upper set of points). The real time ratio says how much faster than reality the simulation runs. If $T(p)$ is how long it takes to compute one second of reality, than the real time ratio is given as

$$RTR = \frac{1\sec}{T(p)}$$

For example, a RTR of 100 means that one simulates 100 seconds of the traffic scenario in one second. – RTR can be obtained from Speed-Up by a vertical shift which is given by the real time ratio of the simulation on a single CPU.

With Ethernet, the computational speed levels out at a real time ratio of about 150. This is caused by the latency of the Ethernet, which is the time necessary to initialize a message. Given a latency of 500 *msec*, two message exchanges per time step, and an average value of six neighbours for $p \to \infty$, this results in $T_{lat} = 6$ *msec* of communication time per time step. The computing time for one time step, $T(p)$, has to be larger than T_{lat}, and therefore for the real time ratio

$$RTR = \frac{1\sec}{T(p)} < \frac{1\sec}{T_{lat}} = 167$$

The consequence of this is fairly drastic: *with Ethernet technology, a parallel simulation that uses a time step of one second and two message exchanges per time step cannot exceed a real time ratio of about 150.* This is a fixed threshold which depends neither on the scenario size nor on the computing speed of the 1-CPU version. It does however depend on the communication hardware, as the better values for the faster Myrinet technology show. Myrinet is a special purpose communication hardware for PC clusters; the current cost (2002) is about $1500 per PC (www.myri.com). Unfortunately, it seems that waiting for better hardware will in this case not solve the problem: although the standard bandwidth for local area networks has increased from 10 Mbit via 100 Mbit to Gbit Ethernet since 1990, latency has not improved similarly.

So far, we have concentrated on the computational performance of the traffic simulation. In fact, with real time ratios of 200 as shown in Figure 9.4, the simulation of 24 hours of traffic takes less than 8 minutes. In that situation, the implementation of agent learning easily becomes the main computational bottle-neck. Our current implementation (Raney and Nagel, 2003), using the public domain data base MySQL (www.mysql.org), needs about 1 hour of computing time per iteration. This is due to the large amount of data that needs to be proc-essed for a simulation with several million agents. A future implementation, which will keep all the data in memory, is expected to be at least a factor of ten faster.

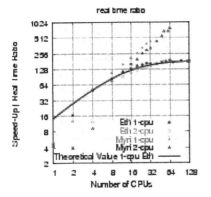
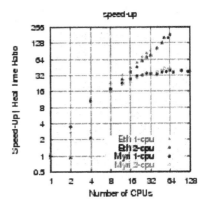

Figure 9.4   Computational Performance of the Queue Micro-simulation on a Computing Cluster using Standard Pentium CPUs. The lower set of points shows the speed-up, the upper set of points the real time ratio (RTR). As one can see, speed-up and real time ratio are related by a simple vertical shift, corresponding to the RTR of the single CPU ver-sion of the code. "Myri" and "Eth" refer to the Myrinet or Ethernet (100 Mbit) communication that was used; "1-CPU" and "2-CPU" de-note if the number of CPUs displayed on the x-axis was recruited by using one or two CPUs per computer (all computers were equipped with dual CPUs). The solid line is a theoretical prediction for the 1-CPU Ethernet situation (the method is described in Nagel and Rickert, 2001; the specific parameters for the Beowulf are described in Cetin and Nagel, 2003).

In summary, one can say that the expected computational speed of a scenario with several millions of agents will be of the order of 15 minutes per iteration for a 24-hour scenario. This makes the agent-based simulation technology truly applicable for large metropolitan areas.

Extensions for Urban Planning Applications

Even if one considers transportation planning alone, some modules are missing from the design outlined above. May be the most important omission is commer-cial traffic, which contributes a considerable fraction of everyday traffic. In terms of systems design, such a module or modules would be straightforward to integrate as long as it would generate, as output, trucks with route plans. For the queue traffic simulation, one would probably not do any changes at all; for simulations with a more realistic traffic dynamics, one would include vehicles with different driving characteristics. Several groups are working on this; we expect that eventually operational modules will become available.

Another important set of modules regards analysis. Basic economic analysis, such as "vehicle miles traveled" or "number of successful trips per person" can be obtained by queries on the simulation results or on the agent database. However, a microscopic simulation system also allows more sophisticated post-processing, such as the computation of emissions. This allows one to add, say, air-flow and air-chemistry models which will compute what will happen to chemical and particular emissions after they have left the vehicles.

After these modules are included, the system should become immediately useful for some questions of land use research, in particular questions which refer to static land use patterns. That is, it will be possible to code a different land use pattern into the system and let the simulation react to it. Since the simulation will be activity-based, it will be able to pick up small-scale differences that may result in the selection of different modes of transportation or even a complete re-organization of daily activity patterns. For example, combining different activity options at one location ("multifunctional land use") may make that location attractive just because the travel patterns become easier, even if there are more attractive activity locations in other places.

If one wants to go beyond analysis where the land use remains static, one has to include elements whose dynamics unfolds on much slower time scales than the transportation dynamics. Figure 9.5 lists many of those elements; corresponding simulation systems are under development in some places (e.g. URBANSIM, see www.urbansim.org; ILLUMAS, see irpud.raumplanung.uni-dortmund.de). From a current perspective, it seems that computational modules for these aspects can be combined with the approach described in this paper. The two integrating entities will be:

- **The spatial substrate.** Changes in the infrastructure or in the buildings will be reflected in the land use data which is used by the other modules.
- **Agents.** Entities of the simulation which can change location will be modeled as agents. This ensures that there is a consistent concept independent from the simulation modules. Each individual module will be able to use information from other modules, and to add its own information. For example, an agent representing a commercial firm will, at the activities level, use information from vehicle ownership and from location choice.

In contrast, a considerable challenge will be to understand the dynamics of a simulation system consisting of so many coupled modules. This is somewhat comparable to the situation in weather forecasting some sixty years ago, when the first ideas about numerical weather forecasting emerged, but the concept of numerical instability was unknown. Similarly, with a simulation system as outlined above, the first challenge will be to understand under which conditions the simulation system is stable and under which it is not, and how these instabilities relate to real world vs. computational issues. For a survey, see, for exaple Bottom (2000).

In addition, while for route assignment it seems to make sense to consider a "relaxed" solution (after many learning steps), this assumption is not correct for the modules that operate on longer time scales: for everything upward from "location choice" in Figure 9.5 it is plausible to assume that a relaxed solution does not represent reality. In consequence, an additional requirement that is less important for route assignment is that the mechanism and speed of adaptation and learning also need to be correct (Waddell et al., 2003).

In summary, one can perhaps say that a consistent agent-based land use simulation seems within reach in terms of computational technology. Several groups are working on this, all with different starting points but a similar ultimate goal. However, even when the first completely consistent simulation packages become available, a long phase of testing should be expected since the dynamics of these integrated systems is completely unknown. Interesting times lie ahead!

Summary

In terms of travelers and trips, a simulation of all of Switzerland, with about five million car trips alone, is comparable to a simulation of a large metropolitan area, such as London or Los Angeles. It is also comparable in size to a molecular dynamics simulation, except that travelers have considerably more "internal intelligence" than molecules, leading to complicated rule-based instead of relatively simple equation-based code. Such multi-agent simulations do not run well on traditional vectorizing supercomputers (e.g. Cray) but run well on distributed workstations, meaning that the computing capabilities for such simulations have virtually exploded over the last decade.

Transport infrastructure	5 yrs	Road network	Public transport			

Buildings	3 yrs	Residential	Industrial	Retail	Office

Life cycles	2 yrs	Persons	Households	Firms		

Location choice	1 yr	Labour	Residential	Industrial	Retail	Services

Vehicle ownership	1 yr	Private	Commercial		

Activities	1 day	*Individual*	Household	Logistics	

Mode/ route choice	1 hr	**Individual travel**	Services	Delivery	Freight	

Transport	1 min	**Passenger cars**	Non-motorized modes	Public transport	Service/ delivery traffic	Freight

Figure 9.5 Modules for a Complete Land Use/Regional Planning Tool (after M. Wegener, personal communication). In a column, the first box names the module aspect, and the second box gives a typical time scale, which is also an indication of how often the corresponding module needs to be called in a simulation. Further boxes to the right give different entities this module needs to be operational for. For example, once every year one would have to re-calculate vehicle ownership, and this needs to be done, presumably by different methods, for private and for commercial fleets. Only the two modules in bold are used for the work described in this text; the module in italics will be added soon. Integration of many more of these modules probably goes beyond the capabilities of any single group and thus needs to be a collaborative effort.

This chapter first describes the general design of such an agent-based simulation for transportation planning purposes, including the most important modules: population generator, activities generator, mode choice and route generator, traffic simulation, and feedback. This is followed by a description of the status of ongoing work of an implementation of all of Switzerland in such a simulation. A single destination scenario is used to verify the plausibility of the replanning set-up. A result of a morning peak-hour simulation of all of Switzerland is shown, including comparisons to field data from automatic counting stations. These results are shown to be at least as good as a static assignment model compared to the same field data.

The same technology can be extended so that it becomes useful for questions related to land use and regional planning. Some extensions are discussed. For the next couple of years, the main challenge is the implementation of these extensions, and how to do this so that the work on them can be divided up between several research groups. Once these simulations are functional, the next big challenge is to understand under which conditions they are stable or not, and how far stability is related to real world dynamics and how far to modeling/implementation issues.

Acknowledgments

We thank the Swiss regional planning authority (Bundesamt f'ur Raumentwicklung) for the original input data. We also thank ETHZ and the Department of Computer Science for making the Beowulf Cluster Xibalba including its Myrinet partition available to us. Marc Schmitt does a great job in maintaining the Linux environment of the cluster. This work was funded by ETHZ core funding and by the ETHZ project "Large scale multi-agent simulation of travel behavior and traffic flow".

References

Axhausen, K.W. (1990), "A simultaneous simulation of activity chains", in Jones, P.M. (ed.), *New Approaches in Dynamic and Activity-based Approaches to Travel Analysis*, Avebury, Aldershot, pp. 206–225.

Barrett, C.L., Jacob, R. and Marathe, M.V. (2000), "Formal-language-constrained path problems", *SIAM J COMPUT*, 30 (3), pp. 809–837.

Beckman, R.J., Baggerly, K.A. and McKay, M.D. (1996), "Creating synthetic base-line populations", *Transportion Research Part A – Policy and Practice*, 30 (6), pp. 415–429.

Ben-Akiva, M. (2001), *Route Choice Models*, presented at the Workshop on "Human Behaviour and Traffic Networks", Bonn.

Ben-Akiva, M. and Lerman, S.R. (1985), *Discrete Choice Analysis*, The MIT Press, Cambridge, Mass.

Bottom, J.A. (2000), *Consistent Anticipatory Route Guidance*, PhD thesis, Massachusetts Institute of Technology, Cambridge, Mass.

Bowman, J.L. (1998), *The Day Activity Schedule Approach to Travel Demand Analysis*, PhD thesis, Massachusetts Institute of Technology, Cambridge.

Bundesamt für Statistik und Dienst für Gesamtverkehrsfragen (1994), Verkehrsverhalten in der Schweiz, Mikrozensus Verkehr, Bern, 1996.
    See also http://www.statistik.admin.ch/news/archiv96/dp96036.htm.

Bundesamt für Strassen (2000), Automatische Strassenverkehrszählung 1999, Bern, Switzerland.

Cascetta, E. and Cantarella, C. (1991), "A day-to-day and within day dynamic stochastic assignment model", *Transportation Research A*, 25A (5), pp. 277–291.

Cayford, R., Lin, W.-H. and Daganzo, C.F. (1997), "The NETCELL simulation package: Technical description", *California PATH Research Report UCB-ITS-PRR-97-23*, University of California, Berkeley.

Cetin, N. and Nagel, K. (2003), "Parallel queue model approach to traffic microsimulations", paper 03-4272, *Transportation Research Board Annual Meeting*, Washington, D.C. Also see sim.inf.ethz.ch/papers.

Charypar, D. (2002) *Genetic Algorithms for Activity Planning. Term Project*, Swiss Federal Institute of Technology (ETH), Zurich, Switzerland.
See www.inf.ethz.ch/ nagel/papers.

Doherty, S.T. and Axhausen, K.W. (1998), "The developement of a unified modelling framework for the household activity-travel scheduling process", in *Verkehr und Mobilität*, number 66 in Stadt Region Land, Institut für Stadtbauwesen, Technical University, Aachen, Germany.

Esser, J. (1998), *Simulation von Stadtverkehr auf der Basis zellularer Automaten*, PhD thesis, University of Duisburg, Germany.

Esser, J. and Nagel, K. (2001), "Iterative demand generation for transportation simulations", in D. Hensher and J. King (eds.), *The Leading Edge of Travel Behavior Research*, Pergamon, pp. 659–681.

Gawron, C. (1998), "An iterative algorithm to determine the dynamic user equilibrium in a traffic simulation model", *International Journal of Modern Physics C*, 9 (3), pp. 393–407.

Gingold, R.A. and Monaghan, J.J. (1997), "Smoothed particle hydrodynamics. Theory and application to non-spherical stars", *Royal Astronomical Society, Monthly Notices*, 181.

Gloor, Chor. (2001), "Modelling of autonomous agents in a realistic road network (in German)", *Diplomarbeit*, Swiss Federal Institute of Technology ETH, Zürich, Switzerland.

Hofbauer, J. and Sigmund, K. (1998), *Evolutionary Games and Replicator Dynamics*, Cambridge University Press.

Holland, J.D. (1992), *Adaptation in Natural and Artificial Systems*, Bradford Books. Reprint edition.

Jacob, R.R., Marathe, M.V. and Nagel, K. (1999), "A computational study of routing algorithms for realistic transportation networks", *ACM Journal of Experimental Algorithms*, 4 (1999es, Article No. 6).

Kaufman, D.E., Wunderlich, K.E. and Smith, R.L. (1991), "An iterative routing/assignment method for anticipatory real-time route guidance", *Technical Report IVHS Technical Report 91-02*, University of Michigan Department of Industrial and Operations Engineering, Ann Arbor MI 48109, May.

Kelly, T. and Nagel, K. (1998), "Relaxation criteria for iterated traffic simulations", *International Journal of Modern Physics C*, 9 (1), pp. 113–132.

McNamara G.R. and Zanetti, G. (1988), "Use of the Boltzmann equation to simulate lattice-gas automata", *Physical Review Letters*, 61 (20), pp. 2332–2335.

Nagel, K. (1995), *High-speed Microsimulations of Traffic Flow*, PhD thesis, University of Cologne, 1994/95. See www.inf.ethz.ch/~nagel/papers.

Nagel, K. and Rickert, M. (2001), "Parallel implementation of the TRANSIMS microsimulation", *Parallel Computing*, 27 (12), pp. 1611–1639.

O'Loan, O.J., Evans, M.R. and Cates, M.E. (1998), "Jamming transition in a homogeneous one-dimensional system: The bus route model", *Physical Review E*, 58, pp. 1404–1418.

Park, D. and Rilett, R.L. (1997), "Identifying multiple and reasonable paths in transportation networks: A heuristic approach", *Transportation Research Records*, 1607, pp. 31–37.

Raney, B., Cetin, N., Völlmy, A., Vrtic, M., Axhausen, K. and Nagel, K. (2003), "An agent-based microsimulation model of Swiss travel: First results", *Paper 03-4267, Transportation Research Board Annual Meeting*, Washington, D.C. Also see sim.inf.ethz.ch/papers.

Raney, B. and Nagel K. (2003), "Truly agent-based strategy selection for transportation simulations", *Paper 03-4258, Transportation Research Board Annual Meeting*, Washington, D.C. Also see sim.inf.ethz.ch/papers.

Rickert, M. (1998), *Traffic Simulation on Distributed Memory Computers*, PhD thesis, University of Cologne, Germany. See www.zpr.uni-koeln.de/~mr/dissertation.

Sahimi, M. (1993), "Flow phenomena in rocks: From continuum models to fractals, percolation, cellular automata, and simulated annealing", *Revue of Modern Physicss*, 65 (4), pp. 1393–1534.

Unger, H. (1998), "An approach using neural networks for the control of the behaviour of autonomous individuals", in A. Tentner (ed.), *High Performance Computing 1998*, The Society for Computer Simulation International, pp. 98–103.

Unger, H. (2002), *Modellierung des Verhaltens autonomer Verkehrsteilnehmer in einer variablen staedtischen Umgebung*, PhD thesis, TU Berlin.

Vrtic, M., Koblo, R. and Vödisch, M. (1999), "Entwicklung bimodales Personenverkehrsmodell als Grundlage für Bahn2000, 2, Etappe, Auftrag 1", *Report to the Swiss National Railway and to the Dienst für Gesamtverkehrsfragen*, Prognos AG, Basel. See www.ivt.baug.ethz.ch/vrp/abl15.pdf for a related report.

Waddell, P., Borning, A., Noth, M., Freier, N., Becke, M. and Ulfarsson, G. (2003), "Microsimulation of urban development and location choices: Design and implementation of UrbanSim", *Networks and Spatial Economics*, in press.

Weinmann, S. *Simulation of Spatial Learning Mechanisms*, PhD thesis, Swiss Federal Institute of Technology ETH, Zürich, Switzerland, in preparation.

Chapter 10

Traffic-related Air Pollution in an Urban Environment: a KBDSS for Improving the Decisional Context

Emilia Conte and Grazia Concilio

Introduction

Recent decades have seen very significant and profound changes to cities. While the changes have been both physical and non-physical in nature, the latter have recently been considered even more important than the former (Boyle, Thomas and Wield, 2000). There are many reasons for these developments and the relationships between them vary according to different contexts, so attempts to define them in a general way are often not very useful. Nevertheless, we can try to highlight some common features with reference to developed countries, although differences do exist between particular cases. A first element is the increasing phenomenon of urbanisation, involving a physical enlargement of cities as well as an improvement in living conditions from every perspective. The arrival of refugees and immigrants from poor countries is at present a main contributory factor in urbanisation, bringing significant socio-cultural changes. A second element can be related to infrastructure networks in cities. They are always of great importance for a city's development and they now face two major needs: to be complemented by near non-physical flows (Internet) and to be improved by means of information technologies (IT). A third element can be identified with the general concept of quality of life, which is rapidly changing over time due to primary needs being met for most people in a city and the increasing potentials being offered by technology.

All these factors are interconnected and it is not easy to describe single characteristics in detail, but we can observe that intangible assets are becoming increasingly important for people. This is also why growing attention is being paid to sustainable development, going beyond its environmental and economic aspects towards its social or, rather, societal aspects – thus including the social as well as the cultural and ethical impacts of sustainability. This situation is also causing significant changes to the way cities are administered, requiring that appropriate political structures evolve for handling new kinds of problems and requiring that different actors at different levels be considered. Policy-making activities must become more sensitive to changes than before. They need to develop an ability to understand problems as well as to foresee them, and consequently to not only interpret but also construct them. Thus, making judgements and acting in a situation become possible through a profound interpretative and sense-making practice, as is the case for most human practices (Soneryd and Uggla, 2000). But since real problems are complex and their management requires a large amount of data and information, interpretation and perception can – and need to – be given as much support as possible so that issues can be evaluated and appropriate decisions taken. This provides an opportunity for effectively using IT within policy-making organisations, as is happening in other kinds of organisation, and improving human abilities to deal with computerised systems.

Referring to cities and their evolving situations, many public and private organisations are called to address city-related problems. They are requested to carry out planning activities at different levels, making decisions both for managing routine situations and for implementing strategies affecting long-term performances. The decision-making process is fundamental in organisations, and strategic decision-making, in particular, is a process that is very intensively based on knowledge and information (Sun and Liu, 2001). Decision-makers within urban management agencies have to improve their behaviour, not only with regard to managing current situations in the short-term, but also being proactive in addressing future situations. To do this, they must combine a range of different types of data, information and knowledge, choosing what is useful for the problem at hand, and using resources effectively without wasting them. If we feel that monitoring and modelling of problems can enhance decision-making activities, it is essential for this to be carried out. Thus, it seems that real decisional contexts at present need decision support by means of effective systems that are able to promote knowledge, so improving the mental models and understanding of decision-makers and consequently improving their decision-making (Nemati et al., 2002). This means we need to build decision support systems (DSS) which are not only based on knowledge but also – and much more importantly – stimulate human learning activity and knowledge creation within organisations.

The Research Framework

The research that we carried out over the last two years and report here was prompted by the underlying situation stated in the introduction. Cities are at present facing a growing problem of air pollution caused by traffic flows. This is an increasingly urgent problem facing the urban environment and demands emergency solutions as well as medium and long-term strategies, thus posing a substantial challenge to the usual decision-making procedures in urban organisations. Air pollution has recently attracted considerable attention from technical experts and policy-makers due to its significant public health consequences, though risks for individual health are relatively small (Künzli et al., 2000). Among other sources of air pollution, road transport must be singled out, since its emissions are released very close to humans, who are receptors; moreover in city centres it is more difficult for pollutants produced by vehicle emissions to naturally dilute or disperse due to buildings located alongside the roads (Colvile et al., 2001). Thus, controlling air pollution caused by traffic has become a major concern of governors and assuring good air quality in cities is a key target of urban policies. In addition to regulations concerning vehicle fuel efficiency and atmospheric pollution, policy-makers are at present shifting towards transport policy itself, trying to address its specific externalities, in the hope that such policies can beneficially affect air pollution externalities (Proost and Van Dender, 2001).

However, the decision-making context is very complex. A predictive process can be carried out based on measurements of air pollutants and weather conditions, together with related information such as traffic flows in the area and other factors affecting source behaviour, and it can also be supported by automation (Kalapani-das and Avouris, 2001). But the issue also relates to how single drivers will behave, since each one is an autonomous agent in the system, and to the large impacts that even small disturbances can cause on the system. Bearing this in mind, a substantial contribution to policy targets can be provided by developing intelligent transportation systems (Middelham, 2001). Many experts are currently involved in carrying out research on intelligent transportation systems and modelling forecasts, with interesting results also for the field of advanced decision support systems (see for example, Brand et al., 2002). Our research had the more modest goal of supporting the daily activity of decision-makers in the municipal offices, dealing first with the problem of controlling and validating the data acquired by the monitoring system, and secondly with the problem of designing local responses for immediate action when necessary, and of developing medium and long-term strategies for the future. This support is supplied by a DSS, whose architectural design was the main operational goal of our research. The system is based on the knowledge available, both documentary and of local experts, and is designed to improve on the relatively modest advances in the effectiveness and extent of DSS usage seen so far (Beynon, Rasmequan and Russ, 2002).

In fact, one of our major concerns in developing the DSS was to make it acceptable, through its usefulness, in the local context for which it was intended. Many efforts in developing DSSs have focused on their ease of use, thinking this would make them more readily accepted. However, a DSS must first be useful. It must therefore be designed so that it will improve the quality of decisions, and also increase willingness to use it (Lu, Yu and Lu, 2001). We can expect that the DSS can be more readily accepted in specific contexts, particularly those characterised by cognitive styles favouring intuitivism and feeling. Moreover it is very important that the DSS models the decision-making process to meet the real needs of its users. Thus, rather than being a fully automated system, a DSS must be interactive with users, so it can be viewed as a cooperative agent in a system where the DSS users are the other participating agents (Wang, Liao and Liao, 2002). We thought that using our DSS in this way could help create a system able to support the decision-making activities of people in the municipal offices, for routine as well as for strategic actions, while also improving their ability to recognise, understand and represent problems. This is the only process by which the DSS can be useful, used, and effective in terms of learning and knowledge production within the organisation. These are essential factors for making decisions aimed at addressing a complex problem such as traffic-related air pollution.

The following sections report on the design of the DSS, considering the related technological and operational issues as well as theoretical questions. In particular, next section briefly outlines the local case study and its decisional context, on which we based the development of the DSS in its prototypal form; the following section describes the DSS architecture, examining the definition and implementation of two modules of the system; the final section considers some final issues deriving from implementation of the prototype, related to the knowledge acquisition question when implementing the DSS and the organisational and machine-learning perspectives.

Developing a DSS Prototype for the City of Bari

The city of Bari, on the Adriatic coast of southern Italy, has significant air pollution and traffic congestion problems and the related decision-making process has a considerable need for expert knowledge and information management. Daily monitoring of air quality in Bari started three years ago and decisions are taken in accordance with international and national regulations which define two threshold levels signalling traffic-management measures: the first is a level of "attention" and the other is a level of "alarm", based on the concentration of chemical pollutants in the air.

Based on daily monitoring of air quality, weather conditions, and city users' behaviour, technicians in the traffic office of Bari make short-term decisions concerning private mobility and its contribution to urban mobility patterns. Medium/long-term strategies must also be designed by means of specific urban traffic plans, currently under construction in many Italian cities, with a major focus on sustainable solutions. Our experimentation mainly involves supporting short-term decision-making, which is heavily dependent on data collected within the Bari urban area by six fixed measurement stations, each responding to regulatory requirements and collecting different data depending on their location in the town.

Semi-structured interviews were carried out with actors involved in the decision process – technicians and administrators in municipal offices – in order to acquire the knowledge related to the problem. This covered both the technical and the policy aspects of decisions connected with the control of polluting urban activities. A first phase of interviews showed us the basic structure of the short-term decision-making procedure, mainly based on: data validation, data management, information transfer and selection of alternatives for traffic limitation. Since data validation is the most demanding task in terms of the expert knowledge to be used, uncertainty management, information processing, and time required, we carried out further semi-structured interviews in order to acquire knowledge to be used when supporting this activity by the DSS.

The DSS architecture we studied has the main aim of supporting the short-term decision-making process related to urban air quality management and, within the decision-making organisation, is the foundation for a long-term planning perspective, which is currently only defined at a high strategic level. The first goal is the most relevant issue within the public department where the decision-making process is carried out by an ad hoc multi-expert group (Commission on Air Quality). The decision process is only partially defined and is still subject to significant changes due to rapidly changing legal requirements. Recently, for example, the use of pollutant diffusion models has been made mandatory.

The changing environment made it possible to carry out wider experimentation to study learning within the decision-making organisation. This issue has recently become a great challenge for system analysts, especially for those working within business organisation environments (Ruhleder, Jordan and Elmes, 1996; Wan and Johnson, 1994): law changes, in fact, induce the need for organisational changes and, subsequently, for learning. Furthermore the introduction of a DSS itself requires significant adaptation within an organisation. This need to adapt can result in learning if IT support is developed together with the organisation itself abandoning a technological top-down approach.

The DSS Architecture

Within the perspectives presented above, the system architecture (Figure 10.1) attempts to represent the decision-making process currently carried out by the group of experts committed to air quality control and implementation of traffic strategies. We have so far focused on constructing a system covering air quality monitoring and the short-term/urgent traffic intervention modules, which are the main constituents of the decision-making process. The medium/long-term strategy module is a system that could possibly be constructed in the future since, as already mentioned, medium/long-term decision-making is linked to the willingness of the municipal administration to consider the traffic problem in a wider context of transport patterns and behaviour.

The decision-making process for short-term traffic interventions is currently centred on the work of one of the experts belonging to the decision-making group, the chemist. This person has been sceptical about introducing an automatic system; his work mainly involves data validation and data analysis. Data validation requires at least three hours of work daily, with the expert having to check all the data supplied by the air pollution measurement system each day. Checking is carried out early each morning for the preceding 24-hour period (7.00a.m. – 7.00a.m.), in accordance with regulatory requirements. The data validation module is described in the following paragraph: the prototype was developed in order to automate just part of the validation process, leaving it interfaced and partially controlled by the expert.

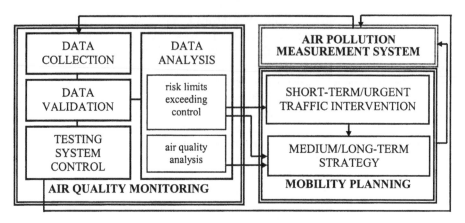

Figure 10.1 The DSS Architecture

Data analysis is carried out through two main activities: risk limits exceeding control and air quality analysis, which were implemented as the first modules of the system. The first activity involves short-term monitoring of pollutants for acute pollution events: exceeding the limits is considered a health and environmental risk by law. The risk limits are divided into two categories, "attention" and "alarm" threshold values, and require short-term/urgent traffic interventions. The short-term/urgent traffic intervention module has been developed within an Expert System (ES) approach which required close links with the data base.

The Data Base (DB) is divided into three sub-modules: the pollutants sub-module, updated daily with the data from the six measurement stations, and split into two parts, non-validated and validated data; the weather forecast sub-module, updated daily through a connection with the weather office (this update is currently carried out by fax), and finally the sub-module summarising the time series of pollution conditions (this information is necessary to declare attention/alarm conditions). The DB structure has been designed to be consistent with the data required for the decision-making and according to the different data sources (Figure 10.2): the first sub-module acquires the non-validated data directly from the measurement stations while the validated data are inputted by the data validation module and/or directly by the expert; the weather condition data are directly supplied by the weather office; finally the past pollution conditions are updated by the short-term traffic intervention module where the pollution conditions are summarised.

The Data Validation Module

Data validation is currently carried out by the human expert with basically three main goals, which avoid the need to assess data correctness: assessment of the correctness of the data trend, so as to improve predictive ability; anticipating failures in the measuring system, so as to reduce the incidence of missing data; and completing the data validation process carried out by the measuring system itself. As already mentioned, data validation takes several hours of work each day; it is mainly characterised by a routine process of data observation, and appears largely capable of being replicated by an automatic algorithm, depending on the kind of validation task and knowledge used. Therefore, the design of the data validation module was developed after acquisition of the expert knowledge.

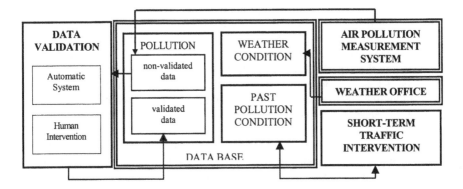

Figure 10.2 The DB Updating System

In order to understand what knowledge the expert uses and how, we carried out some participant observation sessions with him working on data validation. This enabled us to deduce that the whole data validation process is developed in two main phases: first, assessment of data correctness, and second, control of the measurement system. The first phase, which is a routine task, is carried out by the expert on the basis of two different kinds of knowledge. There is an experiential knowledge base linked to the data structure and acquired over a large number of data validation sessions. In the present study we designate it "observation-derived knowledge", because it results from the expert's assessment of the data patterns he observes each day. There is also a more theoretical knowledge, evidently deriving from the expert's education, here named "theoretically-oriented knowledge", because it is strongly independent of data observation.

In order to make the system procedure similar to the expert procedure, we considered the two phases separately and designed the first with a neural network approach, the second with an expert system approach. It is important for the system procedure to be similar to the expert procedure since system behaviour has to be acceptable to the expert: he needs to recognise his own behaviour within the system. In the following the particular role of neural networks is described for the data validation task.

The Neural Network Approach

Neural networks derive their computing power firstly through their massively parallel distributed structure and secondly through their ability to learn and therefore to generalise: they can produce reasonable outputs for inputs not encountered during the training (Haykin, 1998). Knowledge representation in a neural network becomes increasingly compounded when there are multiple sources of information activating the network, and these sources interact with each other. It is potentially a very powerful tool for the present problem being considered due to the strong spatial and time relations between the measured data.

In the problem under consideration, the two learning behaviours typical of neural networks (supervised and unsupervised learning) appear suitable for reproducing the expert's knowledge. Clustering, that is unsupervised learning, can be regarded as a good approach for automatic construction of the observation-derived knowledge used during data validation; supervised learning can be used to reproduce theoretically-oriented knowledge on the basis of training samples of validated data.

In our experimentation, it would be feasible to use expert knowledge, in the form of rules, to carry out the validation task without using a neural network to capture it from data, but since it was important to encourage the expert to accept the system, there was an opportunity to show him how autonomous the system could be in deriving part of the knowledge he uses from data. In unsupervised learning, neural networks show sequential learning ability in recognising spatial and temporal relations. The unsupervised learning procedure can start at the level of one measurement station and a one-week data set; the derived knowledge can be used for subsequent learning procedures on a wider set of data, in order to recognise higher levels of data structure, and extend to recognising the structure related to monthly data and to all six measurement stations. The neural network module is still under construction: a first elaboration was carried out with one-month data of one measurement station, within a possibility approach to clustering (Krishnapuram and Keller, 1993), and the results were presented to the expert for checking. A further clustering elaboration was developed after referring to the expert's comments in order to improve the time discretisation of clusters.

After the clustering, a description of the clusters was built according to two different principles. The clusters were described with reference to their mutual dependency (Table 10.1) and using a qualitative linguistic description obtained by fuzzifying the pollutant concentrations characterising each cluster (Table 10.2). Each description, in the form of multiple ANDs, was considered as the IF part of a rule, while the THEN part identified each single data as a valid/invalid set or a set that has to be checked by the expert.

Table 10.1 The DB Updating System

Cluster #	Description
Cluster 6	Daily
Cluster 7	Daily
Cluster 10	Daily, of transaction between clusters 6 and 7
Cluster 1	Not daily, it alternates with cluster 4
Cluster 2	Not daily, it alternates with cluster 5
Cluster 3	Not daily, it appears before clusters 4 and 1
Cluster 4	Not daily, it alternates with cluster 1
Cluster 5	Not daily, it alternates with cluster 2
Cluster 8	Not daily, it appears after cluster 4
Cluster 9	Not daily, it appears after cluster 5

Table 10.2 Linguistic Description of Pollutant Concentration (First Elaboration)

Description of cluster 8			
SO_2	low	**BENZENE**	medium
NO_x	medium-low	**TOLUENE**	medium-low
NO_2	low	**O-XYLENE**	low
CO	low	**TEMP**	low
O_3	medium	**UMR**	very high
NMHC	medium	**RADS**	low
THC	medium	**PRESS**	medium
CH_4	medium	-	-

The rules built through the first two clustering elaborations were added to some rules describing theoretically-oriented knowledge and derived directly from the shared observation sessions. An ES prototype was developed, following the structure described by Figure 10.3. Due to the high level of uncertainty, the ES module can declare data valid or invalid just when a certain threshold of certainty is reached for a solution. In all the other cases, it leaves solution of the problem to the expert, who is considered the user of the system.

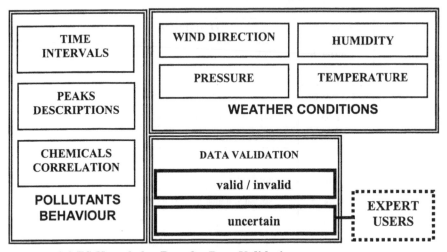

Figure 10.3 ES Knowledge Base for Data Validation

The Module for Controlling Exceeding of Risk Limits: a Normative ES

The Bari Commission on Air Quality produced a report containing both the medium/long-term mobility strategies necessary to improve city air quality and the short-term interventions to be implemented in case of attention or alarm conditions. The report, for the short-term case, recommends interventions be decided within one day of the risk limit exceeding event, depending on the weather forecast. Therefore decisions have to be taken when weather forecasts announce the persistence of pollution levels and the transition into alarm conditions.

The data supplied by the measurement systems therefore need to be related to the weather forecasts for the decision-making process. The report also regulates the procedure through which attention or alarm conditions are declared. The procedure presented in the Commission report is summarised in Figure 10.4 and has been implemented in the DSS as an ES module starting from the short-term traffic intervention ES sub-module, represented in Figure 10.5. The ES module described in Figure 10.4 is a norm-based agent in the DSS and is characterised by a chain of rule-based modules each working on a small sub-problem.

Final Considerations

The research produced a range of different outputs, some related to the cognitive dimension and others to the potential of the DSS approach. The most significant results were those referring to: knowledge acquisition, knowledge representation, formalisation in terms of decision-routine production, and, finally, organisational and machine learning.

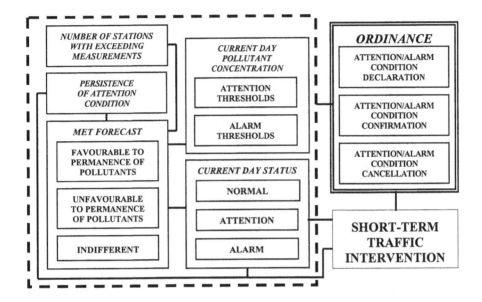

Figure 10.4 ES Module: Air Quality Normative Assessment

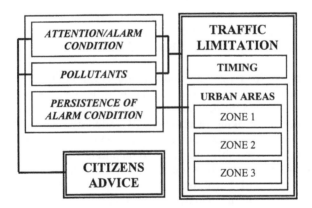

Figure 10.5 ES Module: Short-term Traffic Intervention

Acquiring Knowledge for DSS

The construction of knowledge-based DSSs has to first of all address the question of knowledge acquisition. What portions of the knowledge used during the real, individual or organisational decision-making process have to be considered to ensure effective support to the process itself? Two different aspects of the problem have to be explored. What knowledge is needed to plan the decision support? What knowledge has to be acquired and represented in a certain form (productive or descriptive) in the DSS? It is difficult to answer these questions completely.

The first question certainly poses a problem regarding the effectiveness of the support with respect to both the decision-making process and the system's use within the process itself. Moreover it is necessary to identify the knowledge required for the process observation task. This knowledge cannot be completely acquired before the process has been observed, but has to be built during the observation itself, thus making the observation relevant in terms of the learning process of the knowledge engineer. The knowledge engineer has to distinguish between the knowledge necessary for the design of the DSS and the knowledge to be used by the system. With respect to this problem, our work tried to explore the decision-making process on two levels: the procedural level and the substantive level.

At the procedural level, the observation can be carried out by investigating the organisational aspects of decision-making: what are the decision-making procedures? Who are the decision-makers? Is there a power hierarchy structuring these procedures? What competencies are required? Who has got these competencies? How are they distributed within the decision-making structure?

On the other hand, the second level refers to substantive cognitive aspects, those aspects which are, in some sense, hard to explain. This observational level divides the problem up within the decision process and investigates each segment of the problem separately from the others, without losing overall view of the problem itself.

The second question (what knowledge to implement in the DSS), together with a problem of knowledge representation and formalisation, poses the problem of introducing the DSS into the decision-making organisation and thus reproducing or transforming decision-making mechanisms. We addressed this problem by trying to distinguish routine decisions from those requiring innovative and unusual behaviours, which are less replicable and harder to support using automatic systems.

The issues relating to the above questions have not been investigated separately within the research work but through the identification of relationships, interdependencies, complementarity, and overlap of procedural and substantive elements.

Knowledge Structuring and Formalisation for Decision-making in DSS

If we recognise that decisions are not simple choices among alternatives but complex processes involving the production of alternatives by exploring decision space, then using IT systems to support decision-making requires both structuring of knowledge and "productive" representation of knowledge.

Knowledge structuring is related to the task of exploring and representing a problem and can be considered, within a DSS, as a passive support – that is a support that cannot be immediately put into action. The interface between DSS and users becomes relevant in order to ensure that non-productive cognitive structures are considered; in our case, this problem was addressed by including the air pollution normative base and the interaction of air pollution with human health.

The implementation of knowledge, with the aim of producing decision-making segments, poses the problem of validating the produced decisions. This raises the question of the reliability of decision-making routines, the completeness of knowledge, the system's ability to recognise non-routine conditions, and also representation of the competence domain of automatic systems. This last aspect was not directly addressed during the research work but the outcomes certainly provide a basis for reflecting on it.

Organisational and Machine Learning

The learning issue showed two problem-related levels: the first one involved the support of learning within the decision-making organisation and the second referred to learning as a form of experiential knowledge representation.

Information systems are promising tools for supporting the main organisational activities related to learning processes (acquisition of knowledge and information, distribution of knowledge and information, interpretation of information, adaptation of organisational memory) but it must be remembered that their information and information flow is linear and static whereas human knowledge and the learning processes that characterise organisations are non-linear and adaptive.

Many information systems have been developed for managing extensive knowledge bases and for facilitating communication among organisational components, but no significant change has been observed in knowledge workers' activities following the introduction of these systems. This seems to be related to the traditional top-down approach used when implementing systems devoted to organisational decision-making processes (Kersten, 1999), while bottom-up approaches appear more promising from an organisational learning perspective. Within this perspective, information systems show promising results in terms of deducing knowledge from databases, automatic learning and complex reasoning in general, but are still far from being effective tools for supporting learning in organisational environments, especially in the context of spatial planning and management.

Moreover, the use of information technologies within complex organisations requires at least two main issues to be considered. The first issue is that when developing learning support systems, the form of learning has to be developed collaboratively within the specific decision-making context (Ruhleder, Jordan and Elmes, 1996). The second issue, more directly linked to the effectiveness of the decision process, relates to the conviction that decision-making is not a choice among feasible alternatives but rather, and more realistically, a process of producing alternatives; this implies that decision support has to be oriented to the production of different interpretations of available information, and, therefore, to the use of different kinds of knowledge.

The learning process was a significant reference during the design of the prototype. It was studied so that it could be recognised by the organisation and, consequently, attempt to replicate the real decision process. The prototype, therefore, did not aim to transform the decision process, although substitution of portions of human decision-making by IT systems does represent a transformation and requires the organisation to adapt.

Machine learning, as a form of experiential knowledge representation, is certainly a crucial node when building DSSs. Experiential knowledge can be linked to the ability to recognise recursive phenomena in reality and uses them when critically observing that reality. Experiential knowledge is deeply contextual, it has stable characteristics (it can be confirmed by observation and becomes increasingly significant and, consequently, useful), it is transformable (it can always be restructured so as to adapt itself to emergent phenomena of observed reality) and, in particular conditions, it can be acquired through systematic observations of reality, thus being replicable by automatic systems. Our work addressed this latter aspect by investigating the possibility of representing experiential knowledge through the outputs of automatic learning. Some issues arise from this attempt: the produced knowledge needs to be recognised by the system users (this explains why we needed to translate clusters into linguistic descriptions); and we need to understand how this knowledge differs from the knowledge acquired by the human observers whose behaviour we try to replicate.

Acknowledgments

The authors wish to express their gratitude to the interviewees and particularly to N. Trizio, the chemist/technician in the municipal office, who kindly agreed to be repeatedly interviewed for the case study and observed during his work, and also his staff who were always helpful in promptly providing monitored data.

Note

This chapter is part of a research project co-financed by the Italian Ministry of Scientific Research and the Polytechnic of Bari, "Knowledge Engineering in the Territorial Planning Process", co-ordinated by L. Diappi, Polytechnic of Milan. The local research unit in the Polytechnic of Bari was co-ordinated by E. Conte. The chapter is the result of joint effort: sections 1 and 2 are by Emilia Conte, sections 3, 4 and 5 are by Grazia Concilio.

The experiment was carried out in collaboration with colleagues from the Department of Electronics and Electric Engineering of the Polytechnic of Bari.

References

Beynon, M., Rasmequan, S., Russ, S. (2002), "A new paradigm for computer-based decision support", *Decision Support Systems*, 33, pp. 127-142.
Boyle, G., Thomas, C., Wield, D. (2000), "Beyond single vision", *Futures*, 32, pp. 221-228.

Brand, C., Mattarelli, M., Moon, D., Wolfler Calvo, R. (2002), "STEEDS: A strategic transport-energy-environment decision support", *European Journal of Operational Research*, 139, 416-435.

Colvile, R.N., Hutchinson, E.J., Mindell, J.S., Warren, R.F. (2001), "The transport sector as a source of pollution", *Atmospheric Environment*, 35, pp. 1537-1565.

Haykin, S. (1998), *Neural Networks: A Comprehensive Foundation*, Prentice Hall, Englewood Cliffs, NJ.

Kalapanidas, E., Avouris, N. (2001), "Short-term air quality prediction using a case-based classifier", *Environmental Modelling & Software*, 16, pp. 263-272.

Kersten, G. (1999), *Learning Organisations in the 5th Long Wave: Management, Innovation, Knowledge, and IT*, Seminar held at DAU, Politecnico di Bari.

Krishnapuram, R., Keller, J.M. (1993), "A possibilistic approach to clustering", *IEEE Transactions on Fuzzy Systems*, 1, pp. 98-110.

Künzli, N., Kaiser, R., Medina, S., Studnicka, M., Chanel, O., Filliger, P., Herry, M., Horak, F. Jr, Puybonnieux-Texier, P., Quénel, P., Schneider, J., Seethaler, R., Vergnaud, J-C., Sommer, H. (2000), "Public-health impact of outdoor and traffic-related air pollution: a European assessment", *Lancet*, 356, pp. 795-801.

Lu, H.P., Yu, H.J., Lu, S.S.K. (2001), "The effects of cognitive style and model type on DSS acceptance: An empirical study", *European Journal of Operational Research*, 131, pp. 649-663.

Middelham, F. (2001), "Predictability: some thoughts on modeling", *Future Generation Computer Systems*, 17, pp. 627-636.

Nemati, H.R., Steiger, D.M., Iyer, L.S., Herschel, R.T. (2002), "Knowledge warehouse: an architectural integration of knowledge management, decision support, artificial intelligence and data warehousing", *Decision Support Systems*, 33, pp. 143-161.

Proost, S., Van Dender, K. (2001), "The welfare impacts of alternative policies to address atmospheric pollution in urban road transport", *Regional Science and Urban Economics*, 31, pp. 383-411.

Ruhleder, K., Jordan, B., Elmes, M.B. (1996), "Wiring the 'New Organisations': integrating collaborative technologies and team-based work", *Annual Meeting of the Academy of Management*.

Soneryd, L., Uggla, Y. (2000), "Politics as a struggle over definition – two case studies", *Environmental Science & Policy*, 3, pp. 277-286.

Sun, L., Liu, K. (2001), "A method for interactive articulation of information requirements for strategic decision support", *Information and Software Technology*, 43, pp. 247-263.

Wan, D., Johnson, P.M. (1994), "Computer supported collaborative learning using CLARE: the approach and experimental findings", *Working Paper of the Department of Information and Computer Sciences*, University of Hawaii at Manoa.

Wang, H., Liao, S., Liao, L. (2002), "Modeling constraint-based negotiating agents", *Decision Support Systems*, 33, pp. 201-217.

Chapter 11

The Chaotic Nature of
Urban Neighbourhood Evolution

Chris Webster

Introduction

Neighbourhoods are more than artefacts of urban scholarship. They can be detected from the train window, delineated on maps, priced by real estate agents and discriminated against by homebuyers. The fact that governments make policy for neighbourhoods and that buyers and sellers in property markets are not indifferent to their attributes means that neighbourhoods are *economic entities*. And yet the neighbourhood in planning theory, economic geography and urban economics remains poorly conceptualised. This chapter presents the idea of a neighbourhood as a constantly evolving institution the purpose of which is to govern joint consumption in cities. Neighbourhoods are therefore joint consumption spheres. They are also spheres of joint agreement (or contract) over the allocation rules that govern joint consumption. More formally, contracts may be thought of as emerging to create and protect rights to consume private and public goods and services (referred to as property rights from hereon). Property rights may be *de jure* (legal) or *de facto* (economic) and the former, which may be created by government or by the market and backed up by government authority, evolve to protect the latter.

In this chapter I present a model of the urban neighbourhood that draws on these theoretical ideas and present a computer simulation that demonstrates how voluntarily supplied public realms (spheres of private planning) can emerge naturally through bilateral neighbour agreements.

The discussion and the simulation together show the potential of agent-based simulations in operationalising institutional economic models of the city that are rooted in propositions about the behaviour of individual economic agents. In particular, I show that simulations of individual optimising behaviour can yield well-founded simulations of institutional behaviour when individual decisions are contingent on those of others.

The contingent nature of individual economic behaviour yields a chaotic pattern of neighbourhood evolution. Neighbourhood growth (spread of bi-lateral contracts between neighbouring land-users) can equilibrate in several states: a city-wide stable neighbourhood; fragmented stable neighbourhoods; fragmented unstable neighbourhoods; and fragmented anarchy. In next section elaborates on the ideas of institutional emergence and property rights. The third section presents the behavioural model of voluntary neighbourhood contracts that underlies the simulation and is based on the propositions in the second section. The fourth section presents the simulation. The fifth section discusses the results; and the final section concludes.

Institutional Evolution, Property Rights and Neighbourhood Efficiency

Society chooses between a variety of mechanisms to allocate scarce resources and these include governments, markets, voluntary agreements and anarchy. All are active to some degree in effecting the allocation of the shared territorial goods that make up urban neighbourhoods and the institutions that implement them constantly evolve in shape, size and function. Two important questions underlie many academic and practical discussions about urban management and planning: what are the more efficient institutional forms and what is the efficient size of a particular institutional form? The simulation models presented in this paper and elsewhere by the author (Webster and Wu, 1999a, 1999b, 2001; Wu and Webster, 1998, 2000) allows for simultaneous analysis of both efficiency questions. The interdependence between spatial institutions and spatial attributes (neighbourhood public goods) can be made explicit in the language of property rights theory following Alchian (1965), Cheung (1969), Barzel (1997). On the one hand, access to neighbourhood goods is determined by the nature of the rights governing their consumption and these property rights (*de jure* and *de facto*) therefore shape urban morphology. On the other hand, property rights are determined by urban morphology and it is this that leads to institutional evolution.

Consider the following proposition:

• *Proposition 1*: When the value of a neighbourhood attribute (local public good) changes or the transaction costs of assigning rights to it change there will be a corresponding demand to adjust the assignment of property rights over it.

Britain's highest law-making body, the House of Lords, recently debated a Transport Bill that proposes to grant residents yet more rights over local streets in the form of statutory Quiet Lanes and Home Zones (Hansard, 2000). Locally imposed speed restrictions are one expression of proposition 1 as are road and lane closures and smart-card controls over access to local streets. The raft of local traffic management measures currently being enacted in cities around the world are a response to demands for a reallocation of property rights in the light of (a) rising total value of shared consumption goods (road space) in the sense of more people using (valuing) roads; (b) rising congestion costs (c) falling (transaction) costs of property rights assignment. If roads were not becoming more congested there would not be a widespread demand for greater control. If there had not been a fall in the costs of technology (remote policing, smart-card pricing and cordoning, etc.) or of the political cost of regulations, there would not be a demand by residents for reallocating property rights over access and use. The same may be said of residential club communities such as condominiums and gated suburbs. The rise in the (negative) value of neighbourhood security risk leads to demand for reassignment of property rights over shared space and other facilities. Technological and product innovations (smart-card access, automated security devices, new markets in private neighbourhoods) reduce the costs of such reassignment and thus the institutions governing joint consumption in cities evolve. Proposition 2 is a stronger form of proposition 1, stating that rights over neighbourhood goods will be delimited wherever this is cost-efficient. An interesting and contentious corollary of this is that the *public realm* should be understood as a residual category – the spatial domain over which unassigned rights (public domain) prevail.

- *Proposition 2*: Property rights assignment over neighbourhood attributes is constrained by the high transaction costs of rights delimitation and enforcement, meaning that many neighbourhood attributes remain in the *public domain*.

This helps define a spatial dimension to a theory of institutional evolution, which can be thought of as a behavioural theory of the public realm. Public, private and club realms constantly evolve in response to the shifting demand for property rights. Proposition 3 is even stronger, suggesting that there are real costs of leaving neighbourhood attributes in the public domain. These are the costs that arise when citizens compete to consume congested, shared resources – costs that could be avoided by appropriate assignments of rights over those resources.

- *Proposition 3*: Neighbourhood attributes left in the *public domain* will be subject to competitive behaviour resulting in rent dissipation as citizens expend resources that accrue to no-one.

To the degree that governments, markets or voluntary associations of individuals perceive such costs, institutional innovation and adaptation will occur. If the costs of the innovation (co-ordination costs) exceeds the competition costs that would prevail without property rights assignment then the institutional innovation is inefficient. Government administered property rights reassignments (via statute and policy) arguably run a greater risk of this kind of inefficiency than market reassignments since the latter are shaped by more accurate demand information in the form of prices.

The remainder of the paper examines an interesting class of voluntary institution; one that is crucial to the composition and evolution of cities. The institution is the collective agreement that renders many residential neighbourhoods distinct and stable – or the lack of it that renders them indistinct or unstable. Formally constituted homeowners' associations are competing in a big way with tax-funded local government in the US and China and yet cities the world over contain well-functioning neighbourhoods governed by informal cultures of consumption and undocumented rules of behaviour. This is so with and without effective government regulation of land use and environmental nuisances. *Where collective action is not the cause of these informal neighbourhood norms, then individual action must be and it is worth asking how this works.* As an institutional phenomenon a neighbourhood may be thought of as a joint producer-consumer club in which every household has an incentive to consume and/or produce (home investment "products", etc.) at socially optimal levels. In this sense, the neighbourhood is co-produced. *However, one must ask what the individual incentive is to*

*voluntarily adjust consumption and home-based production when free-riding will
maximise individual payoff.* One answer is that the economists have got it wrong and
that the *prisoner's dilemma* is a fiction. Or perhaps the difference between successful
and unsuccessful neighbourhoods is accounted for by differences in preferences – a
preponderance of public-spirited residents overcome the collective consumption dilemma faced by the more selfish residents of less cohesive neighbourhoods. The idea is
probably worth pursuing and it has obvious links to Tieboutian notions of spatial sort-
ing into homogenous preference groups. However, an alternative explanation of neighbourhood variation is possible that is consistent with the conventional view of residents
as individual maximisers. It is an atomistic theory of neighbourhood formation and
rests only on the assumption that individuals will exploit mutual benefits in bilateral
negotiations. Being an atomistic theory it is easily amenable to simulation using agent-
based models. The following section elaborates this idea.

Voluntary Agreements and Neighbourhood Equilibrium

Figure 11.1 represents three neighbours located along a street. Each derives certain
benefits from certain consumption/production activities such as using their property for
a business, playing music, repairing cars or extending the property. Due to diminishing
returns, the marginal benefits decline as the level of activity increases and these are
represented by the demand curves $\delta\Pi$. Unrestrained, households would pro-
duce/consume $q2$ of the activity – the point at which marginal benefit is zero. However,
each household generates nuisance (externality) costs for its neighbours, represented by
δe and these are assumed to rise with the level of activity. The question arises, what
will happen if neighbours negotiate with full information? The classic analysis is presented in Coase (1960) but in his account, negotiation involves real compensatory
payments (in cash or kind). The case depicted in Figure 11.1 is a special and interesting
case of the general problem since compensation is possible in terms of restraint. Neighbour 1 has the incentive to cut back on an activity that lowers neighbour 2's welfare if
the latter offers compensation in the form of restraint on an activity that lowers neighbour 1's welfare. To simplify exposition, neighbours are assumed to be identical in
preferences. The bargaining problem is *Pareto relevant* in that there are mutual gains
from trade. Between $q2$ and $q1$, the welfare loss of a neighbour due to externalities is
greater than the welfare gain due to consumption/production $(E + F > F)$. A household
will be willing to lose F by voluntary restraint in order to gain $E + F$ from his neighbour's restraint. Since this is true of both parties, both gain from voluntary restraint and
an informal contract can be assumed to emerge, which sets the acceptable level of con-
sumption-production at the social optimum $q2$. By striking a good-neighbour agreement each party gains E and the neighbourhood of two gains $2E$. The analysis has to be
modified slightly when a household negotiates with a neighbour on either side but the
basic principle remains – bilateral "contracts" emerge between adjacent land-users
without collective action problems. The externalities imposed by a neighbour become
something like a shadow price of a household's own polluting activities and faced with
that pricing information the household adjusts to the socially optimal. Once the contract

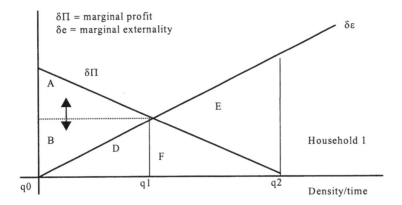

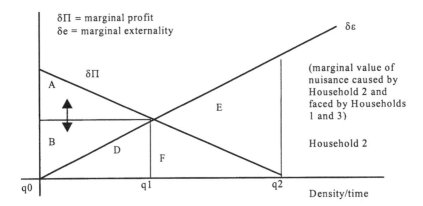

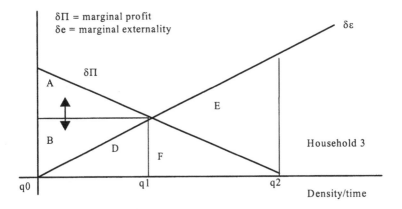

**Figure 11.1 Consumption/Production Decisions by Three Neighbouring
Households**

is in place, the threat of neighbourly retribution if a household reneges has the effect of internalising the externality – external costs become internal costs by reciprocation.

The simulation described in the next section models this theory by making the assumption that voluntary restraining contracts will emerge if at least three adjacent households make simultaneous bids to negotiate for mutual gain. In the one-dimensional case of houses on a street, this assumes that a household requires both neighbours to opt-in to the contract as a condition for opting-in itself. If one neighbour is not offering to restrain (because its other neighbour is not offering) then the contract fails to emerge – or dissolves if it had already emerged. Contracts only emerge, therefore, where households stand to gain. If a neighbour on one side does not comply, the gains from the compliant neighbour are assumed to be wiped out (it only takes one bad neighbour to reduce welfare and once reduced, an additional source of nuisance adds only a small marginal cost). In a two-dimensional neighbourhood in which contracts can be made with households across a street or adjoining to the rear, the simulation models a situation in which a threshold of two others in the immediate joint-consumption sphere is required in order for a household to offer voluntary restraint.

A CA Model of Emergent Neighbourhoods Under Voluntary Governance

The simulation is a very simple conventional Cellular Automata (CA) model in which there are two states (values 1 and 3 represent the same state and are necessary for the algorithm):

State	Description	Bilateral contract	Figure 11.1
1,3	Socially optimal production/consumption	Yes	q1
2	Privately optimal production/consumption	No	q2

The CA is defined with the following five rules (a dot between commas is a wild card):

$$1(1,1,.,.)\text{->}3; 2(1,1,.,.)\text{->}3; 1(.,.,.,.)\text{->}2; 2(.,.,.,.)\text{->}2; 3(.,.,.,.)\text{->}1$$

Reading across: if a cell (household) that is voluntarily restraining at the social optimum has at least two neighbours doing likewise then maintain social optimum. If a cell producing at private optimum has at least two neighbours that are voluntarily restraining then convert to social optimum. If a cell producing at social optimum does not possess at least two neighbours doing likewise then convert back to private optimum. Cells producing at private optimum and not having at least two voluntarily restraining neighbours continue to produce at private optimum. The last rule is purely algorithmic. The simulation starts with a random seeding of households switched to state 1 – modelling some random start point in a neighbourhood's evolution at which a minority of households offer to make mutually beneficial agreements with neighbours. The CA proceeds with a Von Neumann neighbourhood with a radius of one.

Simulation Results

Figure 11.2 shows a city of 122,500 households in three stages of neighbourhood evolution. The bright areas are stable neighbourhoods comprising households who have agreed to voluntarily curtail production/consumption activity to a mutually agreed social optimum. Areas with intermediate brightness are unstable neighbourhoods in which households fluctuate between private and social optimum levels of activities as they make and break agreements. Dark areas are inefficient neighbourhoods in the sense that all households maximise individual welfare but in so doing are individually and collectively worse off (each forgoes a welfare gain equal to the area E in Figure 11.1).

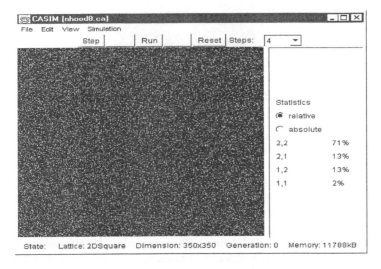

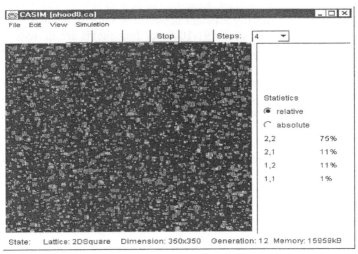

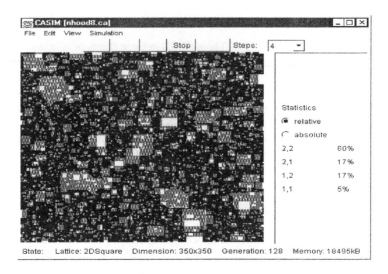

Figure 11.2 Emergence of Neighbourhoods in a City of 122,500 Households

The neighbourhoods in Figure 11.2 have emerged purely as a result of households making bilateral agreements with neighbours. This means of course that the resultant morphology is dependent on the initial spatial distribution of households offering to make good neighbour contracts (the top image in Figure 11.2). Had the starting distribution been different, a very different city might have emerged. This point is illustrated in Table 11.1, which shows the frequency distribution of neighbourhood types emerging in 100 simulations with different initial distributions. The simulated city in Table 11.1 has 2,500 households (50x50) and each simulation is randomly seeded with 375 (15%) households that make an opening bid to make a good neighbour contract. Reading the bottom row of Table 11.1: from a starting point of 15% socially efficient households, the city has a 0.33 chance of equilibrating to a state in which 91-100% of households are in stable efficient neighbourhoods (bottom right cell). The greater probability, however, is that only 0-10% of households will form such neighbourhoods (0.46). Reading the top row, which is also bi-modal, there is a 0.33 chance of the city stabilising with 0-10% of households in neighbourhoods where consumption/production is individually optimal but jointly sub-optimal (inefficient neighbourhoods). The most likely percentage of households in inefficient neighbourhoods at equilibrium, however, is 61-80% (0.43). Reading the middle row, there is a roughly equal chance of 0-10% and 21-30% of households forming unstable alliances as they pursue mutually beneficial contracts.

Table 11.1 Probability of Inefficient, Unstable and Efficient Neighbourhood Formation

| | Percentage of households in three different kinds of neighbourhood | | | | |
	0-10	11-20	21-30	31-40	41-50
Inefficient	0.33	0	0	0.05	0.08
Unstable	0.35	0.17	0.34	0.11	0.03
Efficient	0.46	0.10	0.05	0.03	0.01
	51-60	61-70	71-80	81-90	91-100
Inefficient	0.11	0.22	0.21	0	0
Unstable	0	0	0	0	0
Efficient	0.02	0	0	0	0.33

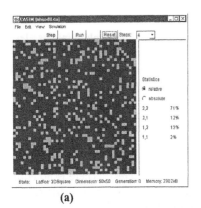

(a)

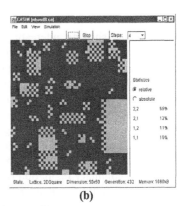

(b)

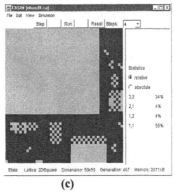

(c)

Figure 11.3 Random Allocation of Neighbourly Contract Offers and Two Contrasting Equilibrium States (bright neighbourhoods are efficient, dark are inefficient and chequered are unstable)

Figure 11.3 shows two examples of neighbourhood emergence at equilibrium. The distributions depicted in (b) and (c) have evolved from a random distribution of contract-offers such as that displayed in (a). Cities (b) and (c) are both at equilibrium but have very different proportions of households living in efficient, inefficient and unstable neighbourhoods. Table 11.1 suggests that there is a 0.46 chance of a neighbourhood pattern like (b) emerging and a 0.2 chance of a more efficient pattern like (c) emerging. Intriguingly, the chance that neighbourhood evolution stabilises with 100% households making mutually beneficial neighbour contracts is higher (0.33) than the chance of stabilising at some lesser percentage, such as the 50% in (c). The most likely neighbourhood pattern emerging from bilateral agreements is either one of two extremes: very few or very many households living in efficient neighbourhoods, with the *very few* outcome being the more probable by a small margin.

Conclusion

These results shed an interesting light on debates about more planning vs. less planning; urban ecological evolution; neighbourhood formation and stability; and many other contemporary urban planning issues. The main substantial point is that neighbourhoods can develop from bilateral action between households that are motivated by individual welfare maximisation. This is a kind of private (voluntary) planning. Areas of common consumption and production behaviour governed by informal rules and norms that might appear to be a spatial expression of collective action can emerge through bilateral action. The simulation also shows that neighbourhoods can be understood to be areas in which individuals agree on behavioural norms and voluntary regulation regimes for mutual self-interest. There is no community spirit (altruistic behaviour) built into the model. This means that neighbourhood stability is fragile and susceptible to individuals breaking faith. There is no incentive for breaking faith in the model once a stable area has evolved but exogenous factors might break the equilibrium and cause knock-on effects in neighbourhood boundaries throughout the city. Real-life experience shows that the stability of a neighbourhood can be affected rapidly by the in-migration of nonconforming neighbours. In a celebrated case in the city of Manchester, England, a stable street in a lower-income area took a sudden dive after two new households moved in. Property values fell from £30,000 to £1,500 in ten years and by 2002 all but five families had cut their losses and exited.

Wu and Webster (1998) demonstrate the more general principle, showing how random changes of land use at the boundaries of same-use zones cause a constant shifting of natural (market) land use zones across the city over time in pursuit of economic efficiency. The simulations in Figure 11.4 show two land uses shifting like oil and water under two regimes: one in which polluting users have the right to pollute without liability and one in which polluted land users have the right to negotiate compensation from polluters. The two institutional frameworks give rise to systematic differences in morphology (larger clusters when the victims of pollution have the right to compensation) but the effect of random trend-bucking land use changes has the same effect in both simulations – to cause the patterns to shift over time.

The use clusters or neighbourhoods in Figure 11.4 form as a result of formal (government) rules governing third party liability for spillover costs (externalities). It might be predicted that the fragility of neighbourhoods formed by *informal* institutions (the bilateral contracts modelled in Figures 11.1-11.3) leads to a demand for more formal neighbourhood contracts as cities evolve over time. Returning to the propositions introduced in the second section, this is more likely the higher the value of the nuisance problems (the higher the δe curves in Figure 11.1 and the larger the triangle E) and the higher the risk of living next to a reneging neighbour. Two outcomes can be predicted: demand for government legislation that grants more powers of control (property rights) over shared neighbourhood facilities to residents; and a rising demand for private neighbourhoods. From one point of view, all forms of micro-neighbourhood governance including devolved municipal powers and proprietary communities (gated suburbs, condominiums, shopping malls, leisure complexes and industrial parks) might be thought of as a response to the capricious nature of voluntary agreements. Even where there is strong planning and environmental nuisance laws, successful residential, commercial and industrial neighbourhoods rely on a good deal of voluntary compliance in the use of public domain attributes. Where this cannot be relied upon there will be a natural evolution towards clearer property rights assignment and greater control whether this is via legal contracts and the market or via government regulation and policing. The exclusive public realms supplied to members of residential clubs (club realms – see Webster, 2002) are a natural market response to secular changes in the demand and supply of neighbourhood goods and the demand for property rights governing the consumption of such goods.

Acknowledgments

In writing this chapter I am grateful for comments made by various colleagues including those present when the work reported here was presented at the World Planning Congress in Shanghai (2001); the International Conference of Economic Geographers held in Singapore (2000); the Milan CA workshop; and the American Association of Geographers conference in New York (2000). I am also grateful to anonymous referees of an earlier version of the paper published in the University of Southern California on-line journal *Planning and Markets*: (http://www-pam.usc.edu/index.html).

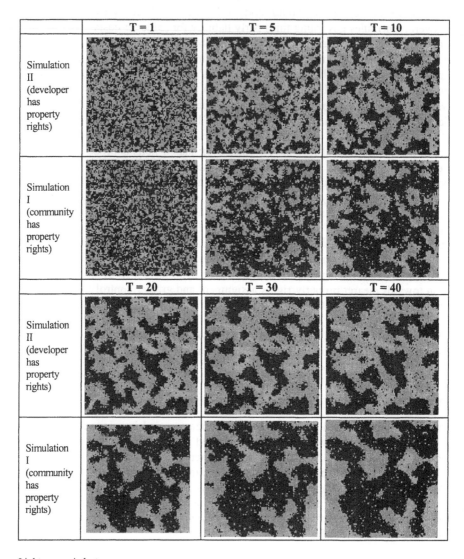

Light grey = industry
Dark grey = residential

Figure 11.4 Two Land Use Morphologies Evolving Over Time in Response to Random Changes in Use on Inter-use Boundaries

References

Alchian, A.A. (1965), "Some economics of property rights", *Il Politico* 30 (4) pp. 816-29, reprinted in Alchian, A.A., *Economic Forces at Work*, Ind. Liberty Press, Indianapolis, 1977.

Barzel, Y. (1997), *Economic Analysis of Property Rights*, 2nd edn., CUP, Cambridge.

Cheung, S.N.S. (1969), *A Theory of Share Tenancy*, University of Chicago Press, Chicago.

Coase, R.H. (1960), "The problem of social cost", *Journal of Law and Economics* 3, pp. 1-44.

Hansard (Lords), 9 November 2000.

Webster, C.J. (2002), "Property rights and the public realm: gates, green belts and gemeinschaft", *Environment and Planning B*, 29, pp. 397-412.

Webster, C.J. and Wu, F. (1999a), "Regulation, land use mix and urban performance. Part 1: Theory", *Environment and Planning A*, 31, pp. 1433-1442.

Webster, C.J. and Wu, F. (1999b), "Regulation, land use mix and urban performance. Part 2: Simulation", *Environment and Planning A*, 31, pp. 1529-1545.

Webster, C.J. and Wu, F. (2001), "Coase, spatial pricing and emergent cities", *Urban Studies* 38 (12), pp. 2037-2054.

Wu, F. and Webster, C.J. (1998), "Simulation of natural land use zoning under free-market and incremental development control regimes", *Computers Environment and Urban Systems*, 22 (3), pp. 241-256.

Wu, F. and Webster, C.J. (2000), "Simulating artificial cities in a GIS environment: urban growth under alternative regulative regimes", *International Journal of Geographical Information Science*, 14 (7), pp. 625-648.

Index